Memories of a Catholic Girlhood

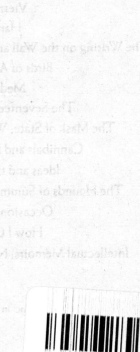

BOOKS BY MARY McCARTHY

The Company She Keeps*
The Oasis
Cast a Cold Eye*
The Groves of Academe*
A Charmed Life*
Sights and Spectacles
Venice Observed*
Memories of a Catholic Girlhood*
The Stones of Florence*
On the Contrary
The Group*
Mary McCarthy's Theatre Chronicles
Vietnam
Hanoi
The Writing on the Wall and Other Literary Essays*
Birds of America*
Medina
The Seventeenth Degree
The Mask of State: Watergate Portraits*
Cannibals and Missionaries*
Ideas and the Novel
The Hounds of Summer and Other Stories
Occasional Prose
How I Grew*
Intellectual Memoirs: New York 1936–1938*

*Available from Harcourt, Inc. in a Harvest paperback edition

Mary McCarthy

MEMORIES OF A
CATHOLIC GIRLHOOD

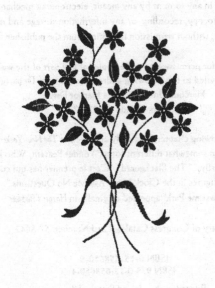

A Harvest Book • Harcourt, Inc.
San Diego   New York   London

Requests for permission to make copies of any part of the work
should be mailed to the following address: Permissions Department,
Harcourt, Inc., 6277 Sea Harbor Drive,
Orlando, Florida 32887-6777.

The following chapters originally appeared in *The New Yorker*,
some of them in somewhat different form: "Yonder Peasant, Who Is He?,"
"A Tin Butterfly," " The Blackguard," "C'est le premier pas qui coûte,"
"The Figures in the Clock," and "Ask Me No Questions."
"Yellowstone Park" appeared originally in *Harper's Bazaar*.

Library of Congress Catalog Card Number: 57-8842

ISBN 0-15-658650-9
ISBN 978-0-15-658650-4

Printed in the United States of America
DOC 30 29 28 27 26 25 24 23

TO REUEL

CONTENTS

CONTENTS

ILLUSTRATIONS

(between pages 118 and 119)

Roy McCarthy and Tess Preston—engagement period
Parents, again, before and after marriage
The Preston family
The McCarthy children in Seattle
Augusta Morganstern Preston with her son Harold
Augusta Morganstern Preston with her grandson Preston
The McCarthy family
The McCarthy children in Minneapolis
Mary, on her way to college

Memories of a Catholic Girlhood

TO THE READER

Memories of a Catholic Childhood

These memories of mine have been collected slowly, over a period of years. Some readers, finding them in a magazine, have taken them for stories. The assumption that I have "made them up" is surprisingly prevalent, even among people who know me. "That Jewish grandmother of yours . . . !" Jewish friends have chided me, skeptically, as though to say, "Come now, you don't expect us to believe that your grandmother was really Jewish." Indeed she was, and indeed I really had a wicked uncle who used to beat me, though more than once, after some public appearance, I have had a smiling stranger invite me to confess that "Uncle Myers" was a hoax. I do not understand the reason for these doubts, I have read about far worse men than my cruel uncle in the newspapers, and many Gentile families possess a Jewish ancestor. Can it be that the public takes for granted that anything written by a professional writer is eo ipso untrue? The professional writer is looked on perhaps as a "storyteller," like a child who has fallen into that habit and is mechanically chidden by his parents even when he protests that this time he is telling the truth.

Many a time, in the course of doing these memoirs, I have wished that I were writing fiction. The temptation to invent has been very strong, particularly where recollection is hazy and I remember the substance of an event but not the details—the color of a dress, the pattern of a carpet, the placing of a picture. Sometimes I have yielded, as in the case of the conversations. My memory is good, but obviously I cannot recall whole passages of dialogue that took place years ago. Only a few single sentences stand out: "They'd make you toe the chalk line," "Perseverance wins the crown," "My child, you must have faith." The conversations, as given, are mostly fictional. Quotation marks indicate that a conversation to this general effect took place, but I do not vouch for the exact words or the exact order of the speeches.

Then there are cases where I am not sure myself whether I am making something up. I think I remember but I am not positive. I wonder, for instance, whether the Mesdames of the Sacred Heart convent really talked as much about Voltaire as I have represented them as doing; all I am sure of is that I first heard of Voltaire from the nuns in the convent. And did they really speak to us of Baudelaire? It seems to me now extremely doubtful, and yet I wrote that they did. I think I must have thrown Baudelaire in for good measure, to give the reader an idea of the kind of poet they exalted while deploring his way of life. The rumor in the convent was that our nuns had a special dispensation to read works on the Index, and that was how we liked to think of them, cool and learned, with their noses in heretical books. When I say "we," however, perhaps I mean only myself and a few other "original" spirits.

I have not given the right names of my teachers or of my fellow students, in the convent and later in boarding school. But all these people are real, they are not composite portraits. In the case of my near relations, I have given real names, and, wherever possible, I have done this with neighbors, servants, and friends of the family, for, to me, this record lays a claim to being historical—that is, much of it can be checked. If there is more fiction in it than I know, *I should like to be set right, in some instances, which I shall call attention to later, my memory has already been corrected.*

One great handicap to this task of recalling has been the fact of being an orphan. *The chain of recollection—the collective memory of a family—has been broken. It is our parents, normally, who not only teach us our family history but who set us straight on our own childhood recollections, telling us that this cannot have happened the way we think it did and that that, on the other hand, did occur, just as we remember it, in such and such a summer when So-and-So was our nurse. My own son, Reuel, for instance, used to be convinced that Mussolini had been thrown off a bus in North Truro, on Cape Cod, during the war. This memory goes back to one morning in 1943 when, as a young child, he was waiting with his father and me beside the road in Wellfleet to put a departing guest on the bus to Hyannis. The bus came through, and the bus driver leaned down to shout the latest piece of news: "They've thrown Mussolini out." Today, Reuel knows that Mussolini was never ejected from a Massachusetts bus, and he also knows how he got that impression. But if his father and I had died the following year, he would have been left with a clear recollection of something that everyone would have assured him was an historical impossibility, and with no way of reconciling his stubborn memory to the stubborn facts on record.*

As an orphan, *I was brought up between two sets of grandparents, all of whom are now dead, beyond questioning, and who knew very little, in any case, of the daily facts of our childhood, either before or after the death of our parents. My aunts and uncles, too, were remote from our family life and took small interest in it, my brother Kevin, whose memory corroborates mine for the period of our stay in Minneapolis, was too young when my parents died to remember much about them. For events of my early childhood, I have had to depend on my own sometimes blurry recollections, on the vague and contradictory testimony of uncles and aunts, on a few idle remarks of my grandmother's, made before she became senile, and on some letters written me by a girlhood friend of my mother's. For the Minneapolis period, I have had the help of Kevin, but for later events, in Seattle, when my brothers and I were separated, I am reduced, again, chiefly to my own memory. What more ancient family history I know has been pieced together from hearsay, from newspaper clippings, old photographs, and a sort of scrapbook journal kept by my great-grandfather, who lived to be ninety-nine. This old man seems to have been the only member of the family who was alive to the interest of history. The grandmother I was closest to, his daughter-in-law (as I will show later), disliked talking about the past.*

Yet the very difficulties in the way have provided an incentive. As orphans, my brother Kevin and I have a burning interest in our past, which we try to reconstruct together, like two amateur archaeologists, falling on any new scrap of evidence, trying to fit it in, questioning our relations, belaboring our own memories. It has been a kind of quest, in which Kevin's wife and my husband and even friends have joined, poring over albums with us, offering conjectures: "Do you think your grandmother could have been jealous of you?" "Could your grandfather have had a nervous breakdown?"

How odd this might seem to an outsider never struck any of us until a week ago. It was a Sunday, and my brother Preston, whom I had not seen for many years, had come up from Wilmington to lunch at Kevin's house in the country, bringing with him his wife and children. There were seven of us, seven adults (for we had brought a friend), having cocktails, when someone—my husband, I think—mentioned Uncle Myers. Did Preston have a snapshot of him? "Who was Uncle Myers?" came the voice of Preston's wife, clear and innocent. All motion ceased, the room was frozen in incredulity. The cocktail shaker in Kevin's hand halted in mid-air, like one of the spits turned by the cook in the story of the Sleeping Beauty. "'WHO WAS UNCLE MYERS?'!" Kevin's wife, Augusta, finally echoed, falling back on her chair in a fit of help-less laughter. "'WHO WAS UNCLE MYERS?'" cried Kevin, mock-indignant. We laughed so hard and long that the children came running in to find out what had happened. "Ann wanted to know who Uncle Myers was," Augusta explained to her little boy, James Kevin. He nodded and ran out again; it was not necessary to explain to him why it was funny; he knew. The idea that any-body could have entered the McCarthy orbit and failed to take notice of Uncle Myers was clearly fantastic.

It was ourselves, of course, we were laughing at—not Ann, though she did not think so. Uncle Myers was our White Whale. Anyone who came near us found they had shipped for the voyage. But it is not Uncle Myers alone; it is our whole family history that exercises a fascination on most people who hear even a little of it. They want to know more, which is precisely our situation; we want to know more than we shall ever find out. But why? What inspires this curiosity, beyond sheer contagion? Our family was not remarkable. There was no special genius, on either side; not even eccentricity. The mentality was probably somewhat above average for several generations, if success is a criterion, but most of my relations were and are today quite typical of their class and kind. It is the conjunction of them that is so curious and that produced such curious results. They were ordinary people who behaved quite oddly, to each other and to us four children, that, I think, is the source of the fascination. One wants to have this explained: to learn either that they were not ordinary or that their behavior was not so odd as it looked. They, certainly, did not think themselves unusual; in their own eyes, they were like every-

one else, and their conduct seemed to them, so far as I can judge, highly natural, just what anyone else would do under the circumstances. It puzzles them—the ones who survive—that anyone else should puzzle over them, and this, surely, is a mark of mediocrity. And it is just this mediocrity, this lack of self-awareness, that leaves one pounding at a closed door.

I was born in Seattle in 1912, the first of four children. My parents had met at a summer resort in Oregon, while my mother was a coed at the University of Washington and my father, a graduate of the University of Minnesota, was in the Washington Law School. His father, J. H. McCarthy, had made a fortune in the grain-elevator business in Duluth and Minneapolis; before that, the family had been farmers in North Dakota and, before that, in Illinois. Originally, some generations back, the McCarthys had settled in Nova Scotia; the story is that they had emigrated for religious reasons and not because of the potato famine. In any case, according to legend, they became "wreckers," a common species of land pirate, off the Nova Scotia coast, tying lanterns at night to their sheep on the rocky cliffs to simulate a beaconing port and lure ships to their destruction, for the sake of plunder, or, as it is sometimes told, for the sake of the salvage contract. Plunder would be more romantic, and I hope that was it. By the time I knew them, the McCarthys had become respectable. Nevertheless, there was a wild strain in the family. The men were extraordinarily good-looking, dark and black-browed as pirates, with very fair skin and queer lit-up grey-green eyes, fringed by the "McCarthy eyelashes," long, black, and thick. There was an oddity in the hair pigmentation: my grandfather McCarthy was white by the time he was twenty, and my father was grey at the same age. The women were pious and plain. My grandmother,

Elizabeth Sheridan, looked like a bulldog. Her family, too, had originally settled in Canada, whence they had come down to Chicago.

All her sons, as if to be ornery, married pretty wives, and all married Protestants. (Her daughter, my aunt Esther, married a widower named Florence McCarthy who, freakishly, was not a Catholic either.) My mother, Therese Preston, always called "Tess" or "Tessie," was a beautiful, popular girl with an attractive, husky singing voice, the daughter of a prominent Seattle lawyer who had a big house overlooking Lake Washington. His family came originally from Vermont, of old New England stock. Harold Preston had run for United States senator and been defeated, as I always heard it, by "the interests." As state senator, he framed the first Workmen's Compensation Act passed in the United States, an act that served as a model for the workmen's compensation laws later enacted throughout the Union. He was supposed to have had a keen legal brain and was much consulted by other lawyers on points of law. He was president of the state and the city Bar Associations. He did not aspire to a judgeship, the salaries, even on the highest level, were too low, he used to say, to attract the most competent men. In professional and business circles in Seattle, his name was a byword for honesty.

The marriage between my mother and my father was opposed by both sides of the family, partly on religious grounds and partly because of my father's health. He had a bad heart, the result, I was told as a child, of playing football, and the doctors had warned him that he might die at any moment. The marriage took place, despite the opposition. It was a small wedding, with chiefly family present, in the house over the lake. My father survived seven years (during which my mother had four children and several miscarriages), but he was never very well. Nor did he make any money. Though he had a law office in the Hoge Building and a shadowy partner, he spent most of his time at home, often in bed, entertaining us children.

It sounds like a gloomy situation, yet in fact it was very gay. My mother's parents were in a state of constant apprehension that she was going to be left a young widow with a handful of children to take care of, but my mother and father seemed to be completely carefree. They were very much in love, everyone agrees, and money never worried my father. He had an allowance of eight or nine hundred dollars a month from his father, and my mother had a hundred from hers. In spite of this, they were always in debt, which was my father's fault. He was a recklessly extravagant man, who lay in bed planning treats and surprises. The reader will hear later of my little diamond rings and my ermine muff and neckpiece. I remember, too, beauty pins, picnics in the back yard, Easter egg hunts, a succession of birthday cakes and ice-cream molds, a glorious May basket my father hung on my doorknob, a hyacinth plant, parties with grab bags and fish ponds, the little electric stove on which my mother made us chocolate and cambric tea in the afternoons. My mother had a strain of extravagance in her family, too. But it was my father who insisted on turning everything into a treat. I remember his showing me how to eat a peach by building a little white mountain of sugar and then dipping the peach into it. And I remember his coming home one night with his arms full of red roses for my mother, and my mother's crying out, "Oh, Roy!" reproachfully because there was no food for dinner. Or did someone tell me this story? If we went without dinner while we were waiting for the monthly allowance, it cannot have happened often; our trouble, on the contrary, was upset stomachs due to "fancy" food, or so I am told —I have no recollection of this myself or of all the enemas and purges we are supposed to have taken. I do remember that we could not keep maids or nurses, those that stayed longest were a raw, red, homely Irishwoman with warts on her hands, the faithful Gertrude, whom I disliked because she was not pretty, and a Japanese manservant who was an artist with the pastry bag.

My father, I used to maintain, was so tall that he could not get through a door without bending his head. This was an exaggeration. He was a tall man, but not remarkably so, as I can see from pictures, like all the McCarthy men, he had a torso that was heavy-boned and a little too long for his legs. He wore his gray hair in a pompadour and carried a stick when he walked. He read to me a great deal, chiefly Eugene Field and fairy tales, and I remember we heard a nightingale together, on the boulevard, near the Sacred Heart convent. But there are no nightingales in North America.

My father was a romancer, and most of my memories of him are colored, I fear, by an untruthfulness that I must have caught from him, like one of the colds that ran round the family. While my grandfather Preston was preternaturally honest, there was mendacity, somewhere, in the McCarthy blood. Many of my most cherished ideas about my father have turned out to be false. There was the legend of his football prowess. For years I believed, and repeated, that he had been captain of the Minnesota football team, but actually it was only a high-school team in Minneapolis. I suppose I must have got this impression from the boasts of my grandmother McCarthy. For years I believed that he was a Deke at college, but I think it was really Delta Upsilon. His gold watch, saved for my brother Kevin, turned out to be plated—a great disappointment. He was at the head of his class in law school, so I always heard, but I do not think this was true. As for the legend that he was a brilliant man, with marked literary gifts, alas, I once saw his diary. It was a record of heights and weights, temperatures and enemas, interspersed with slightly sententious "thoughts," like a schoolboy's, he writes out for himself, laboriously, the definitions of an atheist and an agnostic.

All the same, there was a romantic aura surrounding him, a certain mythic power that made people want to invent stories about him. My grandmother Preston, for instance, who was no special partisan of his, told me that on our fatal journey from Seattle to Minneapolis, my father drew a revolver on the train conductor, who was threatening to put our sick family off somewhere in North Dakota. I wrote this, and the reader will find it, in the memoir titled "Yonder Peasant, Who Is He?" But my uncle Harry, who was on the train, tells me that this never happened. My father, he says, was far too sick to draw a gun on anybody, and who would have told my grandmother, except my uncle Harry himself, since he and his wife were the only adult survivors of our party? Or did my grandmother hear it from some other passenger, on his way east during the great flu epidemic?

My last clear personal recollection of my father is one of sitting beside him on that train trip and looking out the window at the Rocky Mountains. All the rest of the party, as my memory sees it, are lying sick in bed in their compartments or drawing rooms, and I am feeling proud of the fact that my father and I, alone and still well, are riding upright in the Pullman car. As we look up at the mountains, my father tells me that big boulders sometimes fall off them, hitting the train and killing people. Listening, I start to shake and my teeth to chatter with what I think is terror but what turns out to be the flu. How vivid all this is in my mind! Yet my uncle Harry says that it was he, not my father, who was sitting with me. Far from being the last, my father was the first to fall ill. Nor does Uncle Harry recall talking about boulders.

It is the case of the gold watch, all over again. Yet how could I have mistaken my uncle for my father?

"My mother is a Child of Mary," I used to tell other children, in the same bragging spirit that I spoke of my father's height. My mother, not long after her marriage, was converted to Catholicism and though I did not know what a Child of Mary was (actually a member of a sodality of the Ladies of the Sacred Heart), I knew it was something wonderful from the way my mother spoke of it. She was proud and happy to be a convert, and her attitude made us feel that it was a special treat to be a Catholic, the crowning treat and privilege. Our religion was a present to us from God. Everything in our home life conspired to fix in our minds the idea that we were very precious little persons, precious to our parents and to God, too, Who was listening to us with loving attention every night when we said our prayers. "It gave you a basic complaisancy," a psychoanalyst once told me (I think he meant "complacency"), but I do not recall feeling smug, exactly. It was, rather, a sense of wondering, grateful privilege. Later, we heard a great deal about having been spoiled by our parents, yet we lacked that discontent that is the real mark of the spoiled child, to us, our existence was perfect, just the way it was.

My parents' death was brought about by a decision on the part of the McCarthy family. They concluded—and who can blame them?—that the continual drain of money, and my father's monthly appeals for more, had to stop. It was decided that our family should be moved to Minneapolis, where my grandfather and grandmother could keep an eye on what was happening and try to curb my father's expenditures.

At this point, I must mention a thing that was told me, only a few years ago, by my uncle Harry, my father's younger brother. My father, he confided, was a periodical drunkard who had been a family problem from the time of his late teens. Before his marriage, while he was still in Minnesota, a series of trained nurses had been hired to watch over him and keep him off the bottle. But, like all drunkards, he was extremely cunning and persuasive. He eluded his nurses or took them with him (he had a weakness for women, too) on a series of wild bouts that would end, days or weeks later, in some strange Middle Western city where he was hiding. A trail of bad checks would lead the family to recapture him. Or a telegram for money would eventually reveal his whereabouts, though if any money was sent him, he was likely to bolt away again. The nurses having proved ineffective, Uncle Harry was summoned home from Yale to look after him, but my father evaded him also. In the end, the family could no longer handle him, and he was sent out West as a bad job. That was how he came to meet my mother.

I have no idea whether this story is true or not. Nor will I ever know. To me, it seems improbable, for I am as certain as one can be that my father did not drink when I was a little girl. Children are sensitive to such things, their sense of smell, first of all, seems sharper than other people's, and they do not like the smell of alcohol. They are also quick to notice when anything is wrong in a household. I do recall my father's trying to make some homemade wine (this must have been just before Prohibition was enacted) out of some grayish-purple bricks that had been sold him as essence of grape. The experiment was a failure, and he and my mother and their friends did a good deal of laughing about "Roy's wine." But if my father had been a dangerous drinker, my mother would not have laughed. Moreover, if he was a drinker, my mother's family seem not to have known it. I asked my mother's brother whether Uncle Harry's story could possibly be true. His answer was that it was news to him. It is just possible, of course, that my father reformed after his marriage, which would explain why my mother's family did not know of his habits, though as Uncle Harry pointed out, rather belligerently: "You would think they could have looked up their future son-in-

law's history." Periodical drunkards, however, almost never reform, and if they do, they cannot touch wine. It remains a mystery, an eerie and troubling one. Could my father have been
drinking heavily when he came home with those red roses, for
my mother, in his arms? It is a drunkard's appeasing gesture,
certainly, lordly and off-balance. Was that why my mother said,
"Oh, Roy!"?

If my father was a sort of remittance man, sent out West by his
family, it would justify the McCarthys, which was, of course,
Uncle Harry's motive in telling me. He felt I had defamed his
mother, and he wanted me to understand that, from where she sat,
my father's imprudent marriage was the last straw. Indeed, from
the McCarthy point of view, as given by Uncle Harry, my father's
marriage was just another drunkard's dodge for extracting money
from his father, all other means having failed. My mother, "your
lovely mother," as Uncle Harry always calls her, was the innocent lure on the hook. Perhaps so. But I refuse to believe it.
Uncle Harry's derelict brother, Roy, is not the same person as my
father. I simply do not recognize him.

Uncle Harry was an old man, and rather far gone in his cups
himself, when he made these charges, which does not affect the
point, however—in fact, might go to substantiate it. An uncanny
resemblance to my father had come out in him with age, a resemblance that had not existed when he was young: his white
hair stood up in a pompadour, and he had the same gray-green,
electric eyes and the same animal magnetism. As a young man,
Uncle Harry was the white hope of the family, the boy who went
east to school, to Andover and Yale, and made a million dollars
before he was thirty. It was in this capacity, of budding million-
aire and family impresario, that he entrained for Seattle, in 1918,
together with his pretty, social wife, my aunt Zula, to superintend
our move to Minneapolis. They put up at the New Washington

Hotel, the best hotel in those days, and, as my grandmother Preston told it, they brought the flu with them.

We were staying at the hotel, too, since our house had been vacated—a very unwise thing, for the first rule in an epidemic is to avoid public places. Indeed, the whole idea of traveling with a sick man and four small children at the height of an epidemic seems madness, but I see why the risk was taken from an old Seattle newspaper clipping, preserved by my great-grandfather Preston: "The party left for the East at this particular time in order to see another brother, Lewis McCarthy [Louis], who is in the aviation service and had a furlough home." This was the last, no doubt, of my father's headstrong whims. I remember the grave atmosphere in our hotel suite the night before we took the train. Aunt Zula and the baby were both sick, by this time, as I recall it, and all the adults looked worried and uncertain. Nevertheless, we went ahead, boarding the train on a Wednesday, October 30. A week later, my mother died in Minneapolis; my father survived her by a day. She was twenty-nine, he was thirty-nine (a nice difference in age, my grandmother always said).

I sometimes wonder what I would have been like now if Uncle Harry and Aunt Zula had not come on, if the journey had never been undertaken. My father, of course, might have died anyway, and my mother would have brought us up. If they had both lived, we would have been a united Catholic family, rather middle class and wholesome. I would probably be a Child of Mary. I can see myself married to an Irish lawyer and playing golf and bridge, making occasional retreats and subscribing to a Catholic Book Club. I suspect I would be rather stout. And my brother Kevin —would he be an actor today? The fact is, Kevin and I are the only members of the present generation of our family who have done anything out of the ordinary, and our relations at least profess to envy us, while I do not envy them. Was it a good thing, *then, that our parents were "taken away," as if by some higher design? Some of my relations philosophize to this effect, in a somewhat Panglossian style. I do not know myself.*

Possibly artistic talent was already dormant in our heredity and would have come out in any case. What I recall best about myself as a child under six is a passionate love of beauty, which was almost a kind of violence. I used to get cross with my mother when she screwed her hair up on top of her head in the mornings; I could not bear that she should not be beautiful all the time. My only criterion for judging candidates who presented themselves to be our nursemaids was good looks; I remember importuning my mother, when I was about five, to hire one called Harriet—I liked her name, too—and how the world, for the first time, seemed to me cruel and inexplicable, when Harriet, who had been engaged, never materialized. She must have had a bad character, my mother said, but I could not accept the idea that anyone beautiful could be bad. Or rather, "bad" seemed to me irrelevant when put beside beauty, just as the faithful Gertrude's red warts and her ugly name made me deaf to anything alleged to me about her kindness. One of the great shocks connected with the loss of my parents was an aesthetic one; even if my guardians had been nice, I should probably not have liked them because they were so unpleasing to look at and their grammar and accents were so lacking in correctness. I had been rudely set down in a place where beauty was not a value at all. "Handsome is as handsome does," my grandmother McCarthy's chauffeur, Frank, observed darkly, when my uncle Louis married an auburn-haired charmer from New Orleans. I hated him for saying it; it was one of those cunning remarks that throw cold water on life.

The people I was forced to live with in Minneapolis had a positive gift for turning everything sour and ugly. Even our flowers were hideous: we had golden glow and sickly nasturtiums in our yard. I remember one Good Friday planting sweet peas for myself next to the house, and I believe they actually blossomed—a personal triumph. I had not been an especially pretty child (my own looks were one of my few early disappointments), but, between them, my guardians and my grandmother McCarthy turned me into such a scarecrow that I could not look at myself in the mirror without despair. The reader will see in the photographs that follow the transformation effected in me. It was not only the braces and the glasses but a general leanness and sallowness and lankness.

Looking back, I see that it was religion that saved me. Our ugly church and parochial school provided me with my only aesthetic outlet, in the words of the Mass and the litanies and the old Latin hymns, in the Easter lilies around the altar, rosaries, ornamented prayer books, votive lamps, holy cards stamped in gold and decorated with flower wreaths and a saint's picture. This side of Catholicism, much of it cheapened and debased by mass production, was for me, nevertheless, the equivalent of Gothic cathedrals and illuminated manuscripts and mystery plays. I threw myself into it with ardor, this sensuous life, and when I was not dreaming that I was going to grow up to marry the pretender to the throne of France and win back his crown with him, I was dreaming of being a Carmelite nun, cloistered and penitential, I was also much attracted by an order for fallen women called the Magdalens. A desire to excel governed all my thoughts, and this was quickened, if possible, by the parochial-school methods of education, which were based on the competitive principle. Everything was a contest, our schoolroom was divided into teams, with captains, for spelling bees and other feats of learning, and on the playground we organized ourselves in the same fashion. To win, to skip a grade, to get ahead—the nuns' methods were well adapted to the place and time, for most of the little

Catholics of our neighborhood were children of poor immigrants, bent on bettering themselves and also on surpassing the Protestants, whose children went to Whittier, the public school. There was no idea of equality in the parochial school, and such an idea would have been abhorrent to me, if it had existed, equality, a sort of brutal cutting down to size, was what I was treated to at home. Equality was a species of unfairness which the good sisters of St. Joseph would not have tolerated

I stood at the head of my class and I was also the best runner and the best performer on the turning poles in the schoolyard, I was the best actress and elocutionist and the second most devout, being surpassed in this by a blond boy with a face like a saint, who sat in front of me and whom I loved, his name, which sounds rather like a Polish saint's name, was John Klosick. No doubt, the standards of the school were not very high, and they gave me a false idea of myself, I have never excelled at athletics elsewhere. Nor have I ever been devout again. When I left the competitive atmosphere of the parochial school, my religion withered on the stalk.

But in St. Stephen's School, I was not devout just to show off, I felt my religion very intensely and longed to serve God better than anyone else. This, I thought, was what He asked of me. I lived in fear of making a poor confession or of not getting my tongue flat enough to receive the Host reverently. One of the great moral crises of my life occurred on the morning of my first Communion. I took a drink of water. Unthinkingly, of course, for had it not been drilled into me that the Host must be received fasting, on the penalty of mortal sin? It was only a sip, but that made no difference, I knew. A sip was as bad as a gallon, I could not take Communion. And yet I had to. My Communion dress and veil and prayer book were laid out for me, and I was supposed to lead the girls' procession, John Klosick, in a white suit, would be leading the boys'. It seemed to me that I would be failing the school and my class, if, after all the rehearsals, I had to confess what I had done and drop out. The sisters would be angry, my guardians would be angry, having paid for the dress and veil. I thought of the procession without me in it, and I could not bear it. To make my first Communion later, in ordinary clothes, would not be the same. On the other hand, if I took my first Communion in a state of mortal sin, God would never forgive me, it would be a fatal beginning. I went through a ferocious struggle with my conscience, and all the while, I think, I knew the devil was going to prevail: I was going to take Communion, and only God and I would know the real facts. So it came about: I received my first Communion in a state of outward holiness and inward horror, believing I was damned, for I could not imagine that I could make a true repentance—the time to repent was now, before committing the sacrilege, afterward, I could not be really sorry, for I would have achieved what I had wanted.

I suppose I must have confessed this at my next confession, scarcely daring to breathe it, and the priest must have treated it lightly: my sins, as I slowly discovered, weighed heavier on me than they did on my confessors. Actually, it is quite common for children making their first Communion to have just such a mishap as mine: they are so excited on that long-awaited morning that they hardly know what they are doing, or possibly the very taboo on food and water and the importance of the occasion drive them into an unconscious resistance. I heard a story almost identical with mine from Ignazio Silone. Yet the despair I felt that summer morning (I think it was Corpus Christi Day) was in a certain sense fully justified: I knew myself, how I was and would be forever, such dry self-knowledge is terrible. Every subsequent moral crisis of my life, moreover, has had precisely the pattern of this struggle over the first Communion, I have battled, usually *without avail, against a temptation to do something which only I knew was bad, being swept on by a need to preserve outward appearances and to live up to other people's expectations of me. The heroine of one of my novels, who finds herself pregnant, possibly as the result of an infidelity, and is tempted to have the baby and say nothing to her husband, is in the same fix, morally, as I was at eight years old, with that drink of water inside me that only I knew was there. When I supposed I was damned, I was right—damned, that is, to a repetition or endless re-enactment of that conflict between excited scruples and inertia of will.*

I am often asked whether I retain anything of my Catholic heritage. This is hard to answer, partly because my Catholic heritage consists of two distinct strains. There was the Catholicism I learned from my mother and from the simple parish priests and nuns in Minneapolis, which was, on the whole, a religion of beauty and goodness, however imperfectly realized. Then there was the Catholicism practiced in my grandmother McCarthy's parlor and in the home that was made for us down the street— a sour, baleful doctrine in which old hates and rancors had been stewing for generations, with ignorance proudly stirring the pot. The difference can be illustrated by an incident that took place when I stopped off in Minneapolis, on my way to Vassar as a freshman, in 1929. In honor of the occasion, my grandmother McCarthy invited the parish priest to her house; she wanted him to back up her opinion that Vassar was "a den of iniquity." The old priest, Father Cullen, declined to comply with her wishes and, ignoring his pewholder's angry interjections, spoke to me instead of the rare intellectual opportunities Vassar had in store for me.

Possibly Father Cullen was merely more tactful than his parishioner, but I cannot forget my gratitude to him. It was not only that he took my grandmother down a peg. He showed largeness of spirit—a quality rare among Catholics, at least in my experience,

though false *magnanimity* is a common stock in trade with them.
I have sometimes thought that Catholicism is a religion not suited
to the laity, or not suited, at any rate, to the American laity, in
whom it seems to bring out some of the worst traits in human
nature and to lend them a sort of sanctification. *In* the course of
publishing these memoirs in magazines, *I* have received a great
many letters from the laity and also from priests and nuns. *The*
letters from the laity—chiefly women—are all alike, they might
almost have been penned by the same person, *I* have filed them
under the head of "Correspondence, Scurrilous." *They* are frequently full of misspellings, though the writers claim to be educated, and they are all, without exception, menacing. "False,"
"misrepresentation," "lying," "bigotry," "hate," "poison," "filth,"
"trash," "cheap," "distortion"—this is the common vocabulary
of them all. *They* threaten to cancel their subscriptions to the
magazine that published the memoir, they speak of a "great
many other people that you ought to know feel as *I* do," i.e., they
attempt to constitute themselves a pressure group. Some demand
an answer. One lady writes: "*I* am under the impression that the
Law forbids this sort of thing."

In contrast, the priests and nuns who have written me, apropos
the same memoirs, strike a note that sounds almost heretical. *They*
are touched, many of them say, by my "sincerity", some of the
nuns are praying for me, they write, and the priests are saying
masses. One young Jesuit tells me that he has thought of me when
he visited *Forest Ridge* Convent in Seattle and looked over the
rows of girls: "*I* see that the startling brilliance of a slim orphan
girl was fairly matched with fiery resolve and impetuous head-
long drive. *Nor* was it easy for her those days. *I* suppose *I* should
be thinking that technically you are an apostate, in bad standing,
outside the gate. . . ." *An* older priest writes me that *I* am saved
whether *I* know it or not: "*I* do not suggest to you where you

will find your spiritual home—but that you will find it—of that I am certain—the Spirit will lead you to it. Indeed for me you have already found it, although you still must seek it." A Maryknoll nun invites me to visit her mission. None of these correspondents feels obliged to try to convert me, they seem to leave that to God to worry about. Some of them have passed through a period of doubt themselves and write me about that, to show their understanding and sympathy. Each of the letters has its own individuality. The only point of uniformity is that they all begin: "Dear Mary."

I am grateful to these priests and nuns, grateful to them for existing. They must be a minority, though they would probably deny it, even among the clergy. The idea that religion is supposed to teach you to be good, an idea that children have, seems to linger on, like a sweet treble, in their letters. Very few people appear to believe this any more, it is utterly out of style among fashionable neo-Protestants, and the average Catholic perceives no connection between religion and morality, unless it is a question of someone else's morality, that is, of the supposed pernicious influences of books, films, ideas, on someone else's conduct.

From what I have seen, I am driven to the conclusion that religion is only good for good people, and I do not mean this as a paradox, but simply as an observable fact. Only good people can afford to be religious. For the others, it is too great a temptation—a temptation to the deadly sins of pride and anger, chiefly, but one might also add sloth. My grandmother McCarthy, I am sure, would have been a better woman if she had been an atheist or an agnostic. The Catholic religion, I believe, is the most dangerous of all, morally (I do not know about the Moslem), because, with its claim to be the only true religion, it fosters that sense of privilege I spoke of earlier—the notion that not everyone is lucky enough to be a Catholic.

I am not sorry to have been a Catholic, first of all for practical reasons. It gave me a certain knowledge of the Latin language and of the saints and their stories which not everyone is lucky enough to have. Latin, when I came to study it, was easy for me and attractive, too, like an old friend, as for the saints, it is extremely useful to know them and the manner of their martyrdom when you are looking at Italian painting, to know, for instance, that a tooth is the emblem of Saint Apollonia, patron of dentistry, and that Saint Agnes is shown with a lamb, always, and Saint Catherine of Alexandria with a wheel. To read Dante and Chaucer or the English Metaphysicals or even T. S. Eliot, a Catholic education is more than a help. Having to learn a little theology as an adult in order to understand a poem of Donne or Crashaw is like being taught the Bible as Great Literature in a college humanities course, it does not stick to the ribs. Yet most students in America have no other recourse than to take these vitamin injections to make good the cultural deficiency.

If you are born and brought up a Catholic, you have absorbed a good deal of world history and the history of ideas before you are twelve, and it is like learning a language early, the effect is indelible. Nobody else in America, no other group, is in this fortunate position. Granted that Catholic history is biased, it is not dry or dead, its virtue for the student, indeed, is that it has been made to come alive by the violent partisanship which inflames it. This partisanship, moreover, acts as a magnet to attract stray pieces of information not ordinarily taught in American schools. While children in public schools were studying American history, we in the convent in the eighth grade were studying English history down to the time of Lord Palmerston, the reason for this was, of course, that English history, up to Henry VIII, was Catholic history, and, after that, with one or two interludes, it became anti-Catholic history. Naturally, we were taught to

*sympathize with Bloody Mary (never called that in the convent),
Mary Queen of Scots, Philip of Spain, the martyr Jesuits, Charles
I (married to a Catholic princess), James II (married first to a
Protestant and then to Mary of Modena), the Old Pretender,
Bonnie Prince Charlie, interest petered out with Peel and Catholic
Emancipation. To me, it does not matter that this history was one-
sided (this can always be remedied later), the important thing is
to have learned the battles and the sovereigns, their consorts,
mistresses, and prime ministers, to know the past of a foreign
country in such detail that it becomes one's own. Had I stayed
in the convent, we would have gone on to French history, and
today I would know the list of French kings and their wives and
ministers, because French history, up to the Revolution, was
Catholic history, and Charlemagne, Joan of Arc, and Napoleon
were all prominent Catholics.*

*Nor is it only a matter of knowing more, at an earlier age, so
that it becomes a part of oneself, it is also a matter of feeling.
To care for the quarrels of the past, to identify oneself passion-
ately with a cause that became, politically speaking, a losing
cause with the birth of the modern world, is to experience a kind
of straining against reality, a rebellious nonconformity that, again,
is rare in America, where children are instructed in the virtues of
the system they live under, as though history had achieved a
happy ending in American civics.*

*So much for the practical side. But it might be pointed out that
to an American educator, my Catholic training would appear to
have no utility whatever. What is the good, he would say, of
hearing the drone of a dead language every day or of knowing
that Saint Ursula, a Breton princess, was martyred at Cologne,
together with ten thousand virgins? I have shown that such things
proved to have a certain usefulness in later life—a usefulness
that was not, however, intended at the time, for we did not study*

the lives of the saints in order to look at Italian painting or recite our catechism in order to read John Donne. Such an idea would be atrocious blasphemy. We learned those things for the glory of God, and the rest, so to speak, was added to us. Nor would it have made us study any harder if we had been assured that what we were learning was going to come in handy in later life, any more than children study arithmetic harder if they are promised it will help them later on in business. Nothing is more boring to a child than the principle of utility. The final usefulness of my Catholic training was to teach me, together with much that proved to be practical, a conception of something prior to and beyond utility ("Consider the lilies of the field, they toil not, neither do they spin"), an idea of sheer wastefulness that is always shocking to non-Catholics, who cannot bear, for example, the contrast between the rich churches and the poor people of southern Europe. Those churches, agreed, are a folly, so is the life of a dirty anchorite or of a cloistered, non-teaching nun— unprofitable for society and bad for the person concerned. But I prefer to think of them that way than to imagine them as an investment, shares bought in future salvation. I never really liked the doctrine of Indulgences—the notion that you could say five Hail Marys and knock off a year in Purgatory. This seemed to me to belong to my grandmother McCarthy's kind of Catholicism. What I liked in the Church, and what I recall with gratitude, was the sense of mystery and wonder, ashes put on one's forehead on Ash Wednesday, the blessing of the throat with candles on St. Blaise's Day, the purple palls put on the statues after Passion Sunday, which meant they were hiding their faces in mourning because Christ was going to be crucified, the ringing of the bell at the Sanctus, the burst of lilies at Easter—all this ritual, seeming slightly strange and having no purpose (except the throat-blessing), beyond commemoration of a Person Who had died a long time ago. In these exalted moments of altruism the soul was fired with reverence.

Hence, as a lapsed Catholic, I do not trouble myself about the possibility that God may exist after all. If He exists (which seems to me more than doubtful), I am in for a bad time in the next world, but I am not going to bargain to believe in God in order to save my soul. Pascal's wager—the bet he took with himself that God existed, even though this could not be proved by reasoning—strikes me as too prudential. What had Pascal to lose by behaving as if God existed? Absolutely nothing, for there was no counter-Principle to damn him in case God didn't. For myself, I prefer not to play it so safe, and I shall never send for a priest or recite an Act of Contrition in my last moments. I do not mind if I lose my soul for all eternity. If the kind of God exists Who would damn me for not working out a deal with Him, then that is unfortunate. I should not care to spend eternity in the company of such a person.

Yonder Peasant, Who Is He?

WHENEVER we children came to stay at my grandmother's house, we were put to sleep in the sewing room, a bleak, shabby, utilitarian rectangle, more office than bedroom, more attic than office, that played to the hierarchy of chambers the role of a poor relation. It was a room seldom entered by the other members of the family, seldom swept by the maid, a room without pride; the old sewing machine, some cast-off chairs, a shadeless lamp, rolls of wrapping paper, piles of cardboard boxes that might someday come in handy, papers of pins, and remnants of material united with the iron folding cots put out for our use and the bare floor boards to give an impression of intense and ruthless temporality. Thin white spreads, of the kind used in hospitals and charity institutions, and naked blinds at the windows reminded us of our orphaned condition and of the ephemeral character of our visit; there was nothing here to encourage us to consider this our home.

Poor Roy's children, as commiseration damply styled us, could not afford illusions, in the family opinion. Our father had put us beyond the pale by dying suddenly of influenza and taking our young mother with him, a defection that was remarked on with horror and grief commingled, as though our mother had been a pretty secretary with whom he had wantonly absconded into the irresponsible paradise of the hereafter. Our reputation was clouded by this misfortune. There was a prevailing sense, not only in the family but among storekeepers, servants, streetcar conductors, and other satellites of our circle, that my grandfather, a rich man, had behaved with extraordinary munificence in allotting a sum of money for our support and installing us with some disagreeable middle-aged relations in a dingy house two blocks distant from his own. What alternative he had was not mentioned; presumably he could have sent us to an orphan asylum and no one would have thought the worse of him. At any rate, it was felt, even by those who sympathized with us, that we led a privileged existence, privileged because we had no rights, and the very fact that at the yearly Halloween or Christmas party given at the home of an uncle we appeared so dismal, ill clad, and unhealthy, in contrast to our rosy, exquisite cousins, confirmed the judgment that had been made on us—clearly, it was a generous impulse that kept us in the family at all. Thus, the meaner our circumstances, the greater seemed our grandfather's condescension, a view in which we ourselves shared, looking softly and shyly on this old man—with his rheumatism, his pink face and white hair, set off by the rosebuds in his Pierce-Arrow and in his buttonhole—as the font of goodness and philanthropy, and the nickel he occasionally gave us to drop into the collection plate on Sunday (two cents was our ordinary contribution) filled us not with envy but with simple admiration for his potency; this indeed was princely, *this* was the way to give. It did not occur to us to judge him for the disparity of our styles of living. Whatever bitterness we felt was kept for our actual guardians, who, we believed, must be embezzling the money set aside for us, since the standard of comfort achieved in our grandparents' house—the electric heaters, the gas logs, the lap robes, the shawls wrapped tenderly about the old knees, the white meat of chicken and red meat of beef, the silver, the white tablecloths, the maids, and the solicitous chauffeur—persuaded us that prunes and rice pudding, peeling paint and patched clothes were *hors concours* with these persons and therefore could not have been willed by them. Wealth, in our minds, was equivalent to bounty, and poverty but a sign of penuriousness of spirit.

Yet even if we had been convinced of the honesty of our guardians, we would still have clung to that beneficent image of our grandfather that the family myth proposed to us. We were too poor, spiritually speaking, to question his generosity, to ask why he allowed us to live in oppressed chill and deprivation at a long arm's length from himself and hooded his genial blue eye with a bluff, millionairish grey eyebrow whenever the evidence of our suffering presented itself at his knee. The official answer we knew: our benefactors were too old to put up with four wild young children; our grandfather was preoccupied with business matters and with his rheumatism, to which he devoted himself as though to a pious duty, taking it with him on pilgrimages to Ste. Anne de Beaupré and Miami, offering it with impartial reverence to the miracle of the Northern Mother and the Southern sun. This rheumatism hallowed my grandfather with the mark of a special vocation; he lived with it in the manner of an artist or a grizzled Galahad; it set him apart from all of us and even from my grandmother, who, lacking such an affliction, led a relatively unjustified existence and showed, in relation to us children, a sharper and more bellicose spirit. She felt, in spite of everything, that she was open to criticism, and, transposing this feeling with a practiced old hand, kept peering into our characters for symptoms of ingratitude.

We, as a matter of fact, were grateful to the point of servility. We made no demands, we had no hopes. We were content if we were permitted to enjoy the refracted rays of that solar prosperity and come sometimes in the summer afternoons to sit on the shady porch or idle through a winter morning on the wicker furniture of the sun parlor, to stare at the player piano in the music room and smell the odor of whisky in the mahogany cabinet in the library, or to climb about the dark living room examining the glassed-in paintings in their huge gilt frames, the fruits of European travel: dusky Italian devotional groupings, heavy and lustrous as grapes, Neapolitan women carrying baskets to market, views of Venetian canals, and Tuscan harvest scenes—secular themes that, to the Irish-American mind, had become tinged with Catholic feeling by a regional infusion from the Pope. We asked no more from this house than the pride of being connected with it, and this was fortunate for us, since my grandmother, a great adherent of the give-them-an-inch-and-they'll-take-a-yard theory of hospitality, never, so far as I can remember, offered any caller the slightest refreshment, regarding her own conversation as sufficiently wholesome and sustaining. An ugly, severe old woman with a monstrous balcony of a bosom, she officiated over certain set topics in a colorless singsong, like a priest intoning a Mass, topics to which repetition had lent a senseless solemnity: her audience with the Holy Father; how my own father had broken with family tradition and voted the Democratic ticket; a visit to Lourdes; the Sacred Stairs in Rome, bloodstained since the first Good Friday, which she had climbed on her knees; my crooked little fingers and how they meant I was a liar; a miracle-working bone; the importance of regular bowel movements; the wickedness of Protestants; the conversion of my mother to Catholicism; and the assertion that my other grandmother must certainly dye her hair. The most trivial reminiscences (my aunt's having hysterics in a haystack) received from her delivery and from the piety of the context a strongly monitory flavor; they inspired fear and guilt, and one searched uncomfortably for the moral in them, as in a dark and riddling fable.

Luckily, I am writing a memoir and not a work of fiction, and therefore I do not have to account for my grandmother's unpleasing character and look for the Oedipal fixation or the traumatic experience which would give her that clinical authenticity that is nowadays so desirable in portraiture. I do not know how my grandmother got the way she was; I assume, from family photographs and from the inflexibility of her habits, that she was always the same, and it seems as idle to inquire into her childhood as to ask what was ailing Iago or look for the error in toilet-training that was responsible for Lady Macbeth. My grandmother's sexual history, bristling with infant mortality in the usual style of her period, was robust and decisive: three tall, handsome sons grew up, and one attentive daughter. Her husband treated her kindly. She had money, many grandchildren, and religion to sustain her. White hair, glasses, soft skin, wrinkles, needlework— all the paraphernalia of motherliness were hers; yet it was a cold, grudging, disputatious old woman who sat all day in her sunroom making tapestries from a pattern, scanning religious periodicals, and setting her iron jaw against any infraction of her ways.

Combativeness was, I suppose, the dominant trait in my grandmother's nature. An aggressive churchgoer, she was quite without Christian feeling; the mercy of the Lord Jesus had never entered her heart. Her piety was an act of war against the Protestant ascendancy. The religious magazines on her table furnished her not with food for meditation but with fresh pretexts for anger; articles attacking birth control, divorce, mixed marriages, Darwin, and secular education were her favorite reading. The teachings of the Church did not interest her, except as they were a rebuke to

others; "Honor thy father and thy mother," a commandment she
was no longer called upon to practice, was the one most frequently
on her lips. The extermination of Protestantism, rather than
spiritual perfection, was the boon she prayed for. Her mind was
preoccupied with conversion; the capture of a soul for God much
diverted her fancy—it made one less Protestant in the world. Foreign missions, with their overtones of good will and social service,
appealed to her less strongly; it was not a *harvest* of souls that
my grandmother had in mind.

This pugnacity of my grandmother's did not confine itself to
sectarian enthusiasm. There was the defense of her furniture and
her house against the imagined encroachments of visitors. With
her, this was not the gentle and tremulous protectiveness endemic
in old ladies, who fear for the safety of their possessions with a
truly touching anxiety, inferring the fragility of all things from the
brittleness of their old bones and hearing the crash of mortality in
the perilous tinkling of a tea cup. My grandmother's sentiment
was more autocratic: she hated having her chairs sat in or her
lawns stepped on or the water turned on in her basins, for no
reason at all except pure officiousness; she even grudged the mail-
man his daily promenade up her sidewalk. Her home was a center
of power, and she would not allow it to be derogated by easy or
democratic usage. Under her jealous eye, its social properties had
atrophied, and it functioned in the family structure simply as a
political headquarters. Family conferences were held there, con-
sultations with the doctor and the clergy; refractory children
were brought there for a lecture or an interval of thought-taking;
wills were read and loans negotiated and emissaries from the
Protestant faction on state occasions received. The family had no
friends, and entertaining was held to be a foolish and unneces-
sary courtesy as between blood relations. Holiday dinners fell, as
a duty, on the lesser members of the organization: the daughters

and daughters-in-law (converts from the false religion) offered up Baked Alaska on a platter, like the head of John the Baptist, while the old people sat enthroned at the table, and only their digestive processes acknowledged, with rumbling, enigmatic salvos, the festal day.

Yet on one terrible occasion my grandmother had kept open house. She had accommodated us all during those fatal weeks of the influenza epidemic, when no hospital beds were to be had and people went about with masks or stayed shut up in their houses, and the awful fear of contagion paralyzed all services and made each man an enemy to his neighbor. One by one, we had been carried off the train which had brought us from distant Puget Sound to make a new home in Minneapolis. Waving good-by in the Seattle depot, we had not known that we had carried the flu with us into our drawing rooms, along with the presents and the flowers, but, one after another, we had been struck down as the train proceeded eastward. We children did not understand whether the chattering of our teeth and Mama's lying torpid in the berth were not somehow a part of the trip (until then, serious illness, in our minds, had been associated with innovations—it had always brought home a new baby), and we began to be sure that it was all an adventure when we saw our father draw a revolver on the conductor who was trying to put us off the train at a small wooden station in the middle of the North Dakota prairie. On the platform at Minneapolis, there were stretchers, a wheel chair, redcaps, distraught officials, and, beyond them, in the crowd, my grandfather's rosy face, cigar, and cane, my grandmother's feathered hat, imparting an air of festivity to this strange and confused picture, making us children certain that our illness was the beginning of a delightful holiday.

We awoke to reality in the sewing room several weeks later,

to an atmosphere of castor oil, rectal thermometers, cross nurses, and efficiency, and though we were shut out from the knowledge of what had happened so close to us, just out of our hearing—a scandal of the gravest character, a coming and going of priests and undertakers and coffins (Mama and Daddy, they assured us, had gone to get well in the hospital)—we became aware, even as we woke from our fevers, that everything, including ourselves, was different. We had shrunk, as it were, and faded, like the flannel pajamas we wore, which during these few weeks had grown, doubtless from the disinfectant they were washed in, wretchedly thin and shabby. The behavior of the people around us, abrupt, careless, and preoccupied, apprised us without any ceremony of our diminished importance. Our value had paled, and a new image of ourselves—the image, if we had guessed it, of the orphan—was already forming in our minds. We had not known we were spoiled, but now this word, entering our vocabulary for the first time, served to define the change for us and to herald the new order. Before we got sick, we were spoiled; that was what was the matter now, and everything we could not understand, everything unfamiliar and displeasing, took on a certain plausibility when related to this fresh concept. We had not known what it was to have trays dumped summarily on our beds and no sugar and cream for our cereal, to take medicine in a gulp because someone could not be bothered to wait for us, to have our arms jerked into our sleeves and a comb ripped through our hair, to be bathed impatiently, to be told to sit up or lie down quick and no nonsense about it, to find our questions unanswered and our requests un-heeded, to lie for hours alone and wait for the doctor's visit, but this, so it seemed, was an oversight in our training, and my grand-mother and her household applied themselves with a will to remedying the deficiency.

Their motives were, no doubt, good; it was time indeed that

we learned that the world was no longer our oyster. The happy life we had had—the May baskets and the valentines, the picnics in the yard, and the elaborate snowman—was a poor preparation, in truth, for the future that now opened up to us. Our new instructors could hardly be blamed for a certain impatience with our parents, who had been so lacking in foresight. It was to everyone's interest, decidedly, that we should forget the past—the quicker, the better—and a steady disparagement of our habits ("Tea and chocolate, can you imagine, and all those frosted cakes—no wonder poor Tess was always after the doctor") and praise that was rigorously comparative ("You have absolutely no idea of the improvement in those children") flattered the feelings of the speakers and prepared us to accept a loss that was, in any case, irreparable. Like all children, we wished to conform, and the notion that our former ways had been somehow ridiculous and unsuitable made the memory of them falter a little, like a child's recitation to strangers. We no longer demanded our due, and the wish to see our parents insensibly weakened. Soon we ceased to speak of it, and thus, without tears or tantrums, we came to know they were dead.

Why no one, least of all our grandmother, to whose repertory the subject seems so congenial, took the trouble to tell us, it is impossible now to know. It is easy to imagine her "breaking" the news to those of us who were old enough to listen in one of those official interviews in which her nature periodically tumefied, becoming heavy and turgid, like her portentous bosom, like peonies, her favorite flower, or like the dressmaker's dummy, that bombastic image of herself that, half swathed in a sheet for decorum's sake, lent a museumlike solemnity to the sewing room and aroused our first sexual curiosity. The mind's ear frames her sentences, but in reality she did not speak, whether from a hygienic motive (keep the mind ignorant and the bowels open), or from a mistaken kindness, it is difficult to guess. Perhaps really she feared our tears, which might rain on her like reproaches, since the family policy at the time was predicated on the axiom of our virtual insentience, an assumption that allowed them to proceed with us as if with pieces of furniture. Without explanations or coddling, as soon as they could safely get up, my three brothers were dispatched to the other house; they were much too young to "feel" it, I heard the grownups murmur, and would never know the difference "if Myers and Margaret were careful." In my case, however, a doubt must have been experienced. I was six—old enough to "remember"—and this entitled me, in the family's eyes, to greater consideration, as if this memory of mine were a lawyer who represented me in court. In deference, therefore, to my age and my supposed powers of criticism and comparison, I was kept on for a time, to roam palely about my grandmother's living rooms, a dangling, transitional creature, a frog becoming a tadpole, while my brothers, poor little polyps, were already well embedded in the structure of the new life. I did not wonder what had become of them. I believe I thought they were dead, but their fate did not greatly concern me; my heart had grown numb. I considered myself clever to have guessed the truth about my parents, like a child who proudly discovers that there is no Santa Claus, but I would not speak of that knowledge or even react to it privately, for I wished to have nothing to do with it; I would not co-operate in this loss. Those weeks in my grandmother's house come back to me very obscurely, surrounded by blackness, like a mourning card: the dark well of the staircase, where I seem to have been endlessly loitering, waiting to see Mama when she would come home from the hospital, and then simply loitering with no purpose whatever; the winter-dim first-grade classroom of the strange academy I was sent to; the drab treatment room of the doctor's office, where every Saturday I screamed and begged on a table while electric shocks were sent through me, for what purpose I cannot conjecture. But this preferential treatment could not be accorded me forever; it was time that I found my niche. "There is someone here to see you"—the maid met me one afternoon with this announcement and a half-curious, half-knowledgeable smile. My heart bounded; I felt almost sick (who else, after all, could it be?), and she had to push me forward. But the man and woman surveying me in the sun parlor with my grandmother were strangers, two unprepossessing middle-aged people—a great-aunt and her husband, so it seemed—to whom I was now commanded to give a hand and a smile, for, as my grandmother remarked, Myers and Margaret had come to take me home that very afternoon to live with them, and I must not make a bad impression.

Once the new household was running, our parents' death was officially conceded and sentiment given its due. Concrete references to the lost ones, to their beauty, gaiety, and good manners, were naturally not welcomed by our guardians, who possessed none of these qualities themselves, but the veneration of our parents' *memory* was considered an admirable exercise. Our evening prayers were lengthened to include one for our parents' souls, and we were thought to make a pretty picture, all four of us in our pajamas with feet in them, kneeling in a neat line, our hands clasped before us, reciting the prayer for the dead. "Eternal rest grant unto them, oh Lord, and let the perpetual light shine upon them," our thin little voices cried, but this remembrancing, so pleasurable to our guardians, was only a chore to us. We connected it with lights out, washing, all the bedtime coercions, and particularly with the adhesive tape that, to prevent mouth-breathing, was clapped upon our lips the moment the prayer was finished, sealing us up for the night, and that was removed, very painfully, with the help of ether, in the morning. It embarrassed

us to be reminded of our parents by these persons who had superseded them and who seemed to evoke their wraiths in an almost
proprietary manner, as though death, the great leveler, had
brought them within their province. In the same spirit, we were
taken to the cemetery to view our parents' graves; this, in fact,
being free of charge, was a regular Sunday pastime with us, which
we grew to hate as we did all recreation enforced by our guardians
—department-store demonstrations, band concerts, parades, trips
to the Old Soldiers' Home, to the Botanical Gardens, to Minnehaha Park, where we watched other children ride on the ponies, to
the Zoo, to the water tower—diversions that cost nothing, involved long streetcar trips or endless walking or waiting, and that
had the peculiarly fatigued, dusty, proletarianized character of
American municipal entertainment. The two mounds that now
were our parents associated themselves in our minds with Civil
War cannon balls and monuments to the doughboy dead; we con-
templated them stolidly, waiting for a sensation, but these twin
grass beds, with their junior-executive headstones, elicited nothing
whatever; tired of this interminable staring, we would beg to be
allowed to go play in some collateral mausoleum, where the dead
at least were buried in drawers and offered some stimulus to
fancy.

For my grandmother, the recollection of the dead became a
mode of civility that she thought proper to exercise toward us
whenever, for any reason, one of us came to stay at her house.
The reason was almost always the same. We (that is, my brother
Kevin or I) had run away from home. Independently of each
other, this oldest of my brothers and I had evolved an identical
project—to get ourselves placed in an orphan asylum. We had
noticed the heightening of interest that mention of our parentless
condition seemed always to produce in strangers, and this led us
to interpret the word "asylum" in the old Greek sense and to

look on a certain red brick building, seen once from a streetcar near the Mississippi River, as a haven of security. So, from time to time, when our lives became too painful, one of us would set forth, determined to find the red brick building and to press what we imagined was our legal claim to its protection. But sometimes we lost our way, and sometimes our courage, and after spending a day hanging about the streets peering into strange yards, trying to assess the kindheartedness of the owner (for we also thought of adoption), or a cold night hiding in a church confessional box or behind some statuary in the Art Institute, we would be brought by the police, by some well-meaning householder, or simply by fear and hunger, to my grandmother's door. There we would be silently received, and a family conclave would be summoned. We would be put to sleep in the sewing room for a night, or sometimes more, until our feelings had subsided and we could be sent back, grateful, at any rate, for the promise that no reprisals would be taken and that the life we had run away from would go on "as if nothing had happened."

Since we were usually running away to escape some anticipated punishment, these flights at least gained us something, but in spite of the taunts of our guardians, who congratulated us bitterly on our "cleverness," we ourselves could not feel that we came home in triumph as long as we came home at all. The cramps and dreads of those long nights made a harrowing impression on us. Our failure to run away successfully put us, so we thought, at the absolute mercy of our guardians; our last weapon was gone, for it was plain to be seen that they could always bring us back and we never understood why they did not take advantage of this situation to thrash us, as they used to put it, within an inch of our lives. What intervened to save us, we could not guess—a miracle, perhaps; we were not acquainted with any *human* motive that would prompt Omnipotence to desist. We did not suspect that these escapes brought consternation to the family circle, which had acted, so it conceived, only in our best interests, and now saw itself in danger of unmerited obloquy. What would be the Protestant reaction if something still more dreadful were to happen? Child suicides were not unknown, and quiet, asthmatic little Kevin had been caught with matches under the house. The family would not acknowledge error, but it conceded a certain mismanagement on Myers' and Margaret's part. Clearly, we might become altogether intractable if our homecoming on these occasions were not mitigated with leniency. Consequently, my grandmother kept us in a kind of neutral detention. She declined to be aware of our grievance and offered no words of comfort, but the comforts of her household acted upon us soothingly, like an automatic mother's hand. We ate and drank contentedly; with all her harsh views, my grandmother was a practical woman and would not have thought it worthwhile to unsettle her whole schedule, teach her cook to make a lumpy mush and watery boiled potatoes, and market for turnips and parsnips and all the other vegetables we hated, in order to approximate the conditions she considered suitable for our characters. Humble pie could be costly, especially when cooked to order.

Doubtless she did not guess how delightful these visits seemed to us once the fear of punishment had abated. Her knowledge of our own way of living was luxuriously remote. She did not visit our ménage or inquire into its practices, and though hypersensitive to a squint or a dental irregularity (for she was liberal indeed with glasses and braces for the teeth, disfiguring appliances that remained the sole token of our bourgeois origin and set us off from our parochial-school mates like the caste marks of some primitive tribe), she appeared not to notice the darns and patches of our clothing, our raw hands and scarecrow arms, our silence and our elderly faces. She imagined us as surrounded by certain playthings she had once bestowed on us—a sandbox, a wooden swing, a wagon, an ambulance, a toy fire engine. In my grandmother's consciousness, these objects remained always in pristine condition; years after the sand had spilled out of it and the roof had rotted away, she continued to ask tenderly after our lovely sand pile and to manifest displeasure if we declined to join in its praises. Like many egoistic people (I have noticed this trait in myself), she was capable of making a handsome outlay, but the act affected her so powerfully that her generosity was still lively in her memory when its practical effects had long vanished. In the case of a brown beaver hat, which she watched me wear for four years, she was clearly blinded to its matted nap, its shapeless brim, and ragged ribbon by the vision of the price tag it had worn when new. Yet, however her mind embroidered the bare tapestry of our lives, she could not fail to perceive that we felt, during these short stays with her, *some* difference between the two establishments, and to take our wonder and pleasure as a compliment to herself.

She smiled on us quite kindly when we exclaimed over the food and the nice, warm bathrooms, with their rugs and electric heaters. What funny little creatures, to be so impressed by things that were, after all, only the ordinary amenities of life! Seeing us content in her house, her emulative spirit warmed slowly to our admiration: she compared herself to our guardians, and though for expedient reasons she could not afford to deprecate them ("You children have been very ungrateful for all Myers and Margaret have done for you"), a sense of her own finer magnanimity disposed her subtly in our favor. In the flush of these emotions, a tenderness sprang up between us. She seemed half reluctant to part with whichever of us she had in her custody, almost as if she were experiencing a genuine pang of conscience. "Try and be good," she would advise us when the moment for leave-taking came, "and don't provoke your aunt and uncle. We might have made different arrangements if there had been only one of you to consider." These manifestations of concern, these tacit admissions of our true situation, did not make us, as one might have thought, bitter against our grandparents, for whom ignorance of the facts might have served as a justification, but, on the contrary, filled us with love for them and even a kind of sympathy—our sufferings were less terrible if someone acknowledged their existence, if someone were suffering for us, for whom we, in our turn, could suffer, and thereby absolve of guilt.

During these respites, the recollection of our parents formed a bond between us and our grandmother that deepened our mutual regard. Unlike our guardians or the whispering ladies who sometimes came to call on us, inspired, it seemed, by a pornographic curiosity as to the exact details of our feelings ("Do you suppose they remember their parents?" "Do they ever *say* anything?"), our grandmother was quite uninterested in arousing an emotion of grief in us. "She doesn't feel it at all," I used to hear her confide, of me, to visitors, but contentedly, without censure, as if I had been a spayed cat that, in her superior foresight, she had had "attended to." For my grandmother, the death of my parents had become, in retrospect, an eventful occasion upon which she looked back with pleasure and a certain self-satisfaction. Whenever we stayed with her, we were allowed, as a special treat, to look into the rooms they had died in, for the fact that, as she phrased it, "they died in separate rooms" had for her a significance both romantic and somehow self-gratulatory, as though the separation in death of two who had loved each other in life were beautiful in itself and also reflected credit on the chatelaine of the house, who had been able to furnish two master bedrooms for the emergency. The housekeeping details of the tragedy, in fact, were to her of paramount interest. "I turned my house into a hospital," she used to say, particularly when visitors were present. "Nurses were as scarce as hen's teeth, and *high*—you can hardly imagine what those girls were charging an hour." The trays and the special cooking, the laundry and the disinfectants recalled themselves fondly to her thoughts, like items on the menu of some long-ago ball-supper, the memory of which recurred to her with a strong, possessive nostalgia.

My parents had, it seemed, by dying on her premises, become in a lively sense her property, and she dispensed them to us now, little by little, with a genuine sense of bounty, just as, later on, when I returned to her a grown-up young lady, she conceded me a diamond lavaliere of my mother's as if the trinket were an inheritance to which she had the prior claim. But her generosity with her memories appeared to us, as children, an act of the greatest indulgence. We begged her for more of these mortuary reminiscences as we might have begged for candy, and since ordinarily we not only had no candy but were permitted no friendships, no movies, and little reading beyond what our teachers prescribed for us, and were kept in quarantine, like carriers of social contagion, among the rhubarb plants of our neglected yard, these memories doled out by our grandmother became our secret treasures; we never spoke of them to each other but hoarded them, each against the rest, in the miserly fastnesses of our hearts. We returned, therefore, from our grandparents' house replenished in all our faculties; these crumbs from the rich man's table were a banquet indeed to us. We did not even mind going back to our guardians, for we now felt superior to them, and besides, as we well knew, we had no choice. It was only by accepting our situation as a just and unalterable arrangement that we could be allowed to transcend it and feel ourselves united to our grandparents in a love that was the more miraculous for breeding no practical results.

In this manner, our household was kept together, and my grandparents were spared the necessity of arriving at a fresh decision about it. Naturally, from time to time a new scandal would break out (for our guardians did not grow kinder in response to being run away from), yet we had come, at bottom, to despair of making any real change in our circumstances, and ran away hopelessly, merely to postpone punishment. And when, after five years, our Protestant grandfather, informed at last of the facts, intervened to save us, his indignation at the family surprised us nearly as much as his action. We thought it only natural that grandparents should know and do nothing, for did not God in the mansions of Heaven look down upon human suffering and allow it to take its course?

There are several dubious points in this memoir.

"... *we had not known that we had carried the flu with us into our drawing rooms.*" *Just when we got the flu seems to be arguable. According to the newspaper accounts, we contracted it on the trip. This conflicts with the story that Uncle Harry and Aunt Zula had brought it with them. My present memory supports the idea that someone was sick before we left. But perhaps we did not "know" it was the flu.*

"... *we saw our father draw a revolver.*" *If Uncle Harry is right, this is wrong. In any case, we did not "see" it, I heard the story, as I have said, from my other grandmother. When she told me, I had the feeling that I almost remembered it. That is, my mind promptly supplied me with a picture of it, just as it supplied me with a picture of my father standing in the dining room with his arms full of red roses. Actually, I do dimly recall some dispute with the conductor, who wanted to put us off the train.*

"*We awoke to reality in the sewing room several weeks later.*" *We cannot have been sick that long. The newspaper accounts of my parents' death state that "the children are recovering." We must have arrived in Minneapolis on the second or third of November. My parents probably died on the sixth and seventh of*

November, I say "probably" because the two newspaper stories contradict each other and neither my brothers nor I feel sure. I know I was still sick on the day of the false armistice, for I remember bells ringing and horns and whistles blowing and a nurse standing over my bed and saying that this meant the war was over. I was in a strange room and did not understand how I had got there, I only knew that outside, where the noise was coming from, was Minneapolis. Looking back, putting two and two together, it suddenly strikes me that this must have been the day of my parents' funeral. My brother Kevin agrees. Now that I have established this, or nearly established it, I have the feeling of "remembering," as though I had always known it. In any case, I was in bed for some days after this, having had flu and pneumonia. Kevin says we were still in our grandmother's house at Christmas. He is sure because he was "bad" that day: he punched out the cloth grill on the library phonograph with a drumstick.

" 'There is someone here to see you'—the maid met me one afternoon with this announcement." *I believe this is pure fiction. In reality, I had already seen the people who were going to be my guardians sometime before this, while we were convalescent. We were brought down, in our pajamas, one afternoon to my grandmother's sun parlor, to meet two strangers, a man and a woman, who were sitting there with the rest of the family, like a reception committee. I remember sensing that the occasion had some importance, possibly someone had told us that these people were going to look after us while Mama and Daddy were away, or perhaps stress had merely been laid on "good behavior." Or could it have been just that they were all dressed in black? The man evinced a great deal of paternal good humor, taking my brothers, one by one, on his lap and fondling them while he talked with my grandparents. He paid me no attention at all, and I remember the queer ebb of feeling inside me when I saw I was going to be left* out. He did not like me, I noticed this with profound surprise and sorrow. I was not so much jealous as perplexed. After he had played with each of my brothers, we were carried back upstairs to bed. So far as I remember, I did not see him or his wife, following this, for weeks, even months. I cannot recall the circumstances of being moved to the new house at all. But one day I was there, and the next thing I knew, Aunt Margaret was punishing me for having spoiled the wallpaper in my room.

The reader will wonder what made me change this story to something decidedly inferior, even from a literary point of view—far too sentimental, it even sounds improbable. I forget now, but I think the reason must have been that I did not want to "go into" my guardians as individuals here, that was another story, which was to be told in the next chapter. "Yonder Peasant," unlike the chapters that follow, is not really concerned with individuals. It is, primarily, an angry indictment of privilege for its treatment of the underprivileged, a single, breathless, voluble speech on the subject of human indifference. We orphan children were not responsible for being orphans, but we were treated as if we were and as if being orphans were a crime we had committed. Read poor for orphan throughout and you get a kind of allegory or broad social satire on the theme of wealth and poverty. The anger was a generalized anger, which held up my grandparents as specimens of unfeeling behavior.

My uncle Harry argues that I do not give his mother sufficient credit: if she had lifted her little finger, he says, she could have had me cut out of his father's will. He wants me to understand this and be grateful. (I was fourteen or fifteen when my grandfather died.) This is typical McCarthy reasoning, as the reader will recognize: ". . . clearly, it was a generous impulse that kept us in the family at all."

Nevertheless, in one sense, I have been unfair here to my grandmother: I show her, as it were, in retrospect, looking back at her and judging her as an adult. But as a child, I liked my grandmother, I thought her a tremendous figure. Many of her faults—her blood-curdling Catholicism, for example—were not apparent to me as faults. It gave me a thrill to hear her go on about "the Protestants" and the outrages of the Ku Klux Klan; I even liked to hear her tell about my parents' death. In her way, "Aunt Lizzie," as my second cousins used to call her, was a spellbinder. She spent her winters in Florida, but in the summer she would let me come in the afternoon, quite often, and sit on her shaded front porch, watching her sew and listening to her. Afterward, I was allowed to go out and give myself a ride on the turntable in her big garage—a sort of merry-go-round on which the chauffeur turned her cars, so that they never had to be backed in or out. Besides her Pierce-Arrow, for winter use, she had a Locomobile, canvas-topped, for summer, which she sometimes took me driving in, out to Minnetonka or Great Bear Lake or Winona. Once we visited an Ursuline convent, and once we went up to St. Joseph to look at St. Benedict's Academy. On these occasions, in her motoring costume, veils, and high-crowned straw hat, she was an imposing great lady.

You felt she could be "big" when she wanted to. "My mother was square," says Uncle Harry. She also had a worldly side, fancying herself as a woman of fashion and broad social horizons. One summer, she and my grandfather took me with them to a snappy resort in northern Minnesota called Breezy Point. It was run by a man named Billy Fawcett, the editor of Captain Billy's Whiz Bang; there I first saw a woman smoke. On the way back, we stopped to visit my grandfather's brother, my uncle John, just outside Duluth, where the grain-elevator company had its main offices. He had a large country house, with formal gardens and *walks, set in a deep forest. They showed me phosphorescent wood and fireflies, there were fairies in the garden, they said. Before going to bed, I left a note for the fairies in a rose, fully expecting an answer. But the next morning there was only dew in the rose, and I felt very troubled, for this proved to me that fairies didn't exist.*

There was a spaciousness in my grandmother's personality that made her comfortable to be with, even though you were in awe of her. Marshall Field's, she often related, had offered her a thousand dollars for a tapestried chair she had sewn, but she had promised the chair to Uncle Louis, so, naturally, she had had to turn down the offer. This impressed me mightily, though I wondered why she did not just make another one if she had wanted to sell it to Marshall Field's. Whenever I went shopping with her, I felt that she was about to give me a present, though there was nothing, except her manner, to encourage this notion. On my way east to Vassar, she did propose buying me an electric doughnut-maker for my room. Fortunately, I refused, I later discovered that she was in the habit of deducting the presents she gave my brothers from the trust fund that had been left them. Thus her ample character was strangely touched with meanness.

I have stressed the family's stinginess where we were concerned, the rigid double standard maintained between the two houses. Yet my grandfather, according to Uncle Harry, spent $41,700 for our support between the years 1918 and 1923. During this time, the Preston family contributed $300. This peculiar discrepancy I shall have to deal with later. What interests me now is the question of where the money went. Approximately $8,200 a year was not a small sum, for those days, considering, too, that it was tax free and that nothing had to be put aside for savings or life insurance. Could some of the money really have been embezzled, as we children used to think?

With that figure before my eyes, I understand a little more than I did of my grandparents' feelings. In view of his check stubs, my grandfather would have had every reason to assume that we children were being decently taken care of in the house he had bought for us. I do remember his surprise when he found that we were being given only those two pennies to put in the collection plate on Sundays. But he did not see us very often, and when he did, we did not complain. This seems odd, but it is true. I do not think we ever brought our woes to our grandparents. When we finally spoke, it was to our other grandfather, the one we hardly knew. We were afraid of punishment, I suppose. The only form of complaint, from us, that was visible to the family was that silent running away. It was I who spent the night in a confessional and a day hiding behind the statue of Laocoön in the Art Institute. That was as far as I got, for I did not have the carfare that was needed to get me to that red brick orphan asylum. Kevin was hardier. Traveling on a transfer he had somehow acquired, he reached a yellow brick orphan asylum called "The Sheltering Arms" that was run by the Shriners. He did not like it as well, in spite of its name, as the red brick one, and though he peered over the wall for a long time, in the end he was afraid to go in. A householder found him crying, fed him, and eventually the Pierce-Arrow came with Uncle Louis to get him, this made the householder think Kevin a terrible fraud.

The family, I think now, must have been greatly perturbed by our running away. It meant either that we were unhappy or that we were incorrigibly bad. I had stolen a ring from the five-and-ten, and my aunt had had to march me back with it into the manager's office. Kevin had altered his report card when the prize of a dime (no, a nickel) had been offered to the one with the highest marks, and one month I had torn and defaced mine because I was afraid to show a low mark at home. At home, threats of reform

*school hung over us, yet at school, paradoxically, we, or at least
I (I cannot remember about Kevin), stood high in conduct. And
when I went to my weekly confession, I seldom got anything but
the very lightest penance—those little Our Fathers and Hail
Marys were almost a disappointment to me. As my grandmother
must have known, I was a favorite with the parish priests.*

*My present impression is that my grandparents slowly came to
realize the true situation in our household and that they themselves were on the point of acting when my other grandfather intervened. Looking back, I believe my grandmother was planning
to enter me in the Ursuline convent we visited, certainly, that
was the hope her behavior on the trip gave rise to. No doubt, they
blinded themselves as long as possible, for to admit the truth was
to face up to the problem of separating us children and either
putting us in schools to board (for which we were really too
young) or distributing us among the family (which my aunts and
uncles would probably have resisted) or letting the Protestants
get some of us. That was what it always came back to, as the
reader will see in the next chapter.*

A Tin Butterfly

THE MAN we had to call Uncle Myers was no relation to us. This was a point on which we four orphan children were very firm. He had married our great-aunt Margaret shortly before the death of our parents and so became our guardian while still a benedict—not perhaps a very nice eventuality for a fat man of forty-two who has just married an old maid with a little income to find himself summoned overnight from his home in Indiana to be the hired parent of four children, all under seven years old.

When Myers and Margaret got us, my three brothers and me, we were a handful; on this there were no two opinions in the McCarthy branch of the family. The famous flu epidemic of 1918, which had stricken our little household en route from Seattle to Minneapolis and carried off our parents within a day of each other, had, like all God's devices, a meritorious aspect, soon discovered by my grandmother McCarthy: a merciful end had been put to a regimen of spoiling and coddling, to Japanese houseboys, iced cakes, picnics, upset stomachs, diamond rings (imagine!), an ermine muff and neckpiece, furred hats and coats. My grandmother thanked her stars that Myers and her sister Margaret were available to step into the breach. Otherwise, we might have had to be separated, an idea that moistened her hooded grey eyes, or been taken over by "the Protestants"—thus she grimly designated my grandfather Preston, a respectable Seattle lawyer of New England antecedents who, she many times declared with awful emphasis, had refused to receive a Catholic priest in his house! But our Seattle grandparents, coming on to Minneapolis for the funeral, were too broken up, she perceived, by our young mother's death to protest the McCarthy arrangements. Weeping, my Jewish grandmother (Preston, born Morganstern), still a beauty, like her lost daughter, acquiesced in the wisdom of keeping us together in the religion my mother had espoused. In my sickbed, recovering from the flu in my grandmother McCarthy's Minneapolis house, I, the eldest and the only girl, sat up and watched the other grandmother cry, dampening her exquisite black veil. I did not know that our parents were dead or that my sobbing grandmother— whose green Seattle terraces I remembered as delightful to roll down on Sundays—had just now, downstairs in my grandmother McCarthy's well-heated sun parlor, met the middle-aged pair who had come on from Indiana to undo her daughter's mistakes. I was only six years old and had just started school in a Sacred Heart convent on a leafy boulevard in Seattle before the fatal November trek back east, but I was sharp enough to see that Grandmother Preston did not belong here, in this dour sickroom, and vain enough to pride myself on drawing the inference that something had gone awry.

We four children and our keepers were soon installed in the yellow house at 2427 Blaisdell Avenue that had been bought for us by my grandfather McCarthy. It was situated two blocks away from his own prosperous dwelling, with its grandfather clock, tapestries, and Italian paintings, in a block that some time before had begun to "run down." Flanked by two-family houses, it was simply a crude box in which to stow furniture, and lives, like a warehouse; the rooms were small and brownish and for some reason dark, though I cannot think why, since the house was graced by no ornamental planting; a straight cement driveway ran up one side; in the back, there was an alley. Downstairs, there were a living room, a "den," a dining room, a kitchen, and a lavatory; upstairs, there were four bedrooms and a bathroom. The dingy wallpaper of the rooms in which we children slept was promptly defaced by us; bored without our usual toys, we amused ourselves by making figures on the walls with our wet tongues. This was our first crime, and I remember it because the violence of the whipping we got surprised us; we had not known we were doing wrong. The splotches on the walls remained through the years to fix this first whipping and the idea of badness in our minds; they stared at us in the evenings when, still bored but mute and tamed, we learned to make shadow figures on the wall—the swan, the rabbit with its ears wiggling—to while away the time.

It was this first crime, perhaps, that set Myers in his punitive mold. He saw that it was no sinecure he had slipped into. Childless, middle-aged, he may have felt in his slow-turning mind that his inexperience had been taken advantage of by his wife's grandiloquent sister, that the vexations outweighed the perquisites; in short, that he had been sold. This, no doubt, was how it must have really looked from where he sat—in a brown leather armchair in the den, wearing a blue work shirt, stained with sweat, open at the neck to show an undershirt and lion-blond, glinting hair on his chest. Below this were workmen's trousers of a brownish-gray material, straining at the buttons and always gaping slightly, just below the belt, to show another glimpse of underwear, of a yellowish white. On his fat head, frequently, with its crest of bronze curly hair, were the earphones of a crystal radio set, which he sometimes, briefly, in a generous mood, fitted over the grateful ears of one of my little brothers.

A second excuse for Myers' behavior is manifest in this description. He had to contend with Irish social snobbery, which looked upon him dispassionately from four sets of green eyes and set him down as "not a gentleman." "My father was a gentleman and you're not"—what I meant by these categorical words I no longer know precisely, except that my father had had a romantic temperament and was a spendthrift; but I suppose there was also included some notion of courtesy. Our family, like many Irish Catholic new-rich families, was filled with aristocratic delusions; we children were always being told that we were descended from the kings of Ireland and that we were related to General "Phil" Sheridan, a dream of my great-aunt's. More precisely, my great-grandfather on this side had been a streetcar conductor in Chicago.

But at any rate Myers (or Meyers) Shriver (or Schreiber—the name had apparently been Americanized) was felt to be beneath us socially. Another count against him in our childish score was that he was a German, or, rather, of German descent, which made us glance at him fearfully in 1918, just after the armistice. In Minneapolis at that time, there was great prejudice among the Irish Catholics, not only against the Protestant Germans, but against all the northern bloods and their hateful Lutheran heresy. Lutheranism to us children was, first of all, a religion for servant girls and, secondly, a sort of yellow corruption associated with original sin and with Martin Luther's tongue rotting in his mouth as God's punishment. Bavarian Catholics, on the other hand, were singled out for a special regard; we saw them in an Early Christian light, brunette and ringleted, like the Apostles. This was due in part to the fame of Oberammergau and the Passion Play, and in part to the fact that many of the clergy in our diocese were Bavarians; all through this period I confided my sins of disobedience to a handsome, dark, young Father Elderbush. Uncle Myers, however, was a Protestant, although, being too indolent, he did not go to church; he was not one of us. And the discovery that we could take refuge from him at school, with the nuns, at church, in the sacraments, seemed to verify the ban that was on him; he was truly outside grace. Having been impressed with the idea that our religion was a sort of logical contagion, spread by holy books and good example, I could never understand why Uncle Myers, bad as he was, had not caught it; and his obduracy in remaining at home in his den on Sundays, like a somnolent brute in its lair, seemed to me to go against nature.

Indeed, in the whole situation there was something unnatural and inexplicable. His marriage to Margaret, in the first place: he was younger than his wife by three years, and much was made of this difference by my grandmother McCarthy, his wealthy sister-in-law, as though it explained everything in a slightly obscene way. Aunt Margaret, née Sheridan, was a well-aged quince of forty-five, with iron-gray hair shading into black, a stiff carriage, high-necked dresses, unfashionable hats, a copy of *Our Sunday Visitor* always under her arm—folded, like a flail—a tough dry skin with soft colorless hairs on it, like dust, and furrowed and corrugated, like the prunes we ate every day for breakfast. It could be said of her that she meant well, and she meant especially well by Myers, all two hundred and five pounds, dimpled double chin, and small, glinting, gross blue eyes of him. She called him "Honeybunch," pursued him with attentions, special foods, kisses, to which he responded with tolerance, as though his swollen passivity had the character of a male thrust or assertion. It was clear that he did not dislike her, and that poor Margaret, as her sister said, was head over heels in love with him. To us children, this honeymoon rankness was incomprehensible; we could not see it on either side for, quite apart from everything else, both parties seemed to us very old, as indeed they were, compared to our parents, who had been young and handsome. That he had married her for her money occurred to us inevitably, though it may not have been so; very likely it was his power over her that he loved, and the power he had to make her punish us was perhaps her strongest appeal to him. They slept in a bare, ugly bedroom with a tall, cheap pine chiffonier on which Myers' black wallet and his nickels and dimes lay spread out when he was at home—did he think to arouse our cupidity or did he suppose that this stronghold of his virility was impregnable to our weak desires? Yet, as it happened, we did steal from him, my brother Kevin and I—rightfully, as we felt, for we were allowed no pocket money (two pennies were given us on Sunday morning to put into the collection plate) and we guessed that the money paid by our grandfather for the household found its way into Myers' wallet.

And here was another strange thing about Myers. He not only did nothing for a living but he appeared to have no history. He came from Elkhart, Indiana, but beyond this fact nobody seemed to know anything about him—not even how he had met my aunt Margaret. Reconstructed from his conversation, a picture of Elkhart emerged for us that showed it as a flat place consisting chiefly of ball parks, poolrooms, and hardware stores. Aunt Margaret came from Chicago, which consisted of the Loop, Marshall Field's, assorted priests and monsignors, and the black-and-white problem. How had these two worlds impinged? Where our family spoke freely of its relations, real and imaginary, Myers spoke of no one, not even a parent. At the very beginning, when my father's old touring car, which had been shipped on, still remained in our garage, Myers had certain seedy cronies whom he took riding in it or who simply sat in it in our driveway, as if anchored in a houseboat; but when the car went, they went or were banished. Uncle Myers and Aunt Margaret had no friends, no couples with whom they exchanged visits—only a middle-aged, black-haired, small, emaciated woman with a German name and a yellowed skin whom we were taken to see one afternoon because she was dying of cancer. This protracted death had the aspect of a public execution, which was doubtless why Myers took us to it; that is, it was a spectacle and it was free, and it inspired restlessness and depression. Myers was the perfect type of rootless municipalized man who finds his pleasures in the handouts or overflow of an industrial civilization. He enjoyed standing on a curbstone, watching parades, the more nondescript the better, the Labor Day parade being his favorite, and next to that a military parade, followed by the commercial parades with floats and girls dressed in costumes; he would even go to Lake Calhoun or Lake Harriet for doll-carriage parades and competitions of children dressed as Indians. He liked bandstands, band concerts, public parks devoid of grass; skywriting attracted him; he was quick to hear of a department-store demonstration where colored bubbles were blown, advertising a soap, to the tune of "I'm Forever Blowing Bubbles," sung by a mellifluous soprano. He collected coupons and tinfoil, bundles of newspaper for the old rag-and-bone man (thus interfering seriously with our school paper drives), free samples of cheese at Donaldson's, free tickets given out by a neighborhood movie house to the first installment of a serial—in all the years we lived with him, we never saw a full-length movie but only those truncated beginnings. He was also fond of streetcar rides (could the system have been municipally owned?), soldiers' monuments, cemeteries, big, coarse flowers like cannas and cockscombs set in beds by city gardeners. Museums did not appeal to him, though we did go one night with a large crowd to see Marshal Foch on the steps of the Art Institute. He was always weighing himself on penny weighing machines. He seldom left the house except on one of these purposeless errands, or else to go to

a ball game, by himself. In the winter, he spent the days at home
in the den, or in the kitchen, making candy. He often had enor-
mous tin trays of decorated fondants cooling in the cellar, which
leads my brother Kevin to think today that at one time in Myers'
life he must have been a pastry cook or a confectioner. He also
liked to fashion those little figures made of pipe cleaners that were
just then coming in as favors in the better candy shops, but Myers
used *old* pipe cleaners, stained yellow and brown. The bonbons,
with their pecan or almond topping, that he laid out in such perfect rows were for his own use; we were permitted to watch him
set them out, but never—and my brother Kevin confirms this—
did we taste a single one.

In the five years we spent with Myers, the only candy I ever
had was bought with stolen money and then hidden in the bottom
layer of my paper-doll set; the idea of stealing to buy candy and
the hiding place were both lifted from Kevin. Opening my paper-
doll box one day, I found it full of pink and white soft-sugar
candies, which it seemed to me God or the fairies had sent me in
response to my wishes and prayers, until I realized that Kevin
was stealing, and using my paper-doll box for a cache; we had so
few possessions that he had no place of his own to hide things in.
Underneath the mattress was too chancy, as I myself found when
I tried to secrete magazines of Catholic fiction there; my aunt, I
learned, was always tearing up the bed and turning the mattress to
find out whether you had wet it and attempted to hide your crime
by turning it over. Reading was forbidden us, except for schoolbooks and, for some reason, the funny papers and magazine section of the Sunday Hearst papers, where one read about leprosy,
the affairs of Count Boni de Castellane, and a strange disease that
turned people to stone creepingly from the feet up.

This prohibition against reading was a source of scandal to the
nuns who taught me in the parochial school, and I think it was

due to their intervention with my grandmother that finally, toward the end, I was allowed to read openly the Camp Fire Girls series, *Fabiola*, and other books I have forgotten. Myers did not read; before the days of the crystal set, he passed his evenings listening to the phonograph in the living room: Caruso, Harry Lauder, "Keep the Home Fires Burning," "There's a Sweet Little Nest," and "Listen to the Mocking Bird." It was his pleasure to make the four of us stand up in a line and sing to him the same tunes he had just heard on the phonograph, while he laughed at my performance, for I tried to reproduce the staccato phrasing of the sopranos, very loudly and off key. Also, he hated long words, or, rather, words that he regarded as long. One summer day, in the kitchen, when I had been ordered to swat flies, I said, "They disappear so strangely," a remark that he mimicked for years whenever he wished to humiliate me, and the worst of this torture was that I could not understand what was peculiar about the sentence, which seemed to me plain ordinary English, and, not understanding, I knew that I was in perpetual danger of exposing myself to him again.

So far as we knew, he had never been in any army, but he liked to keep smart military discipline. We had frequently to stand in line, facing him, and shout answers to his questions in chorus. "Forward *march!*" he barked after every order he gave us. The Fourth of July was the only holiday he threw himself into with geniality. Anything that smacked to him of affectation or being "stuck-up" was subject to the harshest reprisals from him, and I, being the oldest, and the one who remembered my parents and the old life best, was the chief sinner, sometimes on purpose, sometimes unintentionally.

When I was eight, I began writing poetry in school: "Father Gaughan is our dear parish priest/ And he is loved from west to east." And "Alas, Pope Benedict is dead,/ The sorrowing people said." Pope Benedict at that time was living, and, as far as I know, in good health; I had written this opening couplet for the rhyme and the sad idea; but then, very conveniently for me, about a year later he died, which gave me a feeling of fearsome power, stronger than a priest's power of loosing and binding. I came forward with my poem and it was beautifully copied out by our teacher and served as the school's elegy at a memorial service for the Pontiff. I dared not tell that I had had it ready in my desk. Not long afterward, when I was ten, I wrote an essay for a children's contest on "The Irish in American History," which won first the city and then the state prize. Most of my facts I had cribbed from a series on Catholics in American history that was running in *Our Sunday Visitor*. I worked on the assumption that anybody who was Catholic must be Irish, and then, for good measure, I went over the signers of the Declaration of Independence and added any name that sounded Irish to my ears. All this was clothed in rhetoric invoking "the lilies of France"—God knows why, except that I was in love with France and somehow, through Marshal MacMahon, had made Lafayette out an Irishman. I believe that even Kosciusko figured as an Irishman *de coeur*. At any rate, there was a school ceremony, at which I was presented with the city prize (twenty-five dollars, I think, or perhaps that was the state prize); my aunt was in the audience in her best mallard-feathered hat, looking, for once, proud and happy. She spoke kindly to me as we walked home, but when we came to our ugly house, my uncle silently rose from his chair, led me into the dark downstairs lavatory, which always smelled of shaving cream, and furiously beat me with the razor strop—to teach me a lesson, he said, lest I become stuck-up. Aunt Margaret did not intervene. After her first look of discomfiture, her face settled into folds of approval; she had been too soft. This was the usual tribute she paid Myers' greater discernment—she was afraid of losing his love by weakness. The money was taken, "to keep for me," and that, of course, was the end of it. Such was the fate of anything considered "much too good for her," a category that was rivaled only by its pendant, "plenty good enough."

We were beaten all the time, as a matter of course, with the hairbrush across the bare legs for ordinary occasions, and with the razor strop across the bare bottom for special occasions, like the prize-winning. It was as though these ignorant people, at sea with four frightened children, had taken a Dickens novel—*Oliver Twist*, perhaps, or *Nicholas Nickleby*—for a navigation chart. Sometimes our punishments were earned, sometimes not; they were administered gratuitously, often, as preventive medicine. I was whipped more frequently than my brothers, simply by virtue of seniority; that is, every time one of them was whipped, I was whipped also, for not having set a better example, and this was true for all four of us in a descending line. Kevin was whipped for Preston's misdeeds and for Sheridan's, and Preston was whipped for Sheridan's, while Sheridan, the baby and the favorite, was whipped only for his own. This naturally made us fear and distrust each other, and only between Kevin and myself was there a kind of uneasy alliance. When Kevin ran away, as he did on one famous occasion, I had a feeling of joy and defiance, mixed with the fear of punishment for myself, mixed with something worse, a vengeful anticipation of the whipping *he* would surely get. I suppose that the two times I ran away, his feelings were much the same—envy, awe, fear, admiration, and a certain evil thrill, collusive with my uncle, at the thought of the strop ahead. Yet, strange to say, nobody was beaten on these historic days. The culprit, when found, took refuge at my grandmother's, and a fearful hush lay over the house on Blaisdell Avenue at the thought of the monstrous daring and deceitfulness of the runaway; Uncle Myers, doubtless, was shaking in his boots at the prospect of explanations to the McCarthy family council. The three who remained at home were sentenced to spend the day upstairs, in strict silence. But if my uncle's impartial application of punishment served to make us each other's enemies very often, it did nothing to establish discipline, since we had no incentive to behave well, not knowing when we might be punished for something we had not done or even for something that by ordinary standards would be considered good. We knew not when we would offend, and what I learned from this, in the main, was a policy of lying and concealment; for several years after we were finally liberated, I was a problem liar.

Despite Myers' quite justified hatred of the intellect, of reading and education (for he was right—it *was* an escape from him), my uncle, like all dictators, had one book that he enjoyed. It was *Uncle Remus*, in a red cover—a book I detested—which he read aloud to us in his den over and over again in the evenings. It seemed to me that this reduction of human life to the level of talking animals and this corruption of language to dialect gave my uncle some very personal relish. He knew I hated it and he rubbed it in, trotting my brother Sheridan on his knee as he dwelt on some exploit of Br'er Fox's with many chuckles and repetitions. In *Uncle Remus*, he had his hour, and to this day I cannot read anything in dialect or any fable without some degree of repugnance.

A distinction must be made between my uncle's capricious brutality and my aunt's punishments and repressions, which seem to have been dictated to her by her conscience. My aunt was not a bad woman; she was only a believer in method. Since it was the family theory that we had been spoiled, she undertook energetically to remedy this by quasi-scientific means. Everything we did proceeded according to schedule and in line with an over-all plan. She was very strong, naturally, on toilet-training, and everything in our life was directed toward the after-breakfast session on "the throne." Our whole diet—not to speak of the morning orange juice with castor oil in it that was brought to us on the slightest pretext of "paleness"—was centered around this levee. We had prunes every day for breakfast, and corn-meal mush, Wheatena, or farina, which I had to eat plain, since by some medical whim it had been decided that milk was bad for me. The rest of our day's menu consisted of parsnips, turnips, rutabagas, carrots, boiled potatoes, boiled cabbage, onions, Swiss chard, kale, and so on; most green vegetables, apparently, were too dear to be appropriate for us, though I think that, beyond this, the family had a sort of moral affinity for the root vegetable, stemming, perhaps, from everything fibrous, tenacious, watery, and knobby in the Irish peasant stock. Our desserts were rice pudding, farina pudding, overcooked custard with little air holes in it, prunes, stewed red plums, rhubarb, stewed pears, stewed dried peaches. We must have had meat, but I have only the most indistinct recollection of pale lamb stews in which the carrots outnumbered the pieces of white, fatty meat and bone and gristle; certainly we did not have steak or roasts or turkey or fried chicken, but perhaps an occasional boiled fowl was served to us with its vegetables (for I do remember the neck, shrunken in its collar of puckered skin, coming to me as my portion, and the fact that if you sucked on it, you could draw out an edible white cord), and doubtless there was meat loaf and beef stew. There was no ice cream, cake, pie, or butter, but on rare mornings we had johnnycake or large woolly pancakes with Karo syrup.

We were not allowed to leave the table until every morsel was finished, and I used to sit through half a dark winter afternoon staring at the cold carrots on my plate, until, during one short snowy period, I found that I could throw them out the back window if I raised it very quietly. (Unfortunately, they landed on the tar roofing of a sort of shed next to the back porch, and when the snow finally melted, I met a terrible punishment.) From time to time, we had a maid, but the food was so wretched that we could not keep "girls," and my aunt took over the cooking, with sour enthusiasm, assisted by her sister, Aunt Mary, an arthritic, white-haired, wan, devout old lady who had silently joined our household and earned her keep by helping with the sewing and dusting and who tried to stay out of Myers' way. With her gentle help, Aunt Margaret managed to approximate, on a small scale, the conditions prevailing in the orphan asylums we four children were always dreaming of being let into.

Myers did not share our diet. He sat at the head of the table, with a napkin around his neck, eating the special dishes that Aunt Margaret prepared for him and sometimes putting a spoonful on the plate of my youngest brother, who sat next to him in a high chair. At breakfast, he had corn flakes or shredded wheat with bananas or fresh sliced peaches, thought by us to be a Lucullan treat. At dinner, he had pigs' feet and other delicacies I cannot remember. I only know that he shared them with Sheridan, who was called Herdie, as my middle brother was called Pomps, or Pompsie—childish affectionate nicknames inherited from our dead parents that sounded damp as gravemold in my aunt Margaret's flannelly voice, which reminded one of a chest rag dipped in asafetida to ward off winter throat ailments.

In addition to such poultices, and mustard plasters, and iron pills to fortify our already redoubtable diet, we were subject to other health fads of the period and of my great-aunt's youth. I have told elsewhere of how we were put to bed at night with our mouths sealed with adhesive tape to prevent mouth-breathing; ether, which made me sick, was used to help pull the tape off in the morning, but a grimy, gray, rubbery remainder was usually left on our upper lips and in the identations of our pointed chins when we set off for school in our heavy outer clothes, long underwear, black stockings, and high shoes. Our pillows were taken away from us; we were given a sulphur-and-molasses spring tonic, and in the winter, on Saturdays and Sundays, we were made to stay out three hours in the morning and three in the afternoon, regardless of the temperature. We had come from a mild climate, in Seattle, and at fifteen, twenty, or twenty-four below zero we could not play, even if we had had something to play with, and used simply to stand in the snow, crying, and beating sometimes on the window with our frozen mittens, till my aunt's angry face would appear there and drive us away.

No attempt was made to teach us a sport, winter or summer; we were forbidden to slide in Fairoaks Park nearby, where in winter the poorer children made a track of ice down a hill, which they flashed down sitting or standing, but I loved this daring sport and did it anyway, on the way home from school, until one day I tore my shabby coat on the ice and was afraid to go home. A kind woman named Mrs. Corkerey, who kept a neighborhood candy store across from our school, mended it for me, very skillfully, so that my aunt never knew; nevertheless, sliding lost its lure for me, for I could not risk a second rip.

The neighbors were often kind, surreptitiously, and sometimes they "spoke" to the sisters at the parochial school, but everyone, I think, was afraid of offending my grandparents, who diffused an air of wealth and pomp when they entered their pew at St. Stephen's Church on Sunday. Mrs. Corkerey, in fact, got herself and me in trouble by feeding me in the mornings in her kitchen above the candy store when I stopped to pick up her daughter, Clarazita, who was in my class. I used to lie to Mrs. Corkerey and say that I had had no breakfast (when the truth was that I was merely hungry), and she went to the nuns finally in a state of indignation. The story was checked with my aunt, and I was obliged to admit that I had lied and that they did feed me, which must have disillusioned Mrs. Corkerey forever with the pathos of orphaned childhood. It was impossible for me to explain to her then that what I needed was her pity and her fierce choleric heart. Another neighbor, Mr. Harrison, a well-to-do old bachelor or widower who lived in the corner house, used sometimes to take us bathing, and it was thanks to his lessons that I learned to swim—a strange antiquated breast stroke—copied from an old man with a high-necked bathing suit and a beard. In general, we were not supposed to have anything to do with the neighbors or with other children. It was a rule that other children were not allowed to come into our yard or we to go into theirs, nor were we permitted to walk to school with another boy or girl. But since we were in school most of the day, five days a week, our guardians could not prevent us from making friends despite them; other children were, in fact, very much attracted to us, pitying us for our woebegone condition and respecting us because we were thought to be rich. Our grandmother's chauffeur, Frank, in her winter Pierce-Arrow and summer Locomobile, was well known in the neighborhood, waiting outside church on Sunday to take her home from Mass. Sometimes we were taken, too, and thus our miserable clothes and underfed bodies were associated with high financial status and became a sort of dubious privilege in the eyes of our classmates.

We both had enviable possessions and did not have them. In the closet in my bedroom, high on the top shelf, beyond my reach even standing on a chair, was a stack of cardboard doll boxes, containing wonderful French dolls, dressed by my Seattle grandmother in silks, laces, and satins, with crepe-de-Chine underwear and shoes with high heels. These and other things were sent us every year at Christmastime, but my aunt had decreed that they were all too good for us, so they remained in their boxes and wrappings, *verboten*, except on the rare afternoon, perhaps once in a twelvemonth or so, when a relation or a friend of the family would come through from the West, and then down would come the dolls, out would come the baseball gloves and catchers' masks and the watches and the shiny cars and the doll houses, and we would be set to playing with these things on the floor of the living room while the visitor tenderly looked on. As soon as the visitor left, bearing a good report of our household, the dolls and watches and cars would be whisked away, to come out again for the next emergency. If we had been clever, we would have refused this bait and paraded our misery, but we were too simple to do anything but seize the moment and play out a whole year's playtime in this gala hour and a half. Such techniques, of course, are common in concentration camps and penal institutions, where the same sound calculation of human nature is made. The prisoners snatch at their holiday; they trust their guards and the motto *"Carpe diem"* more than they do the strangers who have come to make the inspection. Like all people who have been mistreated, we were wary of being taken in; we felt uneasy about these visitors—Protestants from Seattle—who might be much worse than our uncle and aunt. The latter's faults, at any rate, we knew. Moreover, we had been subjected to propaganda: we had been threatened with the Seattle faction, time and again, by our uncle, who used to jeer and say to us, *"They'd* make you toe the chalk line."

The basis, I think, of my aunt's program for us was in truth totalitarian: she was idealistically bent on destroying our privacy. She imagined herself as enlightened in comparison with our parents, and a super-ideal of health, cleanliness, and discipline softened in her own eyes the measures she applied to attain it. A nature not unkindly was warped by bureaucratic zeal and by her subservience to her husband, whose masterful autocratic hand cut through our nonsense like a cleaver. The fact that our way of life resembled that of an orphan asylum was not a mere coincidence; Aunt Margaret strove purposefully toward a corporate goal. Like most heads of institutions, she longed for the eyes of Argus. To the best of her ability, she saw to it that nothing was hidden from her. Even her health measures had this purpose. The aperients we were continually dosed with guaranteed that our daily processes were open to her inspection, and the monthly medical checkup assured her, by means of stethoscope and searchlight and tongue depressor, that nothing was happening inside us to which she was not privy. Our letters to Seattle were written under her eye, and she scrutinized our homework sharply, though her arithmetic, spelling, and grammar were all very imperfect. We prayed, under supervision, for a prescribed list of people. And if we were forbidden companions, candy, most toys, pocket money, sports, reading, entertainment, the aim was not to make us suffer but to achieve efficiency. It was simpler to interdict other children than to inspect all the children with whom we might want to play. From the standpoint of efficiency, our lives, in order to be open, had to be empty; the books we might perhaps read, the toys we might play with figured in my aunt's mind, no doubt, as what the housewife calls "dust catchers"—around these distractions, dirt might accumulate. The inmost folds of consciousness, like the belly button, were regarded by her as unsanitary. Thus, in her spiritual outlook, my aunt was an early functionalist.

Like all systems, my aunt's was, of course, imperfect. Forbidden to read, we told stories, and if we were kept apart, we told them to ourselves in bed. We made romances out of our schoolbooks, even out of the dictionary, and read digests of novels in the *Book of Knowledge* at school. My uncle's partiality for my youngest brother was a weakness in him, as was my aunt Mary's partiality for me. She was supposed to keep me in her room, sewing on squares of cheap cotton, making handkerchiefs with big, crude, ugly hems, and ripping them out and making them over again, but though she had no feeling for art or visual beauty (she would not even teach me to darn, which is an art, or to do embroidery, as the nuns did later on, in the convent), she liked to talk of the old days in Chicago and to read sensational religious fiction in a magazine called the *Extension*, which sometimes she let me take to my room, with a caution against being caught. And on the Sunday walks that my uncle headed, at the end of an interminable streetcar ride, during which my bigger brothers had to scrunch down to pass for under six, there were occasions on which he took us (in military order) along a wooded path, high above the Mississippi River, and we saw late-spring harebells and, once, a coral-pink snake. In Minnehaha Park, a favorite resort, we were allowed to play on the swings and to examine the other children riding on the ponies or on a little scenic railway. Uncle Myers always bought himself a box of Cracker Jack, which we watched him eat and delve into, to find the little favor at the bottom—a ritual we deeply envied, for, though we sometimes had popcorn at home (Myers enjoyed popping it) and even, once or twice, homemade popcorn balls with molasses, we had never had more than a taste of this commercial Cracker Jack, with peanuts in it, which seemed to us the more valuable because *he* valued it and would often come home eating a box he had bought at a ball game. But one Sunday, Uncle Myers, in full, midsummer mood, wearing his new pedometer, bought my brother Sheridan a whole box for himself.

Naturally, we envied Sheridan—the only blond among us, with fair red-gold curls, while the rest of us were all pronounced brunets, with thick black brows and lashes—as we watched him, the lucky one, munch the sticky stuff and fish out a painted tin butterfly with a little pin on it at the bottom. My brothers clamored around him, but I was too proud to show my feelings. Sheridan was then about six years old, and this butterfly immediately became his most cherished possession—indeed, one of the few he had. He carried it about the house with him all the next week, clutched in his hand or pinned to his shirt, and my two other brothers followed him, begging him to be allowed to play with it, which slightly disgusted me, at the age of ten, for I knew that I was too sophisticated to care for tin butterflies and I felt in this whole affair the instigation of my uncle. He was relishing my brothers' performance and saw to it, strictly, that Sheridan clung to his rights in the butterfly and did not permit anybody to touch it. The point about this painted tin butterfly was not its intrinsic value; it was the fact that it was virtually the only toy in the house that had not been, so to speak, socialized, but belonged privately to one individual. Our other playthings—a broken-down wooden swing, an old wagon, a dirty sandbox, and perhaps a fire engine or so and some defaced blocks and twisted second-hand train tracks in the attic—were held by us all in common, the velocipedes we had brought with us from Seattle having long ago foundered, and the skipping rope, the jacks, the few marbles, and the pair of rusty roller skates that were given us being decreed to be the property of all. Hence, for a full week this butterfly excited passionate emotions, from which I held myself stubbornly apart, refusing even to notice it, until one afternoon, at about four o'clock, while I was doing my weekly chore of dusting the woodwork, my white-haired aunt Mary hurried softly into my room and, closing the door behind her, asked whether I had seen Sheridan's butterfly.

The topic wearied me so much that I scarcely lifted my head, answering no, shortly, and going on with my dusting. But Aunt Mary was gently persistent: Did I know that he had lost it? Would I help her look for it? This project did not appeal to me, but in response to some faint agitation in her manner, something almost pleading, I put down my dustcloth and helped her. We went all over the house, raising carpets, looking behind curtains, in the kitchen cupboards, in the Victrola, everywhere but in the den, which was closed, and in my aunt's and uncle's bedroom. Somehow—I do not know why—I did not expect to find the butterfly, partly, I imagine, because I was indifferent to it and partly out of the fatalism that all children have toward lost objects, regarding them as irretrievable, vanished into the flux of things. At any rate I was right: we did not find it and I went back to my dusting, vindicated. Why should I have to look for Sheridan's stupid butterfly, which he ought to have taken better care of? "Myers is upset," said Aunt Mary, still hovering, uneasy and diffident, in the doorway. I made a slight face, and she went out, plaintive, remonstrant, and sighing, in her pale, high necked, tight-buttoned dress.

It did not occur to me that I was suspected of stealing this toy, even when Aunt Margaret, five minutes later, burst into my room and ordered me to come and look for Sheridan's butterfly. I protested that I had already done so, but she paid my objections no heed and seized me roughly by the arm. "Then do it again, Miss, and mind that you find it." Her voice was rather hoarse and her whole furrowed iron-gray aspect somewhat tense and disarrayed, yet I had the impression that she was not angry with me but with something in outer reality—what one would now call fate or contingency. When I had searched again, lackadaisically, and again found nothing, she joined in with vigor, turning everything upside down. We even went into the den, where Myers was sitting, and searched all around him, while he watched us with an ironical expression, filling his pipe from a Bull Durham sack. We found nothing, and Aunt Margaret led me upstairs to my room, which I ransacked while she stood and watched me. All at once, when we had finished with my bureau drawers and my closet, she appeared to give up. She sighed and bit her lips. The door cautiously opened and Aunt Mary came in. The two sisters looked at each other and at me. Margaret shrugged her shoulders. "She hasn't got it, I do believe," she said.

She regarded me then with a certain relaxing of her thick wrinkles, and her heavy-skinned hand, with its wedding ring, came down on my shoulder. "Uncle Myers thinks you took it," she said in a rusty whisper, like a spy or a scout. The consciousness of my own innocence, combined with a sense of being let into the confederacy of the two sisters, filled me with excitement and self-importance. "But I didn't, Aunt Margaret," I began proclaiming, making the most of my moment. "What would I want with his silly old butterfly?" The two sisters exchanged a look. "That's what I said, Margaret!" exclaimed old Aunt Mary sententiously. Aunt Margaret frowned; she adjusted a bone hairpin in the coiled rings of her unbecoming coiffure. "Mary Therese," she said to me, solemnly, "if you know anything about the butterfly, if one of your brothers took it, tell me now. If we don't find it, I'm afraid Uncle Myers will have to punish you." "He *can't* punish me, Aunt Margaret," I insisted, full of righteousness. "Not if I didn't do it and *you* don't think I did it." I looked up at her, stagily trustful, resting gingerly on this solidarity that had suddenly appeared between us. Aunt Mary's pale old eyes watered. "You mustn't let Myers punish her, Margaret, if you don't think she's done wrong." They both glanced up at the Murillo Madonna that was hanging on my stained wall. Intelligence passed between them and I was sure that, thanks to our Holy Mother, Aunt Margaret would save me. "Go along, Mary Therese," she said hoarsely. "Get yourself ready for dinner. And don't you say a word of this to your uncle when you come downstairs."

When I went down to dinner, I was exultant, but I tried to

hide it. Throughout the meal, everyone was restrained; Herdie was in the dumps about his butterfly, and Preston and Kevin were silent, casting covert looks at me. My brothers, apparently, were wondering how I had avoided punishment, as the eldest, if for no other reason. Aunt Margaret was rather flushed, which improved her appearance slightly. Uncle Myers had a cunning look, as though events would prove him right. He patted Sheridan's golden head from time to time and urged him to eat. After dinner, the boys filed into the den behind Uncle Myers, and I helped Aunt Margaret clear the table. We did not have to do the dishes, for at this time there was a "girl" in the kitchen. As we were lifting the white tablecloth and the silence pad, we found the butterfly —pinned to the silence pad, right by my place.

My hash was settled then, though I did not know it. I did not catch the significance of its being found at *my* place. To Margaret, however, this was grimly conclusive. She had been too "easy," said her expression; once again Myers had been right. Myers went through the formality of interrogating each of the boys in turn ("No, sir," "No, sir," "No, sir") and even, at my insistence, of calling in the Swedish girl from the kitchen. Nobody knew how the butterfly had got there. It had not been there before dinner, when the girl set the table. My judges therefore concluded that I had had it hidden on my person and had slipped it under the tablecloth at dinner, when nobody was looking. This unanimous verdict maddened me, at first simply as an indication of stupidity—how could they be so dense as to imagine that I would hide it by my own place, where it was sure to be discovered? I did not really believe that I was going to be punished on such ridiculous evidence, yet even I could form no theory of how the butterfly had come there. My first base impulse to accuse the maid was scoffed out of my head by reason. What would a grownup want with a silly six-year-old's toy? And the very unfairness of the condemnation that rested on me made me reluctant to transfer it to one of my brothers. I kept supposing that the truth somehow would out, but the interrogation suddenly ended and every eye avoided mine.

Aunt Mary's dragging step went up the stairs, the boys were ordered to bed, and then, in the lavatory, the whipping began. Myers beat me with the strop, until his lazy arm tired; whipping is hard work for a fat man, out of condition, with a screaming, kicking, wriggling ten-year-old in his grasp. He went out and heaved himself, panting, into his favorite chair and I presumed that the whipping was over. But Aunt Margaret took his place, striking harder than he, with a hairbrush, in a businesslike, joyless way, repeating, "Say you did it, Mary Therese, say you did it." As the blows fell and I did not give in, this formula took on an intercessory note, like a prayer. It was clear to me that she was begging me to surrender and give Myers his satisfaction, for my own sake, so that the whipping could stop. When I finally cried out "All right!" she dropped the hairbrush with a sigh of relief; a new doubt of my guilt must have been visiting her, and my confession set everything square. She led me in to my uncle, and we both stood facing him, as Aunt Margaret, with a firm but not ungentle hand on my shoulder, whispered, "Just tell him, 'Uncle Myers, I did it,' and you can go to bed." But the sight of him, sprawling in his leather chair, complacently waiting for this, was too much for me. The words froze on my tongue. I could not utter them to *him*. Aunt Margaret urged me on, reproachfully, as though I were breaking our compact, but as I looked straight at him and assessed his ugly nature, I burst into yells. "I didn't! I didn't!" I gasped, between screams. Uncle Myers shot a vindictive look at his wife, as though he well understood that there had been collusion between us. He ordered me back to the dark lavatory and symbolically rolled up his sleeve. He laid on the strop decisively, but this time I was beside myself, and when Aunt Margaret hurried in and tried to reason with me, I could only answer with wild cries as Uncle Myers, gasping also, put the strop back on its hook. "You take her," he articulated, but Aunt Margaret's hairbrush this time was perfunctory, after the first few angry blows that punished me for having disobeyed her. Myers did not take up the strop again; the whipping ended, whether from fear of the neighbors or of Aunt Mary's frail presence upstairs or sudden guilty terror, I do not know; perhaps simply because it was past my bedtime.

I finally limped up to bed, with a crazy sense of inner victory, like a saint's, for I had not recanted, despite all they had done or could do to me. It did not occur to me that I had been unchristian in refusing to answer a plea from Aunt Margaret's heart and conscience. Indeed, I rejoiced in the knowledge that I had *made* her continue to beat me long after she must have known that I was innocent; this was her punishment for her condonation of Myers. The next morning, when I opened my eyes on the Murillo Madonna and the Baby Stuart, my feeling of triumph abated; I was afraid of what I had done. But throughout that day and the next, they did not touch me. I walked on air, incredulously and, no doubt, somewhat pompously, seeing myself as a figure from legend: my strength was *as* the strength of ten because my *heart* was pure! Afterward, I was beaten, in the normal routine way, but the question of the butterfly was closed forever in that house.

In my mind, there was, and still is, a connection between the butterfly and our rescue, by our Protestant grandfather, which took place the following year, in the fall or early winter. Already defeated, in their own view, or having ceased to care what became of us, our guardians, for the first time, permitted two of us, my brother Kevin and me, to be alone with this strict, kindly lawyer,

as we walked the two blocks between our house and our grandfather McCarthy's. In the course of our walk, between the walls
of an early snow, we told Grandpa Preston everything, over-
coming our fears and fixing our minds on the dolls, the baseball
gloves, and the watches. Yet, as it happened, curiously enough,
albeit with a certain aptness, it was not the tale of the butterfly
or the other atrocities that chiefly impressed him as he followed
our narration with precise legal eyes but the fact that I was not
wearing my glasses. I was being punished for breaking them in a
fall on the school playground by having to go without; and I
could not see why my account of this should make him flush up
with anger—to me it was a great relief to be free of those disfiguring things. But he shifted his long, lantern jaw and, settling
our hands in his, went straight as a writ up my grandfather Mc-
Carthy's front walk. Hence it was on a question of health that
this good American's alarms finally alighted; the rest of what we
poured out to him he either did not believe or feared to think of,
lest he have to deal with the problem of evil.

On health grounds, then, we were separated from Uncle Myers,
who disappeared back into Elkhart with his wife and Aunt Mary.
My brothers were sent off to the sisters in a Catholic boarding
school, with the exception of Sheridan, whom Myers was permitted to bear away with him, like a golden trophy. Sheridan's stay,
however, was of short duration. Very soon, Aunt Mary died,
followed by Aunt Margaret, followed by Uncle Myers; within
five years, still in the prime of life, they were all gone, one, two,
three, like ninepins. For me, a new life began, under a happier
star. Within a few weeks after my Protestant grandfather's visit,
I was sitting in a compartment with him on the train, watching
the Missouri River go westward to its source, wearing my white-
gold wrist watch and a garish new red hat, a highly nervous
child, fanatical against Protestants, who, I explained to Grandpa

Preston, all deserved to be burned at the stake. In the dining car, I ordered greedily, lamb chops, pancakes, sausages, and then sat, unable to eat them. "Her eyes," observed the waiter, "are bigger than her stomach."

Six or seven years later, on one of my trips east to college, I stopped in Minneapolis to see my brothers, who were all together now, under the roof of a new and more indulgent guardian, my uncle Louis, the handsomest and youngest of the McCarthy uncles. All the old people were dead; my grandmother McCarthy, but recently passed away, had left a fund to erect a chapel in her name in Texas, a state with which she had no known connection. Sitting in the twilight of my uncle Louis' screened porch, we sought a common ground for our reunion and found it in Uncle Myers. It was then that my brother Preston told me that on the famous night of the butterfly, he had seen Uncle Myers steal into the dining room from the den and lift the tablecloth, with the tin butterfly in his hand.

Uncle Harry tells me that twice in my father's diary, on February 28 and November 7, 1916, the single word, "butterfly," is written over a whole page. Like most of Uncle Harry's contributions, this gave me quite a jar. Inexplicable, I thought, until I remembered that my father, as a boy, collected butterflies. My grandmother had a case of his specimens. That is the only light I can throw on the notation.

As for Uncle Myers, Uncle Harry writes that this "mountain of blubber" claimed to have been a pickle-buyer around Terre Haute, Indiana. I never heard of his being a pickle-buyer, but it goes with him, certainly. On the other hand, those trays of candy did have a professional look. My feeling is that he had not worked at anything since marrying my aunt. According to Uncle Harry, the family firm gave Uncle Myers a job, soliciting grain shipments on the road, with a salary of $250 a month, mileage books, and an expense account. The job was supposed to keep him in western South Dakota, North Dakota, and eastern Montana, where living was cheap. His expense accounts—lunch checks of three and four dollars on transcontinental trains—were a stunner to Uncle Harry, who had thought up the idea of sending him into this semi-arid territory.

If he was on the road, how can he have been at home all the time? I cannot reconcile this, and Uncle Harry's suggestion— that there might have been two of him—does not really help. He was at home all the time, my brother Kevin agrees. The only exception was a short period when he had jury duty, he used to leave the house in the mornings then, wearing a black bowler hat. I like to think of Uncle Myers as a juror. Kevin believes he may have gone away once on a brief trip—to Elkhart, we would have thought. But this may have represented the time of his employ- ment with the Capital Elevator Company, for I cannot suppose that the firm kept him on very long.

Kevin adds a note about Uncle Myers and ball games. With my little brothers, Uncle Myers used to stand outside the ball park until the seventh-inning stretch, when the bleachers were thrown open and anyone could come in, free. Thus they saw only the ends of ball games, as we saw only the beginnings of movies. There was a superb consistency in our life, like that of a work of art. That is why even I find it sometimes incredible. A small correction, however, is necessary: I did once see a full-length feature. It was in the church basement or school auditorium, and the name of the film was The Seal of the Confessional. *I recall a scene in which an atheist who defied God was struck by lightning. Naturally, it was free.*

About the tin butterfly episode, I must make a more serious correction or at least express a doubt. An awful suspicion oc- curred to me as I was reading it over the other day. I suddenly remembered that in college I had started writing a play on this subject. Could the idea that Uncle Myers put the butterfly at my place have been suggested to me by my teacher? I can almost hear her voice saying to me, excitedly: "Your uncle must have done it!" (She was Mrs. Hallie Flanagan, later head of the Federal Theatre.) And I can visualize a stage scene, with Uncle Myers tiptoeing in and pinning the butterfly to the silence pad. After a struggle with my conscience (the first Communion again), I sent for Kevin and consulted him about my doubts. He remembers the butterfly episode itself and the terrible whipping; he remembers the scene on Uncle Louis' screened porch when we four, reunited, talked about Uncle Myers. But he does not remember Preston's saying that Uncle Myers put the butterfly there. Preston, consulted by long-distance telephone, does not remember either saying it or seeing it. (He cannot have been more than seven when the incident happened and would be unlikely, therefore, to have preserved such a clear and dramatic recollection.) It still seems to me certain that we at least discussed the butterfly affair on Uncle Louis' porch, and I may have put forward Mrs. Flanagan's theory, to which Preston may have agreed, warmly. He may even, says Kevin, have thought, for the moment, he remembered, once the idea was suggested to him. But this is all conjecture, I do not know, really, whether I took the course in Playwriting before or after the night on Uncle Louis' porch. The most likely thing, I fear, is that I fused two memories. Mea culpa. The play, by the way, was never finished. I did not get beyond the first act, which was set in my grandmother's sun parlor and showed our first meeting with our guardians. It was thinking about that meeting, obviously, that nagged me into remembering Mrs. Flanagan and the play. But who did put the butterfly by my place? It may have been Uncle Myers after all. Even if no one saw him, he remains a suspect: he had motive and opportunity. "I'll bet your uncle did it!"—was that what she said?

It was fall or early winter, I wrote, when my grandfather Preston arrived from Seattle and listened to our tale. Kevin thinks it was spring. We both remember the snow. Probably he is right, for he recalls a sequel to this story that took place in summer, after I had gone and the household had been broken up. He and Preston were taken, temporarily, to stay at my grandmother McCarthy's house. For the first time, they enjoyed the freedom of the streets; up to then, we had all been kept behind our iron fence. He and Preston borrowed a wagon from a neighbor girl named Nancy and rode up and down Blaisdell Avenue, past the house we had lived in. To their surprise, Uncle Myers was still there, sitting on the front porch with Sheridan on his lap. The two little boys rode the borrowed wagon along the sidewalk on the other side of the street, screaming names and taunts at Uncle Myers, reveling like demons in their freedom and his powerlessness to harm them: "Yah, yah, yah!" Uncle Myers made no response; he simply sat there, a passive target, with Sheridan on his knee. No doubt, all the neighbors were watching. For Kevin, as he tells it, Uncle Myers' helplessness slowly took the pleasure out of this victory parade; he felt embarrassed for the motionless fat man and drove the wagon away.

A few days later, they went past the house again. It was empty. Something tempted them to try to get in, and they climbed through a basement window that was open. The house looked very strange; all the furniture had been removed. Suddenly, a fury seized them; they began ripping off the wallpaper—the wallpaper we had been punished for spoiling. They tore it off in strips and then they flung open the medicine cabinet. Someone had forgotten to empty it, and all the family medicines were there, together with an empty jar of Aunt Mary's beef tea. They threw the medicine bottles at the walls, smashing them; a horrible orange color—the prevailing tone of the medicines—was splattered over everything. They were revenging themselves on the house. After they had wrecked it to the limit of their powers, they climbed out through the basement window.

When what they had done was discovered, my grandmother

undertook to punish Kevin. She spanked him, in her bathroom, with her hairbrush, pulling him firmly over her knee. It interested him to find that her spanking did not hurt. Prone in her grasp, he howled dutifully, but inwardly he was smiling at her efforts. He thought of Aunt Margaret's hairbrush and Uncle Myers' razor strop and felt a tenderness for my grandmother—the tenderness of experience toward innocence. That fall, he and Preston were sent to St. Benedict's Academy, after a summer stay at Captain Billy Fawcett's Breezy Point.

A final note on Aunt Margaret's health regimen. I have a perfect digestion and very good health, I suppose I owe it to Aunt Margaret. It is true that we children were sick a great deal before we came to her, and no doubt she hardened us with her prunes and parsnips and no pillow and five-mile hikes. Kevin used to have two snapshots, one taken by Aunt Margaret and one by Uncle Myers, they were inscribed "Before the Five Mile Hike" and "After the Five Mile Hike." The one showing Uncle Myers, in a cap, has mysteriously disappeared during the last year or so. My brother Preston thought he had a photo of him, but that, too, is gone. It is as if Uncle Myers himself had contrived to filch away the proof that he had existed corporeally.

One of the family photographs that has recently come to light shows the four of us children, looking very happy, with a pony on which Preston and Sheridan are sitting. We are all dressed up, I am not wearing my glasses, and my straight hair is softly curled. That pony was a stage prop. He used to be led up and down our street by an itinerant photographer, soliciting trade. The photograph, of course, was sent out west to the Preston family, who were in no position to know that this was the only time we had ever been close to a pony. It was found among my grandmother Preston's effects.

I should have supposed that Uncle Myers and Aunt Margaret were unusual, even unique people. But I had a letter from a reader in Chicago who told me that Myers was so like his father that he was tempted to believe in reincarnation. And Aunt Margaret's regimen was almost precisely that followed in this reader's household fifteen years later: the same menus, with the addition of codfish balls, the same prolonged sessions on "the throne," the same turning over of the mattress to make sure it had not been wet, the same putting away of presents on the grounds that they were "much too good." There was the razor strop, too, and the dream of being admitted to an orphan asylum, and the threat that some other members of the family (possibly Protestants) would "make you toe the chalk line." This man and his sister had lost only their mother, the neighbors used to feed them, too.

Even more curious was a letter from Australia from a woman of sixty, telling me that reading "Yonder Peasant" had been "probably the most uncanny experience" of her life. She and her four brothers and sisters had lost both their parents, and their childhood, she said, was an almost complete replica of mine. "Had I your gift of writing . . . I should have written long ago, and written a story that would have been disbelieved, because it would have been so unbelievable—and yet every word of it would have been starkly true. That was why I read and reread your article which . . . was so like our experience . . . that it seemed I was writing and not you."

This woman had been born a Catholic, like the man in Chicago. Her father had married a Protestant.

The Blackguard

WERE HE LIVING today, my Protestant grandfather would be displeased to hear that the fate of his soul had once been the occasion of intense theological anxiety with the Ladies of the Sacred Heart. While his mortal part, all unaware, went about its eighteen holes of golf, its rubber of bridge before dinner at the club, his immortal part lay in jeopardy with us, the nuns and pupils of a strict convent school set on a wooded hill quite near a piece of worthless real estate he had bought under the impression that Seattle was expanding in a northerly direction. A sermon delivered at the convent by an enthusiastic Jesuit had disclosed to us his danger. Up to this point, the disparity in religion between my grandfather and myself had given me no serious concern. The death of my parents, while it had drawn us together in many senses, including the legal one (for I became his ward), had at the same time left the gulf of a generation between us, and my grandfather's Protestantism presented itself as a natural part of the grand, granite scenery on the other side. But the Jesuit's sermon destroyed this ordered view in a single thunderclap of doctrine.

As the priest would have it, this honest and upright man, a great favorite with the Mother Superior, was condemned to eternal torment by the accident of having been baptized. Had he been a Mohammedan, a Jew, a pagan, or the child of civilized unbelievers, a place in Limbo would have been assured him; Cicero and Aristotle and Cyrus the Persian might have been his companions, and the harmless souls of unbaptized children might have frolicked about his feet. But if the Jesuit were right, all baptized Protestants went straight to Hell. A good life did not count in their favor. The baptismal rite, by conferring on them God's grace, made them also liable to His organizational displeasure. That is, baptism turned them Catholic whether they liked it or not, and their persistence in the Protestant ritual was a kind of asseverated apostasy. Thus my poor grandfather, sixty years behind in his Easter duty, actually reduced his prospects of salvation every time he sat down in the Presbyterian church.

The Mother Superior's sweet frown acknowledged me, an hour after the sermon, as I curtsied, all agitation, in her office doorway. Plainly, she had been expecting me. Madame MacIllvra, an able administrator, must have been resignedly ticking off the names of the Protestant pupils and parents all during the concluding parts of the morning's service. She had a faint worried air, when the conversation began, of depreciating the sermon: doctrinally, perhaps, correct, it had been wanting in delicacy; the fiery Jesuit, a missionary celebrity, had lived too long among the Eskimos. This disengaged attitude encouraged me to hope. Surely this lady, the highest authority I knew, could find a way out for my grandfather. She could see that he was a special case, outside the brutal rule of thumb laid down by the Jesuit. It was she, after all, in the convent, from whom all exemptions flowed, who created arbitrary holidays (called *congés* by the order's French tradition); it was she who permitted us to get forbidden books from the librarian and occasionally to receive letters unread by the convent censor. (As a rule, all slang expressions, violations of syntax, errors of spelling, as well as improper sentiments, were blacked out of our friends' communications, so unless we moved in a circle of young Addisons or Burkes, the letters we longed for came to us as fragments from which the original text could only be conjectured.) To my twelve-year-old mind, it appeared probable that Madame MacIllvra, our Mother Superior, had the power to give my grandfather *congé*, and I threw myself on her sympathies.

How could it be that my grandfather, the most virtuous person I knew, whose name was a byword among his friends and colleagues for a kind of rigid and fantastic probity—how could it be that this man should be lost, while I, the object of his admonition, the despair of his example—I, who yielded to every impulse, lied, boasted, betrayed—should, by virtue of regular attendance at the sacraments and the habit of easy penitence, be saved?

Madame MacIllvra's full white brow wrinkled; her childlike blue eyes clouded. Like many headmistresses, she loved a good cry, and she clasped me to her plump, quivering, middle-aged bosom. She understood; she was crying for my grandfather and the injustice of it too. She and my grandfather had, as a matter of fact, established a very amiable relation, in which both took pleasure. The masculine line and firmness of his character made an aesthetic appeal to her, and the billowy softness and depth of the Mother Superior struck him favorably, but, above all, it was their difference in religion that salted their conversations. Each of them enjoyed, whenever they met in her straight, black-and-white little office, a sense of broadness, of enlightenment, of transcendent superiority to petty prejudice. My grandfather would remember that he wrote a check every Christmas for two Sisters of Charity who visited his office; Madame MacIllvra would perhaps recall her graduate studies and Hume. They had long, liberal talks which had the tone of *performances*; virtuoso feats of magnanimity were achieved on both sides. Afterward, they spoke of each other in nearly identical terms: "A very fine woman," "A very fine man."

All this (and possibly the suspicion that her verdict might be repeated at home) made Madame MacIllvra's answer slow. "Perhaps God," she murmured at last, "in His infinite mercy . . ." Yet this formulation satisfied neither of us. God's infinite mercy we believed in, but its manifestations were problematical. Sacred history showed us that it was more likely to fall on the Good Thief or the Woman Taken in Adultery than on persons of daily virtue and regular habits, like my grandfather. Our Catholic thoughts journeyed and met in a glance of alarmed recognition. Madame MacIllvra pondered. There were, of course, she said finally, other loopholes. If he had been improperly baptized . . . a careless clergyman . . . I considered this suggestion and shook my head. My grandfather was not the kind of man who, even as an infant, would have been guilty of a slovenly baptism.

It was a measure of Madame MacIllvra's intelligence, or of her knowledge of the world, that she did not, even then, when my grandfather's soul hung, as it were, pleadingly between us, suggest the obvious, the orthodox solution. It would have been ridiculous for me to try to convert my grandfather. Indeed, as it turned out later, I might have dropped him into the pit with my innocent traps (the religious books left open beside his cigar cutter, or "Grandpa, won't you take me to Mass this Sunday? I am so tired of going alone"). "Pray for him, my dear," said Madame MacIllvra, sighing, "and I will speak to Madame Barclay. The point may be open to interpretation. She may remember something in the Fathers of the Church. . . ."

A few days later, Madame MacIllvra summoned me to her office. Not only Madame Barclay, the learned prefect of studies, but the librarian and even the convent chaplain had been called in. The Benedictine view, it seemed, differed sharply from the Dominican, but a key passage in Saint Athanasius seemed to point to my grandfather's safety. The unbeliever, according to this generous authority, was not to be damned unless he rejected the true Church with sufficient knowledge and full consent of the will. Madame MacIllvra handed me the book, and I read the passage over. Clearly, he was saved. Sufficient knowledge he had not. The Church was foreign to him; he knew it only distantly, only by repute, like the heathen Hiawatha, who had heard strange stories of missionaries, white men in black robes who bore a Cross. Flinging my arms about Madame MacIllvra, I blessed for the first time the insularity of my grandfather's character, the long-jawed, shut face it turned toward ideas and customs not its own. I resolved to dismantle at once the little altar in my bedroom at home, to leave off grace before meals, elaborate fasting, and all ostentatious practices of devotion, lest the light of my example shine upon him too powerfully and burn him with sufficient knowledge to a crisp.

Since I was a five-day boarder, this project had no time to grow stale, and the next Sunday, at home, my grandfather remarked on the change in me, which my feeling for the dramatic had made far from unobtrusive. "I hope," he said in a rather stern and ironical voice, "that you aren't using the *irreligious* atmosphere of this house as an excuse for backsliding. There will be time enough when you are older to change your beliefs if you want to." The unfairness of this rebuke delighted me. It put me solidly in the tradition of the saints and martyrs; Our Lord had known something like it, and so had Elsie Dinsmore at the piano. Nevertheless, I felt quite angry and slammed the door of my room behind me as I went in to sulk. I almost wished that my grandfather would die at once, so that God could furnish him with the explanation of my behavior—certainly he would have to wait till the next life to get it; in this one he would only have seen in it an invasion of his personal liberties.

As though to reward me for my silence, the following Wednesday brought me the happiest moment of my life. In order to understand my happiness, which might otherwise seem perverse, the reader must yield himself to the spiritual atmosphere of the convent. If he imagines that the life we led behind those walls was bare, thin, cold, austere, sectarian, he will have to revise his views; our days were a tumult of emotion. In the first place, we ate, studied, and slept in that atmosphere of intrigue, rivalry, scandal, favoritism, tyranny, and revolt that is common to all girls' boarding schools and that makes "real" life afterward seem a long and improbable armistice, a cessation of the true anguish of activity. But above the tinkling of this girlish operetta, with its clink-clink of changing friendships, its plot of smuggled letters, notes passed from desk to desk, secrets, there sounded in the Sacred Heart convent heavier, more solemn strains, notes of a great religious drama, which was also all passion and caprice, in which salvation was the issue and God's rather sultanlike and elusive favor was besought, scorned, despaired of, connived for, importuned. It was the paradoxical element in Catholic doctrine that lent this drama its suspense. The Divine Despot we courted could not be bought, like a piece of merchandise, by long hours at the *prie-dieu*, faithful attendance at the sacraments, obedience, reverence toward one's superiors. These solicitations helped, but it might well turn out that the worst girl in the school, whose pretty, haughty face wore rouge and a calm, closed look that advertised even to us younger ones some secret knowledge of men, was in the dark of her heart another Mary of Egypt, the strumpet saint in our midst. Such notions furnished a strange counterpoint to discipline; surely the Mother Superior never could have expelled a girl without recalling, with a shade of perplexity, the profligate youth of Saint Augustine and of Saint Ignatius of Loyola.

This dark-horse doctrine of salvation, with all its worldly wisdom and riddling charm, was deep in the idiom of the convent. The merest lay sister could have sustained with spiritual poise her end of a conversation on the purification through sin with Mr. Auden, Herr Kafka, or *Gospodin* Dostoevski; and Madame MacIllvra, while she would have held it bad taste to bow down, like Father Zossima, before the murder in Dmitri Karamazov's heart, would certainly have had him in for a series of long, interesting talks in her office.

Like all truly intellectual women, these were in spirit romantic desperadoes. They despised organizational heretics of the stamp of Luther and Calvin, but the great atheists and sinners were the heroes of the costume picture they taught as a subject called history. Marlowe, Baudelaire—above all, Byron—glowed like terrible stars above their literature courses. Little girls of ten were reciting "The Prisoner of Chillon" and hearing stories of Claire Clairmont, Caroline Lamb, the Segatti, and the swim across the Hellespont. Even M. Voltaire enjoyed a left-handed popularity. The nuns spoke of him with horror and admiration mingled: "A great mind, an unconquerable spirit—and what fearful use they were put to." In Rousseau, an unbuttoned, middle-class figure, they had no interest whatever.

These infatuations, shared by the pupils, were brought into line with official Catholic opinion by a variety of stratagems. The more highly educated nuns were able to accept the damnation of these great Luciferian spirits. A simple young nun, on the other hand, who played baseball and taught arithmetic to the sixth and seventh grades, used to tell her pupils that she personally was convinced that Lord Byron in his last hours must have made an act of contrition.

It was not, therefore, unusual that a line from the works of this dissipated author should have been waiting for us on the black-board of the eighth-grade rhetoric classroom when we filed in that Wednesday morning which remains still memorable to me. "*Zoe mou, sas agapo*": the words of Byron's last assurance to the Maid of Athens stood there in Madame Barclay's French-looking script, speaking to us of the transiency of the passions. To me, as it happened, it spoke a twice-told tale. I had read the poem before, alone in my grandfather's library; indeed, I knew it by heart, and I rather resented the infringement on my private rights in it, the democratization of the poem which was about to take place. Soon, Madame Barclay's pointer was rapping from word to word: "My . . . life . . . I . . . love . . . you," she sharply translated. When the pointer started back for its second trip, I retreated into hauteur and began drawing a picture of the girl who sat next to me. Suddenly the pointer cracked across my writing tablet.

"You're just like Lord Byron, brilliant but unsound."

I heard the pointer being set down and the drawing being torn crisply twice across, but I could not look up. I had never felt so flattered in my life. Throughout the rest of the class, I sat motion-less, simulating meekness, while my classmates shot me glances of wonder, awe, and congratulation, as though I had suddenly been struck by a remarkable disease, or been canonized, or trans-figured. Madame Barclay's pronouncement, which I kept repeat-ing to myself under my breath, had for us girls a kind of final and majestic certainty. She was the severest and most taciturn of our teachers. Her dark brows met in the middle; her skin was a pure olive; her upper lip had a faint mustache; she was the iron and authority of the convent. She tolerated no infractions, overlooked nothing, was utterly and obdurately fair, had no favorites; but her rather pointed face had the marks of suffering, as though her famous discipline had scored it as harshly as one of our papers. She had a bitter and sarcastic wit, and had studied, it was said, at the Sorbonne. Before this day, I had once or twice dared to say to myself that Madame Barclay liked me. Her dark, quite handsome eyes would sometimes move in my direction as her lips prepared an aphorism or a satiric gibe. Yet hardly had I estimated the look, weighed and measured it to store it away in my memory book of requited affections, when a stinging penalty would recall me from my dream and I could no longer be sure. Now, however, there was no doubt left. The reproof was a declaration of love as plain as the sentence on the blackboard, which shimmered slightly before my eyes. My happiness was a confused exaltation in which the fact that I was Lord Byron and the fact that I was loved by Madame Barclay, the most puzzling nun in the convent, blended in a Don Juanesque triumph.

In the refectory that noon, publicity was not wanting to enrich this moment. Insatiable, I could hardly wait for the week end, to take Madame Barclay's words home as though they had been a prize. With the generosity of affluence, I spoke to myself of sharing this happiness, this honor, with my grandfather. Surely, *this* would make up to him for any worry or difficulty I had caused him. At the same time, it would have the practical effect of explaining me a little to him. Phrases about my prototype rang in my head: "that unfortunate genius," "that turbulent soul," "that gifted and erratic nature."

My grandfather turned dark red when he heard the news. His forehead grew knotty with veins; he swore; he looked strange and young; it was the first time I had ever seen him angry. Argument and explanation were useless. For my grandfather, history had interposed no distance between Lord Byron and himself. Though the incestuous poet had died forty years before my grandfather was born, the romantic perspective was lacking. That

insularity of my grandfather's that kept him intimate with morals
and denied the reality of the exotic made him judge the poet as
he judged himself or one of his neighbors—that is, on the merit of
his actions. He was on the telephone at once, asking the Mother
Superior in a thundering, courtroom voice what right one of her
sisters had to associate his innocent granddaughter with that de-
generate blackguard, Byron. On Monday, Madame Barclay, with
tight-drawn lips, told her class that she had a correction to make:
Mary McCarthy did not resemble Lord Byron in any particular;
she was neither brilliant, loose-living, nor unsound.

The interviews between my grandfather and Madame Mac-
Illvra came to an end. To that remarkable marriage of minds the
impediment had at last been discovered. But from this time on,
Madame Barclay's marks of favor to me grew steadily more distinct, while the look of suffering tightened on her face, till some
said she had cancer (a theory supported by the yellowness of her
skin) and some said she was being poisoned by an antipathy to
the Mother Superior.

This account is highly fictionalized. A Jesuit did preach such a sermon, and I really became concerned for my grandfather's soul, I was still very devout, in a childish way, and extremely suggestible. I suppose I was still "nervous" as a result of my Minneapolis experiences. I did take the problem to the Acting Mother Superior, who was finally able to reassure me with the promise that my grandfather could be saved if he did not know the Catholic Church was the true Church. This was "invincible ignorance." The nun I call Madame Barclay did tell me I was like Byron, brilliant but unsound. But what provoked her to say it, I don't remember. And I did tell my grandfather, and he did demand an apology from the Acting Mother Superior, which made me utterly furious. In short, the story is true in substance, but the details have been invented or guessed at.

"My grandfather," I say, "reduced his prospects of salvation every time he sat down in the Presbyterian church." He cannot have reduced them very greatly, since I do not recall his ever attending church, except for weddings and funerals. But when I asked him what his religion was, he said he was a Presbyterian. I was the only churchgoer in the family, every Sunday the car took me to Mass and brought me home again. When I left Minneapolis, my grandmother McCarthy had supplied me with some works of Catholic propaganda which she instructed me to leave about the house, in the hope of effecting a conversion. But I soon saw this was out of the question. The reader may wonder why the priest's sermon did not cause me to worry about my grandmother Preston, too. The answer is simple, she was Jewish. In other words, she had not been baptized.

This technical point about baptism was what I had seized on in the priest's sermon. Possibly he had touched only incidentally on Protestants, but in doing so he had riveted my attention. His theme may have been that the sacrament of Baptism was at once wonderful and dangerous, it conferred duties as well as privileges. Only a baptized person could be saved, but if such a person (e.g., a Protestant) refused to avail himself of the grace conferred by the sacrament, he could be damned simply for that. I knew, of course, that anyone—i.e., anyone who had been baptized—could be saved, no matter what he had done or left undone, by reciting an Act of Contrition in his last moments. But my grandfather did not know the Act of Contrition: "Oh, my God, I am heartily sorry for having offended Thee, through my fault, through my fault, through my most grievous fault . . ."

True repentance would doubtless have suffed, but as a child I thought you would have to start saying the Act itself as rapidly as possible if you were hit, say, by an automobile while in a state of mortal sin. Great stress was laid on the prescribed forms by the priests and nuns who taught us. I speak of "an improper baptism." We had been studying about this in our Catechism class. Baptism was the only sacrament that could be administered by a lay person, could be administered, in fact, by anyone, providing it was done correctly and that the person had the intention to baptize. (You could not be baptized accidentally.) But if a mistake were made, if the prescribed form were not followed, the baptism did not "take." Thus not all Protestant baptisms were recognized by the Church. I have forgotten many of the finer points, but I know it was essential to use water (ice would not do), and I remember our taking up such curiously hypothetical questions as: "If a Mohammedan administered baptism would it be valid?" The answer, I believe, would be: "Yes, providing it was done correctly, and that the Mohammedan had the intention of baptizing."

In the Catholic Church, even the most remote eventualities are discussed with pedantic literalness. The question of what happens in the hereafter to Protestants who have lived a good life has been a common subject of debate in the Church, and different answers have been accepted as authoritative at different times and places. "Extra ecclesiam, nulla salus"—this was the Jesuit's position, which was orthodox enough at the time, though it was not the only position that a priest in good standing could take. Not long ago, Father Feeney and a small circle of Boston Catholics were excommunicated for preaching that there was no salvation outside the Church; their reply was that it was they who were orthodox and that those who condemned them were in error. In recent years, and in Protestant countries, the Church has pulled in its horns. But in Spain, if I am not mistaken, "extra ecclesiam, nulla salus," would be the accepted belief. Many Catholics have written to protest that such a sermon as I have described could not have been preached, I agree that it could not be preached here today— not since the Father Feeney case brought matters to a head. An American priest, however, would still be free to believe privately that Protestants are damned, good and bad alike.

As it happens, I remember the missionary priest very well because, before he went to work among the Eskimos, he had been the popular pastor of the white frame church I had gone to as a little girl, before the death of my parents. He was a very handsome, dark, greying man, who must have been about forty when he came to talk to us in the convent. I recall feeling that he had grown much rougher and blunter during his stay in the North. A priest like that blew into our convent like a rude wind. At some point, he preached a retreat for us. He was a forceful speaker, and he had the power, common to retreat preachers, of making his audience feel uneasy. Every word he uttered seemed to apply to me personally.

Toward the end of the retreat, he delivered us a sermon on unchastity that transfixed me in my seat; afterward, as I recall it, he offered to hear the confessions of any who were in special need. I signed up, or lined up, to confess to him; the sermon had made it clear to me (what I had not guessed before) that my soul was in a precarious state. This is the only one of all the confessions I made that I can remember almost verbatim. I knelt down in the confessional trembling with fear. "Father, I have committed a sin of impurity." "How many times?" Three times, five times, I have forgotten the exact figure. "Was it with a boy?" This question startled me. "Oh, no, Father." "Was it with yourself or with another girl?" "Both, Father." The priest made a noise that sounded like a click of satisfaction. Then he settled back to draw out of me the details of what I had done, but I was so mortified that my admissions came very slowly. I had been looking up words like "breast" in the big school dictionary and in a medical book at home and discussing them with my fellow pupils. "You looked up these words in a book, you say, and talked to other girls about them?" "Yes, Father." "Is that all?" His voice sounded positively indignant. "Yes, Father." "You mean to tell me that this is your only sin of impurity?" "Yes." Before I knew it, he had pronounced absolution, and the door of the confessional grate was shut almost with a bang, as though I had been imposing on his valuable time. This experience mystified and annoyed me, all through his sermon he had been dwelling on the terrible offense given to God by an impure thought. And what was it that he supposed I might have done with a boy? Or with myself or another girl, beyond what I had confessed? My curiosity was awakened.

I must have been eleven at this time, and I now think I was eleven, not twelve, at the time of "The Blackguard." In the next chapter, I am a year older, by the calendar, and though I am still suggestible, I have begun to exploit this quality and play, deliberately, to the gallery.

C'est le Premier Pas Qui Coûte

Like the jesuits, to whom they stand as nieces, the Ladies of the Sacred Heart are a highly centralized order, versed in clockwork obedience to authority. Their institutions follow a pattern laid down for them in France in the early nineteenth century—clipped and pollarded as a garden and stately as a minuet. All Sacred Heart convent schools are the same—the same blue serge dresses, usually, with white collars and cuffs, the same blue and green and pink moire ribbons awarded for good conduct, the same books given as prizes on Prize Day, the same recitation of "Lepanto" by an English actor in a piped vest, the same *congés*, or holidays, announced by the *Mère Supérieure*, the same game of *cache-cache*, or hide-and-seek, played on these traditional feast days, the same *goûter*, or tea, the same retreats and sermons, the same curtsies dipped in the hall, the same early-morning chapel with processions of girls, like widowed queens, in sad black-net veils, the same *prie-dieu*, the same French hymns (*"Oui, je le crois"*), the same glorious white-net veils and flowers and gold vessels on Easter and Holy Thursday and on feasts peculiar to the order. In the year I came to the Seattle *Mesdames*, at four o'clock on any weekday afternoon in Roscrea, Ireland, or Roehampton, England, or Menlo Park, California, the same tiny old whiskered nun was reading, no doubt, from *Emma* or *A Tale of Two Cities* to a long table of girls stitching French seams or embroidering bureau scarves with wreaths of flowers. "Charles Evrémonde, called Darnay!"—the red-rimmed old black eye leveled and raked us all, summarily, with the grapeshot of the Terror.

I was eleven years old, a seventh-grader, when I was first shown into the big study hall in Forest Ridge Convent and issued my soap dish, my veil, and my napkin ring. The sound of the French words awed me, the luster of the wide moire ribbons cutting, military-wise, across young bosoms, the curtained beds in the dormitories, the soft step of the girls, the curtsies to the floor, the white hands of the music master (a Swedish baron in spats), the cricket played in the playground, the wooden rattle of the *surveillante's* clapper. I could not get used to the idea that here were nuns who did not lose their surnames, as all normal nuns did, becoming Sister Mary Aloysia or Sister Josepha, but were called Madame Barclay or Madame Slattery, or *Ma Mère* or Mother for short. They were not *ordinary* nuns, it was scornfully explained to me, but women of good family, cloistered ladies of the world, just as Sacred Heart girls were not *ordinary* Catholics but daughters of the best families. And my new subjects were not ordinary subjects, like spelling and arithmetic, but rhetoric, French, literature, Christian doctrine, English history. I was fresh from a Minneapolis parochial school, where a crude "citizenship" had been the rule, where we pledged allegiance to the flag every morning, warbled "My Country, 'Tis of Thee," said "grievious" instead of "grievous," competed in paper drives and citywide spelling contests, drew hatchets for Washington's Birthday and log cabins for Lincoln's, gave to foreign missions for our brown and yellow brothers, feared the Ku Klux Klan, sold chances and subscriptions to periodicals, were taken on tours of flour mills and water works; I looked upon my religion as a branch of civics and conformity, and the select Sacred Heart atmosphere took my breath away. The very austerities of our life had a mysterious aristocratic punctilio: the rule of silence so often clapped down on us at mealtimes, the pitcher of water and the bowl for washing at our bedsides, the supervised Saturday-night bath in the cold bathroom, with a red-faced nun sitting on a stool behind a drawn curtain with our bath towel in her lap. I felt as though I stood on the outskirts and observed the ritual of a cult, a cult of fashion and elegance in the sphere of religion.

And, thanks to the standardization of an archaic rule, the past still vibrated in the convent, a high, sweet note. It was the France of the Restoration that was embalmed in the Sacred Heart atmosphere, like a period room in a museum with a silken cord drawn across it. The quarrels of the *philosophes* still echoed in the classrooms; the tumbrils had just ceased to creak, and Voltaire grinned in the background. Orthodoxy had been re-established, Louis XVIII ruled, but there was a hint of Orleanism in the air and a whisper of reduced circumstances in the pick-pick of our needles doing fine darning and turning buttonholes. Byron's great star had risen, and, across the sea, America beckoned in the romances of Chateaubriand and Fenimore Cooper and the adventures of the *coureurs de bois*. Protestantism did not trouble us; we had made our peace with the Huguenots. What we feared was skepticism, deism, and the dread spirit of atheism—France's Lucifer. Monthly, in the study hall, the Mother Superior, Madame Mac-Illvra, adjured us, daughters of dentists and lawyers, grocers and realtors, heiresses of the Chevrolet agency and of Riley & Finn, contractors, against the sin of doubt, that curse of fine intellects. Her blue eyes clouded and her fair white brow ruffled under her snowy coif as she considered, with true feminine sympathy, the awful fate of Shelley, a young man of good family who had contracted atheism at Oxford.

These discourses of Madame MacIllvra's fascinated me, peopling the world with new characters and a new sort of hero-villain, alone, noble, bereft; I watched the surge and billow of her bosom, and pulsed with pity and terror. During that first year, I was very unhappy in the convent, or, to be more accurate, I felt like a lorn new soul come to Paradise, elated and charmed by what I saw— by the ranging hierarchies, the thrones and dominions—but unable to get a nod from any of the angels as they brushed by me on errands of bliss. As a revelation of the aristocratic principle, the convent overwhelmed me. The beauty and poise of the middling and older girls were like nothing I had seen on earth. If not like angels, they were like the kings' paramours I had read about in history or like Olympian goddesses, tall and swift of tread. Each of these paragons moved in an aureole of mysterious self-sufficiency; each had her pledged admirers among the younger and plainer girls, and disputes about them raged among us as though someone had thrown the apple of discord. In the intensity of the convent light, even a rather ordinary girl could acquire this penumbra of beauty, by gravity and dignity of person; it was a sort of calling, a still hearkening to inward voices, which brought a secret, cool smile to the lips of the one elected.

From the first, of course, I longed to become a member of this exquisite company, if only as a favored satellite or maid-in-waiting. But instead I stepped straight into that fatality that in every school awaits the newcomer who has not learned the first law of social dynamics: be suspicious of tenders of assistance. Around me, from the very first day, as I arranged my books in my desk, circled the rusty rejects of the school system, hungry as crows for friendship, copious with invitations, pointers, and sweets from home to be shared. Every school, every college, every office, every factory has its complement of these miserable creatures, of whom I was soon to be one. No doubt they exist in Heaven, just inside the gate, peering over Saint Peter's shoulder for the advent of a new spirit, whom they can show the ropes; Hell must have them, too, and if I were Dante, for example, knowing what I know today, I would have been a *little* more leery of Vergil and that guided tour. In any case, I fell; I accepted with thanks those offers of aid and companionship. I learned the way to the refectory, how to fold my papers properly, how to stitch on my collars and cuffs, how to pin my veil, and, in return, I found myself the doomed companion of girls with flat, broad faces and huge collections of freckles, girls with dandruff on their uniforms, with spots and gaping seams, wrinkled black stockings, chilblains, owl-like glasses, carrot-colored hair—damp, confidential souls with quantities of younger brothers and sisters just like themselves. And I was one of them, too. On Saturday afternoons (we were all five-day boarders, which gave us "a lot in common"), I was the intimate of their mah-jongg parties, eating brick ice cream and frosted cupcakes, curtsying to their mothers, suspiciously hospitable dames with stout golfing legs who were pressing with second helpings, prizes, and "Didn't I know your mother?" On Monday mornings, at recess, Nemesis exacted its price; we wretches all loyally "stuck together," like pieces of melting candy in the linty recesses of a coat pocket. At the time, I thought I was alone in my impulses of savage withdrawal, but now I think that all of us, except those of subnormal mentality, bitterly hated each other and had each other's measure.

I felt the shock of all this the more acutely because nothing had prepared me for it. I had come to the convent anticipating a ready acceptance—or, rather, not even anticipating it, so completely had I taken it for granted. In the parochial school, I had led the class in scholarship and athletics; the fact that I was an orphan and the strange circumstances of my home life, led between rich grandparents and a set of harsh, miserly guardians, had given me a unique social position. Waking up now sometimes in my cubicle at six-thirty in the morning to hear the nuns singing their office, far off in the chapel, I could look back, half unbelieving, to a time when the leading boys and girls in my classroom had positively vied for my favors. I thought of my confirmation, which had been the great event of 6A in St. Stephen's School—what a stir it had made when it was known that Mary McCarthy, who was only ten years old, was going to be confirmed with the seventh- and eighth-graders. I remembered how my friends, full of curiosity and awe, had hung around outside the rectory one afternoon while I went in alone to tackle Father Gaughan, the old parish priest, and persuade him to confirm me, because I was such a prodigy of theological lore. In the dining room, next to the parlor, the priest's housekeeper was rattling the dishes and making angry noises, to indicate that I should go, that the Father's dinner was ready, as I could perfectly well smell for myself. Yet I had lingered, stubbornly, refusing to be put off, reciting passages from the catechism, till finally the old priest had patted my head and said to me, "Perseverance wins the crown," and I had run out into the street, jubilating, to meet my amazed classmates. "Perseverance wins the crown, perseverance wins the crown," I had sung over and over, just under my breath. This maxim and the triumph it capped fortified me now in the convent; I argued that it was only a question of time before I would be noticed by the superior girls with whom I rightfully belonged.

It was the idea of being noticed that consumed all my attention; the rest, it seemed to me, would come of itself. Those goddesses whose society I craved had only to look down, once, to discern

among the seventh-graders one who was different from the rest
of the speckled crew. The sprinkling of freckles across the bridge
of my own turned-up nose I regarded as ornamental; I rather
fancied myself as a burning tiger lily among the roses and Easter
lilies and Parma violets of the school. But despite my haughty
manner, my new jeweled barrettes, my week-end applications of
cucumber cream, my studied insolence to my friends, nobody
seemed able to distinguish me. Even those very friends, who
ought, by this time, to have known better (for I could make them
cry whenever I wanted to), treated me comfortably as one of
themselves. Only the nuns recognized the difference, and this with
a certain sorrow and gentle disapprobation. When I shaved off
half my eyebrows, I was given a lecture on vanity, but within the
convent no one was permitted to mention my extraordinary appearance. It was thought that I was getting ideas too old for my
age, and my library list was examined; following the eyebrow
episode, I was given a weekly dose of Fenimore Cooper as a cor-
rective. When I finally refused this as childish, I was started on
John L. Stoddard's Lectures.

Though I often stood first in my studies, the coveted pink ribbon for good conduct never came my way. I suppose this was
because of my meanness, in particular the spiteful taunts I
directed at a supercilious fat girl, the petted daughter of a rich
meat packer, with heavy rings on her fingers and a real fur coat,
who was my principal rival for honors in the classroom, but at
the time I could not understand why the ribbon was denied me.
I never broke any of the rules, and was it my fault if she blub-
bered when I applied, perfectly accurately, a term I had heard
mothers whisper—*nouveau riche*? Wasn't it *true*, I argued, when
I was rebuked by Madame Barclay, our mistress of studies, and
wasn't fat Beryl always boasting of her money and curling her
baby lip at girls whose mothers had to work? It wasn't kind of

me, replied Madame Barclay, but I did not think it kind of her
when she passed me over for Beryl in casting the class play. Everyone could see that I was much the better actress, and the leading
role of haughty Lady Spindle was precisely suited to my style.
I did not believe Madame Barclay when she explained that in the
tryout I sounded too fierce and angry for a comedy; the nuns in
the parochial school had never said so. I could see, darkly, that I
was being punished, with that inverted favoritism so typical of
authority ("Whom the Lord loveth, He chastiseth"), for everyone
detested Beryl, even the nuns. Up to the last moment, I could not
think they would really do this to me; I knew the part by heart
and practiced the lines privately against the time when they would
recognize their error and send for me to rescue them. But, in-
credibly, the play went on without me, and my only satisfaction,
as I sat in the audience, was to watch Pork Barrel forget her lines;
I supplied them, to my neighbors, in a vindictive whisper, till
somebody told me to hush.

Nobody cared, apparently; nobody knew what they had
missed; to them, it was just a silly seventh-grade play. My con-
tempt for the seventh grade was stiffened by this experience; I
resolved to cut myself off from them. At this time, for reasons of
discipline, my desk in study hall was changed, and for the remainder of the term I was put next to an eighth-grader, the
vivacious one of a pair of very popular twins; this girl was being
punished for chattering with her former deskmate. The gulf between the grades was very wide, and it was reasoned, correctly,
that she would have no incentive to repeat her sin with me. Yet
the mistress of discipline who put us together must have had a
taste for visual punning, for the strange fact was that this girl and
I resembled each other far more startlingly than she resembled
her studious sister. We had the same brows, the same noses, the
same fair skin and dark hair, the same height; the only difference

was in the way we parted our hair and in the color of our eyes, hers being hazel and mine green. Louise, unlike me, had a kind disposition but little curiosity, and even the likeness between us, so much remarked on by the nuns, was not enough to focus her merry eye on me for more than a wondering instant. As a twin, doubtless, she had grown indifferent to the oddities of Nature's ways. In any case, she paid me no heed, and the very thing that might have drawn us together underlined the disparity between us. One day, as we sat side by side, bitterness overcame me to see her, my double, exchanging notes with her eighth-grade friends and acting as though I were not there. I took a piece of paper and wrote, "In my other school, I was popular too," and shoved it over onto her desk. She read it and lifted her eyes with a look of quizzical astonishment. "Tell me," she wrote back, and I replied with a dazzling essay on the friends I had had, the contests I had won, the boys who had had crushes on me. As I watched her read, I felt a tremendous satisfaction: I had at last got the facts on record. It had come to me, suddenly, that I was neglected because the convent did not know *who I was*. Once the truth was discovered, I would receive my due, like royalty traveling incognito when it is recognized by someone in the crowd and the whole populace falls on its knees. "It must be very hard," she wrote back, sympathetically. And that, to my amazement, was the end of it. I had only made her vaguely sorry for me, so that she smiled at me from time to time, with looks of encouragement. I was forced to accept the fact that my former self was dead.

But my resolve was not softened. I came back in the fall, as a full-time boarder, with a certain set to my jaw, determined to go it alone. A summer passed in thoughtful isolation, rowing on a mountain lake, diving from a pier, had made me perfectly reckless. I was going to get myself recognized at whatever price. It was in this cold, empty gambler's mood, common to politicians and adolescents, that I surveyed the convent setup. If I could not win fame by goodness, I was ready to do it by badness, and I looked to the past for precedents. Anything that had happened once in a Sacred Heart convent became, so to speak, fossilized in the institutions of the order. Once, long ago, perhaps here or in Bruges or Chicago or nineteenth-century France, a girl had eloped with the music master, so now our piano lessons were chaperoned by a fat sister, one of the domestics, who reclined, snoring gently, in a chair just behind the Baron's. For a few weeks during the fall, the prospect of an elopement held first claim on my thoughts. My twelve-year-old hands trembled with hope whenever, in the stretch of an octave, they grazed the white hands of the professor; he had a few little blond glinting hairs on his plump fingers, which seemed to hint of virility dormant but vibrato, like the sleeping nun. I grew faint when my laced shoe encountered his spatted Oxford on the loud pedal. Examples of child marriages among the feudal nobility crowded through my head, as if to encourage the Baron, but at length I had to bow to the force of American custom and face it: he probably thought I was too young.

The decision to lose my faith followed swiftly on this disappointment. People are always asking me how I came to lose my faith, imagining a period of deep inward struggle. The truth is the whole momentous project simply jumped at me, ready-made, out of one of Madame MacIllvra's discourses. I had decided to do it before I knew what it was, when it was merely an interweaving of words, lose-your-faith, like the ladder made of sheets on which the daring girl had descended into the arms of her Romeo. "Say you've lost your faith," the devil prompted, assuring me that there was no risk if I chose my moment carefully. Starting Monday morning, we were going to have a retreat, to be preached by a stirring Jesuit. If I lost my faith on, say, Sunday, I could regain it during the three days of retreat, in time for Wednesday confessions. Thus there would be only four days in which my soul would be in danger if I should happen to die suddenly. The only real sacrifice would be forgoing Communion on Sunday. He who hesitates is lost; *qui ne risque rien n'a rien,* observed the devil, lapsing into French, as is his wont. If I did not do it, someone else might—that awful Beryl, for instance. It was a miracle that someone had not thought of it already, the idea seemed so obvious, like a store waiting to be robbed.

Surprised looks were bent on me Sunday morning in the chapel when the line formed for Communion and I knelt unmoving in my pew. I was always an ostentatious communicant. Now girls clambered over me, somebody gave me a poke, but I shook my head sorrowfully, signifying by my expression that I was in a state of mortal sin and dared not approach the table. At lunch, eating little, I was already a center of attention at my table; I maintained a mournful silence, rehearsing what I would say to Madame MacIllvra in her office as soon as the meal was over. Having put in my request for an appointment, I was beginning to be slightly frightened. After lunch, as I stood waiting outside her door, I kept licking my lips. Yet this fear, I argued, was a token of sincerity; naturally you would be frightened if you had just lost your faith.

"*Ma Mère,* I have lost my faith." At her roll-top desk, Madame MacIllvra started; one plump white hand fluttered to her heart. She gave me a single searching look. Evidently, my high standing in my studies had prepared her for this catastrophe, for she did not ransack me further as I stood there quaking and bowing and trying to repress a foolish giveaway grin. I had been expecting a long questioning, but she reached, sighing, for the telephone, as though I had appendicitis or the measles.

"Pray, my child," she murmured as she summoned Father Dennis, our chaplain, from the neighboring Jesuit college. "I can't pray," I promptly responded. A classical symptom of unbelief was the inability to pray, as I knew from her own lectures. Madame MacIllvra nodded, turning a shade paler; she glanced at the watch in her bosom. "Go to your room," she said perturbedly. "You are not to speak to anyone. You will be sent for when Father Dennis comes. I will pray for you myself."

Some of her alarm had communicated itself to me. I had not realized that what I had said was so serious. I felt quite frightened now by what I had done and by the prospect of a talk with Father Dennis, who was an old, dry, forbidding man, very different from the handsome missionary father who was going to preach our retreat. The idea of backing down presented itself with more and more attraction, but I did not see how I could do this without being convicted of shallowness. Moreover, I doubted very much that Madame MacIllvra would believe me if I said now that I had got my faith back all at once. She would make me talk to Father Dennis anyway. Once the convent machinery had got into motion, there was no way of stopping it, as I knew from horrendous experience. It was like the mills of the gods.

By the time I reached my cubicle I was thoroughly scared. I saw that I was going to have to go through with this or be exposed before them all as a liar, and for the first time it occurred to me that I would have to have arguments to make my doubts sound real. At the same shaken moment I realized that I knew nothing whatever of atheism. If I were out in the world, I could consult the books that had been written on the subject, but here in the convent, obviously, there could be no access to atheistic literature. From the playground outside floated the voices of the girls, laughing. I went to the window and looked down at them, feeling utterly cut off and imprisoned within my own emptiness. There was no one to turn to but God, yet this was one occasion when prayer would be unavailing. A prayer for atheistic arguments (surely?) would only bring out the stern side of God. What was I going to do?

I sat down on my bed and tried to count my resources. After all, I said to myself suddenly, I did know something about skepticism, thanks to Madame MacIllvra herself. The skeptics' arguments were based on science—false science, said Madame MacIllvra—which reasoned that there was no God because you could not see Him. This was a silly materialistic "proof," to which, unfortunately, I knew the answer. Could you see the wind? And yet its touch was everywhere, like God's invisible grace blowing on our souls. Skeptics denied the life after death and said there was no Heaven, only the blue of space in the celestial vault. Science proved that, they said, and science proved, too, that there was no Hell burning under the earth. We had had the answer to that one, only last week in Christian Doctrine, in Saint Paul's steely words, which we had had to memorize: "That eye hath not seen, nor ear heard, neither hath it entered into the heart of man, what things God hath prepared for them that love Him." I sank into a dull despair. Was I going to have to offer "proofs" that any fool could see through? Any fool knew that man's scientific calipers could not grasp God directly. Hell and Heaven were not contradictory to science but something different altogether, beyond science. But what about miracles?

I sat up suddenly. Miracles were not invisible. They were supposed to happen right here on earth, today. They were attested in the photographs of Lourdes by all the crutches hanging up in token of thankfulness for cures. Nevertheless, I said to myself delightedly, *I* had never seen a miracle, and perhaps all these people were lying or deluded. Christian Science claimed cures, too, and we knew that that was just imagination. Voltaire was an intelligent man and he had laughed at miracles. Why not I?

As I sat there searching my memory, doubts that I had hurriedly stowed away, like contraband in a bureau drawer, came back to me, reassuringly. I found that I had always been a little suspicious of the life after death. Perhaps it was really true that the dead just rotted and I would never rejoin my parents in Heaven? I scratched a spot on my uniform, watching it turn white under my thumbnail. Another memory was tapping at my consciousness: the question of the Resurrection of the Body. At the last trump, all the bodies of men, from Adam onward, were supposed to leap from their graves and rejoin the souls that had left them; this was why the Church forbade cremation. But some- where, not so long ago, I had heard a priest quote scornfully a materialistic argument against this. The materialist said (yes, that was it!) that people rotted and turned into fertilizer, which went into vegetables, and then other people ate the vegetables, so that when the Resurrection came there would not be enough bodies to go around. The priest answered that for God, anything was pos- sible; if God made man from clay, He could certainly make some extra bodies. But in that case, I thought, pouncing, why did He object to cremation? And in any case they would not be the *same* bodies, which was the whole point. And I could think of an even stronger instance: What about cannibals? If God divided the cannibal into the component bodies he had digested, what would become of the cannibal? God could start with whatever flesh the cannibal had had when he was a baby, before he began eating missionaries, but if his father and mother had been cannibals too, what flesh would he really have that he could call his own?

At that time, I did not know that this problem had been treated by Aquinas, and with a child's pertinacity, I mined away at the foundations of the Fortress Rock. Elation had replaced fear. I could hardly wait now to meet Father Dennis and confront him with these doubts, so remarkable in one of my years. Parallels with the young Jesus, discoursing with the scribes and doctors,

bounded through my head: "And all that heard Him were astonished at His Wisdom and His answers." No one now, I felt
certain, would dare accuse me of faking. I strolled along proudly
with the messenger who had come to fetch me; just as her knock
sounded, I had reached the stage of doubting the divinity of
Christ. I could see in the wondering looks this Iris was shedding
on me that already I was a credit to the milieu.

In the dark parlor, the priest was waiting, still in his cassock
—a wrinkled, elderly man with a hairless face and brown, dead
curly hair that looked like a wig. He had a weary, abstracted air
as he turned away from the window, as though he had spent his
life in the confessional box. His voice was hollow; everything
about him was colorless and dry. As chaplain to Madame Mac-
Illvra, he must have become a sort of spiritual factotum, like an
upper servant in an apron, and there was despondency in his
manner, as though his *Nunc Dimittis* would never be pronounced.
It was clear that he did not have the resilience of our clever nuns.
"You have doubts, Mother says," he began in a low, listless
voice, pointing me to a straight chair opposite him and then seating himself in an armchair, with half-averted face, as priests do
in the confessional. I nodded self-importantly. "Yes, Father," I
recited. "I doubt the divinity of Christ and the Resurrection of
the Body and the real existence of Heaven and Hell." The priest
raised his scanty eyebrows, like two little wigs, and sighed. "You
have been reading atheistic literature?" I shook my head. "No
Father. The doubts came all by themselves." The priest cupped
his chin in his hand. "So," he murmured. "Let us have them
then."

I was hurt when he interrupted me right in the middle of the
cannibals. "These are scholastic questions," he said curtly. "Beyond the reach of your years. Believe me, the Church has an

answer for them." A feeling of disappointment came over me; it seemed to me that I had a right to know the answer to the cannibal question, since I had thought it up all by myself, but my "Why can't I know nows" were brushed aside, just as though I had been asking about how babies were born. "No," said Father Dennis, with finality. My first excitement was punctured and I began to be suspicious of him, in the manner of adolescents. What, I asked myself shrewdly, was the Church trying to hide from me?

"Let us come to more important matters." He leaned forward in his chair, with the first sign of interest he had given. "You doubt the divinity of Our Lord?" I felt a peculiar avidity in his question that made me wish to hold back. A touch of fear returned to me. "I *think* so," I said dubiously, half ready to abandon my ground. "*Think!* Don't you know?" he demanded, raising his voice like a frail thunderbolt. Quailing, I produced my doubt— I was one of those cowards who are afraid not to be brave. Nevertheless, I spoke hurriedly, in gulps, as if swallowing medicine. "We are supposed to know that He was God because He rose from the dead—that was His sign to us that He was more than man. But you can't prove that He rose from the dead. That's only what the Apostles said. How do we know they were telling the truth? They were very ignorant, superstitious men—just fishermen, weren't they? People like that nowadays believe in fairies and spirits." I looked appealingly up at him, half begging recognition for my doubt and half waiting for him to settle it.

The priest passed a hand across his forehead. "You consider Our Lord a liar, then?" he said in a sepulchral tone. "You think He deceived the poor, ignorant Apostles by pretending to be the Son of God. That is what you are saying, my child, though you do not know it yourself. You are calling Our Blessed Saviour a liar and a cheat." "He might have been mistaken," I objected,

feeling rather cross. "He might have *thought* He was God." Father
Dennis closed his eyes. "You must have faith, my child," he said
abruptly, rising from his chair and taking a few quick steps, his
cassock bobbing.

I gazed at him in humble perplexity. For the first time, he
seemed to me rather holy, as if the word "faith" had elicited
something sweet and sanctified from his soul, but by the same
token he seemed very remote from me, as if he were feeling something that I was unable to feel. Yet he was not answering my
arguments; in fact, he was looking down at me with a grave,
troubled expression, as if he, too, were suddenly conscious of a
gulf between us, a gulf that could not be bridged by words. The
awesome thought struck me that perhaps I *had* lost my faith.
Could it have slipped away without my knowing it? "Help me,
Father," I implored meekly, aware that this was the right thing
to say but meaning it nevertheless.

I seemed to have divided into two people, one slyly watching
as the priest sank back into the armchair, the other anxious and
aghast at the turn the interview was taking. "The wisdom and
goodness of Jesus," Father Dennis said slowly, "as we find it in
His life and teachings—do you think mere man was capable of
this?" I pondered. "Why not?" I queried, soberly. But the priest
glanced at me with reproach, as if I were being fresh. "You don't
know your history, I see. Among the prophets and the pagans,
among the kings and philosophers, among the saints and scholars,
was there ever such a One?" A little smile glinted in the corners
of his mouth. "No," I admitted. The priest nodded. "There, you
see, my child. Such a departure from our ordinary human nature
signifies the Divine intervention. If we had only Christ's teaching,
we could know that He was God. But in addition we have His
miracles, the firm assurance of tradition, and the Living Church,
the Rock on which He built and which survived the buffets of the

Parents, again, before and after marriage

(infant is Mary)

Harold Preston

mon Manly Preston

Augusta Morganstern Preston, her son
Harold, her daughter, Tess,
her sister Rose Gottstein

ugusta Morganstern Preston
ith her daughter, Tess

The McCarthy children in Seattle

Mary, Kevin, Preston, Mother, Sheridan

Mary, Kevin, Preston

Japanese houseboy with snowman
(child is Kevin)

Augusta Morganstern Preston
with her son Harold

Augusta Morganstern Preston
with her grandson Preston

The McCarthy family

*Roy McCarthy; Kevin; J. H. McCarthy; Mary; Lizzie Sheridan
McCarthy; Sheridan; Tess McCarthy; Preston*

Lizzie McCarthy in her sun parlor

The McCarthy children in Minneapolis

Mary in her
First Communion dress

Mary dressed as
a flower for
a school play

Kevin

Aunt Margaret with Preston,
Mary, Kevin, Sheridan

On the pony,
Preston and Sheridan;
standing, Mary and Kevin

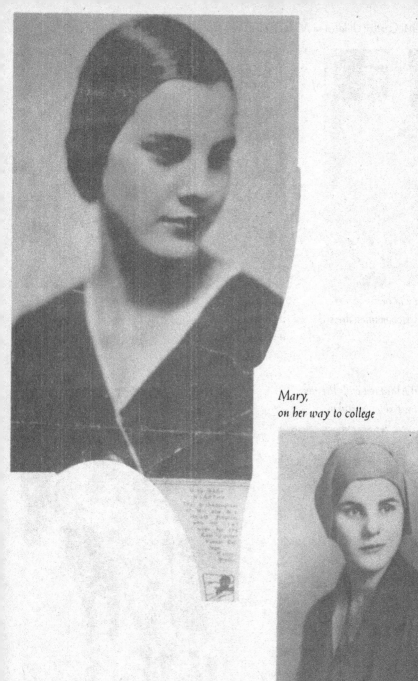

Mary,
on her way to college

ages, where the false religions foundered and were lost to the mind of man."

He took out his watch and peered at it in the dusk. My pride, again, was offended. "It's not only good things that survive," I said boldly. "There's sin, for instance." "The devil is eternal," said Father Dennis, sighing, with a quick glance at me.

"But then the Church could be the instrument of the devil, couldn't it?" Father Dennis swooped. "Then the teachings of Jesus, which it guards, are of diabolical origin?" I flushed. "Other religions have lasted," I said, retreating. "The Jewish religion and Mohammedanism. Is that because they are diabolic?" I spoke with an air of ingenuousness, but I knew I had him in a corner; there were Jewish girls in the convent. "They have a partial truth," Father Dennis murmured. "Hence they have been preserved." I became impatient with this sparring, which was taking me away from a real point I had glimpsed. "Yes, Father," I said. "But still I don't see that the fact that Christ was an exception proves that He was God." "There are no exceptions in nature," retorted Father Dennis. "Oh, Father!" I cried. "I can think of lots."

I was burning to pursue this subject, for it had come to me, slowly, that Christ really *could* have been a man. The idea of Christ as simply man had something extraordinary and joyous about it that was different, I perceived, from the condescension of God to the flesh. I was glad I had started this discussion, for I was learning something new every second. All fear had left me and all sense of mere willful antagonism. I was intent on showing Father Dennis the new possibilities that opened; my feeling for him was comradely.

But once more he shut me off. "You must accept what I tell you," he said, almost sharply. "You are too young to understand these things. You must have faith." "But you're supposed to give me faith, Father," I protested. "Only God can do that," he answered. "Pray, and He will grant it." "I can't pray," I said automatically. "You know your prayers," he said. "Say them." He rose, and I made my curtsy. "Father!" I cried out suddenly, in desperation at the way he was leaving me. "There's something else!"

He turned back, fatiguedly, but the wild look on my face must have alarmed him. "What is it, my child?" He came a little nearer, peering at me with a concerned, kindly expression. "My child," he said gravely, "do you doubt the existence of God?" "Yes," I breathed, in exultant agony, knowing that it was true.

He sat down with me again and took my hand. Very gently, seeing that this was what I seemed to want of him, he recited for me the five *a posteriori* proofs of God's existence: the argument of the unmoved Mover, the argument of efficient causes, the argument of the Necessary Being implied by contingent beings, the argument of graduated perfections, the argument of the wonderful order and design in the universe. Most of what he said I did not understand, but the gist was clear to me. It was that every effect must have a cause and the cause was, of course, God. The universe could not exist unless some self-sufficient Being had created it and put it in motion. I listened earnestly, trying to test what he said, almost convinced and yet not quite. It was as though the spirit of doubt had wormed its way into the very tissue of my thinking, so that axioms that had seemed simple and clear only an hour or so before now became perplexing and murky. "Why, Father," I asked finally, "does everything *have* to have a cause? Why couldn't the universe just be there, causing itself?"

Father Dennis lit the lamp on the table beside him; the bell rang for *goûter*, a girl poked her head in and hurriedly withdrew. "Because," he said patiently, "I have just explained to you, every effect must have a proportionate cause." I turned this over in my head, reminding myself that I was a child and that he probably thought I did not comprehend him. "Except God," I repeated helpfully. The priest nodded. "But Father," I cried, with a sudden start of discovery, "why can't the universe be self-sufficient if God can? Why can't something in matter be the uncaused cause? Like electricity?"

The priest shook his head sorrowfully. "I cannot tell you, my child." He dropped into a different tone, caustic and reproachful. "I cannot open eyes that blindly refuse to see. Can inert matter give birth to spirit? Did inert matter give you your conscience? Who deny causal necessity make the world a chaos where vice and anarchy reign!" His hollow voice reverberated as if he were addressing a whole dockful of secular philosophers, arraigned in a corner of the room. "Oh, my child," he concluded, rising, ' give up reading that atheistic filth. Pray to God for faith and make a good confession." He left the room swiftly, his cassock swelling behind him.

Father Dennis's failure made a great impression on the convent. Wherever I went, eyes regarded me respectfully: there went the girl that a Jesuit had failed to convince. The day girls and five day boarders, returning on Monday, quickly heard the news. Little queens who had never noticed my existence gathered round me at recess and put me whispered questions, for we were not supposed to talk during the retreat. The coincidence of the holy fervor of the retreat with my unsanctified state heightened the sense of the prodigious. It was thought that Father Heeney, the curly-haired, bronzed missionary who had got such results among the Eskimos, was pitting his oratory against me. In her office, at a second interview, Madame MacIllvra wiped the corners of her eyes with her plain cambric handkerchief. She felt that she had betrayed a trust reposed in her, from Heaven, by my dead mother. Tears came readily to her, as to most pretty lady principals, especially when she felt that the *convent* might be open to criticism. By Wednesday, the third time she saw me, we had come to a serious pass. My deskmate, Louise, had bet me that I would not get my faith back by Wednesday; as one fiery sermon followed another and I remained unswayed, a sort of uneasiness settled down over the convent. It was clear to everyone, including me, that I would *have* to get my faith back to put an end to this terrible uncertainty.

I was as much concerned now as Madame MacIllvra herself. I was trying, with all my power, to feel faith, if only as a public duty, but the more I tapped and tested myself, the more I was forced to recognize that there was no belief inside me. My very soul had fled, as far as I could make out. Curiously enough, for the first time, seeing what I had wrought, I had a sense of obligation to others and not to my own soul or to God, which was a proof in itself that I had lost God, for our chief obligation in life was supposed to be to please Him. God (if there was a God) would certainly not be pleased if I *pretended* to regain my faith to satisfy Madame MacIllvra and Madame Barclay and my new friend and double, Louise, who was mischievous but a good Catholic. Yet this was the decision I came to after a second unfruitful session in the parlor, this time with Father Heeney, who could convert me, I felt leadenly, if anybody could. He had said all the same things that Father Dennis had said, though calling me by my first name and laugning when I told him that my father and grandfather were lawyers, as though my serious doubts were part of what he called the gift of gab. He, too, seemed convinced that I had been reading atheistic literature and warned me, jestingly, of the confessional when I denied it. These priests, I thought bitterly, seemed to imagine that you could do nothing for yourself, that everything was from inheritance and reading, just as they imagined that Christ could not have been a "mere man," and just, for that matter, as they kept saying that you must have "faith," a word that had become more and more irritating to me during the past few days. "Natural reason, Mary," expatiated Father Heeney, "will not take you the whole way today. There's a little gap that we have to fill with faith." I looked up at him measuringly. So there *was* a gap, then. How was it that they had never mentioned this interesting fact to us before?

As I left the parlor, I decided to hold Father Heeney personally responsible for the deception he was forcing me into. "I'll see you in the confessional," he called after me in his full, warm voice, but it was not me, I promised myself, that he was going to see but a mere pious effigy of myself. By failing to convert me and treating my case so lightly—calling me Thomasina, for instance, in a would-be funny reference to doubting Thomas—he was driving me straight into fraud. Thanks to his incompetence, the only thing left for me to do was to enact a simulated conversion. But I had no intention of giving him the credit. I was going to pretend to be converted in the night, by a dream.

And I did not feel a bit sorry, even on Thursday morning, kneeling in my white veil at the altar railing to receive the Host. Behind me, the nuns, I knew, were rejoicing, as good nuns should, over the reclamation of a soul. Madame MacIllvra's blue eyes were probably misting. Beside me, Pork Barrel was bursting her seams with envy. Louise (I had just informed her in the veiling room) had invited me to spend the night with her during Christmas vacation. My own chief sensation was one of detached surprise at how far I had come from my old mainstays, as once, when learning to swim, I had been doing the dead-man's float and looked back, raising my doused head, to see my water wings drifting, far behind me, on the lake's surface.

This story is so true to our convent life that I find it almost impossible to sort out the guessed-at and the half-remembered from the undeniably real. The music master, the old snoring nun, the English actor reciting "Lepanto," the embroidery, A Tale of Two Cities, Emma, Lady Spindle (the other character in this playlet was Mrs. Dwindle), all this is just as it was. I am not absolutely certain of the chronology, the whole drama of my loss of faith took place during a very short space of time, and I believe it was during a retreat. The conversations, as I have warned the reader, are mostly fictional, but their tone and tenor are right. That was the way the priests talked, and those, in general, were the arguments they brought to bear on me. Even though I wrote this myself, I smile in startled recognition as I read it.

The proofs of God's existence are drawn from the Catholic Encyclopedia. My own questions are a mixture of memory and conjecture. One bit of dialogue was borrowed from an Episcopal clergyman: "There's a little gap that we have to fill with faith." My son, Reuel, came home one day and quoted this from his Sacred Study teacher. I laughed (it was so like the way my priests had talked) and put it in.

Actually, it now seems to me that my interview with the first priest took place not in the convent parlor but in the old priest's study. Where this study was and how I got there, I have no idea. As for the second priest, whom I call Father Heeney, this may have been the missionary father from "The Blackguard" or it may have been someone else whom I have mixed up with him. All I really remember was that his attitude toward my supposed doubts was much more brusque and summary than the old priest's. He did not take them seriously, which annoyed me, partly for reasons of vanity, but mainly because, by this time, they had become serious and I was frightened. This priest, if it was the same one, had small patience with girls.

The McCarthy family always held my grandfather responsible for the "atheistic ideas" I had imbibed in Seattle. Yet of my three brothers, all of whom were secured from his influence, only one, the youngest, remains in the Church. In my mother's generation, the Church made three recruits. All the Protestant daughters-in-law became converts; Uncle Florrie, Aunt Esther's husband, held out to the end—he would drive his family to Sunday Mass and stay outside, himself, in the car, exciting wonder and envy in the children. In my generation, at least three (I am not sure about my cousins) were lost to the Faith.

Contrary to what the McCarthys believed, my grandfather Preston made it his duty to see that I kept up my religion. It was a pact between us that I would continue to go to church on Sundays until I was a little older. But he never questioned my sincerity. When I told him I had lost my faith (and by then it was true), he did not treat it as a dodge for getting out of Mass. Most families, I think, would have done this. That a person, even a child, was acting from conscientious motives seemed to him natural and fitting. His fair-mindedness rested on this assumption. Many years later, when I became a radical in my early twenties, he received this news with the same searching gravity; the car that had once taken me to church, or, rather, its replacement, now took me to meetings at the Labor Temple, by my grandfather's orders.

I shall describe the Preston family life in subsequent chapters. At this period, while I was still in the convent, I was something of an alien at home. My school friends were all Catholics, and their parents, for the most part, were unknown to my grandparents, who were separated from them not only by religion but by the difference of a generation. None of these children ever came to my house, though I was taken to theirs. My chief interest was the stage, the wish to play a part and attract notice, together with a quick memory, had persuaded me that I was born for the footlights. At home, I was always giving recitations and inviting the Preston family to listen to them. My favorite pieces were "Lord Ullin's Daughter" and "The Inchcape Rock." My new uncles and my aunt and grandmother found these recitations hilarious, but for a long time I did not suspect this. Then I would not recite for them any more.

To the family, I was a curio, and so I was looked on by some of the girls in the convent, as the reader will see in the next chapter. As a child, I had had no self-consciousness; my seriousness prevented me from seeing that other people might be laughing at me. Now I had to learn this.

Names

Aᴺᴺᴀ Lyons, Mary Louise Lyons, Mary von Phul, Emilie von Phul, Eugenia McLellan, Marjorie McPhail, Marie-Louise L'Abbé, Mary Danz, Julia Dodge, Mary Fordyce Blake, Janet Preston—these were the names (I can still tell them over like a rosary) of some of the older girls in the convent: the Virtues and Graces. The virtuous ones wore wide blue or green moire good-conduct ribbons, bandoleer-style, across their blue serge uniforms; the beautiful ones wore rouge and powder or at least were reputed to do so. Our class, the eighth grade, wore pink ribbons (I never got one myself) and had names like Patricia ("Pat") Sullivan, Eileen Donohoe, and Joan Kane. We were inelegant even in this respect; the best name we could show, among us, was Phyllis ("Phil") Chatham, who boasted that her father's name, Ralph, was pronounced "Rafe" as in England.

Names had a great importance for us in the convent, and foreign names, French, German, or plain English (which, to us, were foreign, because of their Protestant sound), bloomed like prize roses among a collection of spuds. Irish names were too common in the school to have any prestige either as surnames (Gallagher, Sheehan, Finn, Sullivan, McCarthy) or as Christian names (Kathleen, Eileen). Anything exotic had value: an "olive" complexion, for example. The pet girl of the convent was a fragile Jewish girl named Susie Lowenstein, who had pale red-gold hair and an exquisite retroussé nose, which, if we had had it, might have been called "pug." We liked her name too and the name of a child in the primary grades: Abbie Stuart Baillargeon. My favorite name, on the whole, though, was Emilie von Phul (pronounced "Pool"); her oldest sister, recently graduated, was called Celeste. Another name that appealed to me was Genevieve Albers, Saint Genevieve being the patron saint of Paris who turned back Attila from the gates of the city.

All these names reflected the still-pioneer character of the Pacific Northwest. I had never heard their like in the parochial school in Minneapolis, where "foreign" extraction, in any case, was something to be ashamed of, the whole drive being toward Americanization of first name and surname alike. The exceptions to this were the Irish, who could vaunt such names as Catherine O'Dea and the name of my second cousin, Mary Catherine Anne Rose Violet McCarthy, while an unfortunate German boy named Manfred was made to suffer for his. But that was Minneapolis. In Seattle, and especially in the convent of the Ladies of the Sacred Heart, foreign names suggested not immigration but emigration— distinguished exile. Minneapolis was a granary; Seattle was a port, which had attracted a veritable Foreign Legion of adventurers— soldiers of fortune, younger sons, gamblers, traders, drawn by the fortunes to be made in virgin timber and shipping and by the Alaska Gold Rush. Wars and revolutions had sent the defeated out to Puget Sound, to start a new life; the latest had been the Russian Revolution, which had shipped us, via Harbin, a Russian colony, complete with restaurant, on Queen Anne Hill. The English names in the convent, when they did not testify to direct English origin, as in the case of "Rafe" Chatham, had come to us from the South and represented a kind of internal exile; such girls as Mary Fordyce Blake and Mary McQueen Street (a class ahead of me; her sister was named Francesca) bore their double-barreled first names like titles of aristocracy from the ante-bellum South. Not all our girls, by any means, were Catholic; some of the very prettiest ones—Julia Dodge and Janet Preston, if I remember rightly—were Protestants. The nuns had taught us to behave with special courtesy to these strangers in our midst, and the whole effect was of some superior hostel for refugees of all the lost causes of the past hundred years. Money could not count for much in such an atmosphere; the fathers and grandfathers of many of our "best" girls were ruined men.

Names, often, were freakish in the Pacific Northwest, particularly girls' names. In the Episcopal boarding school I went to later, in Tacoma, there was a girl called De Vere Utter, and there was a girl called Rocena and another called Hermoine. Was Rocena a mistake for Rowena and Hermoine for Hermione? And was Vere, as we called her, Lady Clara Vere de Vere? Probably. You do not hear names like those often, in any case, east of the Cascade Mountains; they belong to the frontier, where books and libraries were few and memory seems to have been oral, as in the time of Homer.

Names have more significance for Catholics than they do for other people; Christian names are chosen for the spiritual qualities of the saints they are taken from; Protestants used to name their children out of the Old Testament and now they name them out of novels and plays, whose heroes and heroines are perhaps the new patron saints of a secular age. But with Catholics it is different. The saint a child is named for is supposed to serve, literally, as a model or pattern to imitate; your name is your fortune and it tells you what you are or must be. Catholic children ponder their names for a mystic meaning, like birthstones; my own, I learned, besides belonging to the Virgin and Saint Mary of Egypt, originally meant "bitter" or "star of the sea." My second name, Therese, could dedicate me either to Saint Theresa or to the saint called the Little Flower, Soeur Thérèse of Lisieux, on whom God was supposed to have descended in the form of a shower of roses. At Confirmation, I had added a third name (for Catholics then rename themselves, as most nuns do, yet another time, when they take orders); on the advice of a nun, I had taken "Clementina," after Saint Clement, an early pope—a step I soon regretted on account of "My Darling Clementine" and her number nine shoes. By the time I was in the convent, I would no longer tell anyone what my Confirmation name was. The name I had nearly picked was "Agnes," after a little Roman virgin martyr, always shown with a lamb, because of her purity. But Agnes would have been just as bad, I recognized in Forest Ridge Convent—not only because of the possibility of "Aggie," but because it was subtly, indefinably *wrong*, in itself. Agnes would have made me look like an ass.

The fear of appearing ridiculous first entered my life, as a governing motive, during my second year in the convent. Up to then, a desire for prominence had decided many of my actions and, in fact, still persisted. But in the eighth grade, I became aware of mockery and perceived that I could not seek prominence without attracting laughter. Other people could, but I couldn't. This laughter was proceeding, not from my classmates, but from the girls of the class just above me, in particular from two boon companions, Elinor Heffernan and Mary Harty, a clownish pair—oddly assorted in size and shape, as teams of clowns generally are, one short, plump, and baby-faced, the other tall, lean, and owlish —who entertained the high-school department by calling attention to the oddities of the younger girls. Nearly every school has such a pair of satirists, whose marks are generally low and who are tolerated just because of their laziness and non-conformity; one of them (in this case, Mary Harty, the plump one) usually appears to be half asleep. Because of their low standing, their indifference to appearances, the sad state of their uniforms, their clowning is taken to be harmless, which, on the whole, it is, their object being not to wound but to divert; such girls are bored in school. We in the eighth grade sat directly in front of the two wits in study hall, so that they had us under close observation; yet at first I was not afraid of them, wanting, if anything, to identify myself with their laughter, to be initiated into the joke. One of their specialties was giving people nicknames, and it was considered an honor to be the first in the eighth grade to be let in by Elinor and Mary on their latest invention. This often happened to me; they would tell me, on the playground, and I would tell the others. As their intermediary, I felt myself almost their friend and it did not occur to me that I might be next on their list.

I had achieved prominence not long before by publicly losing my faith and regaining it at the end of a retreat. I believe Elinor and Mary questioned me about this on the playground, during recess, and listened with serious, respectful faces while I told them about my conversations with the Jesuits. Those serious faces ought to have been an omen, but if the two girls used what I had revealed to make fun of me, it must have been behind my back. I never heard any more of it, and yet just at this time I began to feel something, like a cold breath on the nape of my neck, that made me wonder whether the new position I had won for myself in the convent was as secure as I imagined. I would turn around in study hall and find the two girls looking at me with speculation in their eyes.

It was just at this time, too, that I found myself in a perfectly absurd situation, a very private one, which made me live, from month to month, in horror of discovery. I had waked up one morning, in my convent room, to find a few small spots of blood on my sheet; I had somehow scratched a trifling cut on one of my legs and opened it during the night. I wondered what to do about this, for the nuns were fussy about bedmaking, as they were about our white collars and cuffs, and if we had an inspection those spots might count against me. It was best, I decided, to ask the nun on dormitory duty, tall, stout Mother Slattery, for a clean bottom sheet, even though she might scold me for having scratched my leg in my sleep and order me to cut my toenails. You never know what you might be blamed for. But Mother Slattery, when she bustled in to look at the sheet, did not scold me at all; indeed, she hardly seemed to be listening as I explained to her about the cut. She told me to sit down: she would be back in a minute. "You can be excused from athletics today," she added, closing the door. As I waited, I considered this remark, which seemed to me strangely munificent, in view of the unimportance of the cut. In a moment, she returned, but without the sheet. Instead, she produced out of her big pocket a sort of cloth girdle and a peculiar flannel object which I first took to be a bandage, and I began to protest that I did not need or want a bandage; all I needed was a bottom sheet. "The sheet can wait," said Mother Slattery, succinctly, handing me two large safety pins. It was the pins that abruptly enlightened me; I saw Mother Slattery's mistake, even as she was instructing me as to how this flannel article, which I now understood to be a sanitary napkin, was to be put on.

"Oh, no, Mother," I said, feeling somewhat embarrassed. "You don't understand. It's just a little cut, on my leg." But Mother, again, was not listening; she appeared to have grown deaf, as the nuns had a habit of doing when what you were saying did not fit in with their ideas. And now that I knew what was in her mind, I was conscious of a funny constraint; I did not feel it proper to name a natural process, in so many words, to a nun. It was like trying not to think of their going to the bathroom or trying not to see the straggling iron-grey hair coming out of their coifs (the common notion that they shaved their heads was false). On the whole, it seemed better just to show her my cut. But when I offered to do so and unfastened my black stocking, she only glanced at my leg, cursorily. "That's only a scratch, dear," she said. "Now hurry up and put this on or you'll be late for chapel. Have you any pain?" "No, no, Mother!" I cried. "You don't understand!" "Yes, yes, I understand," she replied soothingly, "and you will too, a little later. Mother Superior will tell you about it some time during the morning. There's nothing to be afraid of. You have become a woman."

"I know all about that," I persisted. "Mother, please listen. I just cut my leg. On the athletic field. Yesterday afternoon." But the more excited I grew, the more soothing, and yet firm, Mother Slattery became. There seemed to be nothing for it but to give up and do as I was bid. I was in the grip of a higher authority, which almost had the power to persuade me that it was right and I was wrong. But of course I was not wrong; that would have been too good to be true. While Mother Slattery waited, just outside my door, I miserably donned the equipment she had given me, for there was no place to hide it, on account of drawer inspection. She led me down the hall to where there was a chute and explained how I was to dispose of the flannel thing, by dropping it down the chute into the laundry. (The convent arrangements were very old-fashioned, dating back, no doubt, to the days of Louis Philippe.)

The Mother Superior, Madame MacIllvra, was a sensible woman, and all through my early morning classes, I was on pins and needles, chafing for the promised interview with her which I trusted would clear things up. "*Ma Mère*," I would begin, "Mother Slattery thinks . . ." Then I would tell her about the cut and the athletic field. But precisely the same impasse confronted me when

I was summoned to her office at recess-time. I talked about my cut, and *she* talked about becoming a woman. It was rather like a round, in which she was singing "Scotland's burning, Scotland's burning," and I was singing "Pour on water, pour on water." Neither of us could hear the other, or, rather, I could hear her, but she could not hear me. Owing to our different positions in the convent, she was free to interrupt me, whereas I was expected to remain silent until she had finished speaking. When I kept breaking in, she hushed me, gently, and took me on her lap. Exactly like Mother Slattery, she attributed all my references to the cut to a blind fear of this new, unexpected reality that had supposedly entered my life. Many young girls, she reassured me, were frightened if they had not been prepared. "And you, Mary, have lost your dear mother, who could have made this easier for you." Rocked on Madame MacIllvra's lap, I felt paralysis overtake me and I lay, mutely listening, against her bosom, my face being tickled by her white, starched, fluted wimple, while she explained to me how babies were born, all of which I had heard before.

There was no use fighting the convent. I had to pretend to have become a woman, just as, not long before, I had had to pretend to get my faith back—for the sake of peace. This pretense was decidedly awkward. For fear of being found out by the lay sisters downstairs in the laundry (no doubt an imaginary contingency, but the convent was so very thorough), I reopened the cut on my leg, so as to draw a little blood to stain the napkins, which were issued me regularly, not only on this occasion, but every twenty-eight days thereafter. Eventually, I abandoned this bloodletting, for fear of lockjaw, and trusted to fate. Yet I was in awful dread of detection; my only hope, as I saw it, was either to be released from the convent or to become a woman in reality, which might take a year, at least, since I was only twelve. Getting out of athletics once a month was not sufficient compensation for the farce

I was going through. It was not my fault; they had forced me into it; nevertheless, it was I who would look silly—worse than silly; half mad—if the truth ever came to light.

I was burdened with this guilt and shame when the nickname finally found me out. "Found me out," in a general sense, for no one ever did learn the particular secret I bore about with me, pinned to the linen band. "We've got a name for you," Elinor and Mary called out to me, one day on the playground. "What is it?" I asked, half hoping, half fearing, since not all their sobriquets were unfavorable. "Cye," they answered, looking at each other and laughing. " 'Si'?" I repeated, supposing that it was based on Simple Simon. Did they regard me as a hick? "C.Y.E.," they elucidated, spelling it out in chorus. "The letters stand for something. Can you guess?" I could not and I cannot now. The closest I could come to it in the convent was "Clean Your Ears." Perhaps that was it, though in later life I have wondered whether it did not stand, simply, for "Clever Young Egg" or "Champion Young Eccentric." But in the convent I was certain that it stood for something horrible, something even worse than dirty ears (as far as I knew, my ears were clean), something I could never guess because it represented some aspect of myself that the world could see and I couldn't, like a sign pinned on my back. Everyone in the convent must have known what the letters stood for, but no one would tell me. Elinor and Mary had made them promise. It was like halitosis; not even my best friend, my deskmate, Louise, would tell me, no matter how much I pleaded. Yet everyone assured me that it was "very good," that is, very apt. And it made everyone laugh.

This name reduced all my pretensions and solidified my sense of *wrongness*. Just as I felt I was beginning to belong to the convent, it turned me into an outsider, since I was the only pupil who was not in the know. I liked the convent, but it did not like me, as people say of certain foods that disagree with them. By this, I do not mean that I was actively unpopular, either with the pupils or with the nuns. The Mother Superior cried when I left and predicted that I would be a novelist, which surprised me. And I had finally made friends; even Emilie von Phul smiled upon me softly out of her bright blue eyes from the far end of the study hall. It was just that I did not fit into the convent pattern; the simplest thing I did, like asking for a clean sheet, entrapped me in consequences that I never could have predicted. I was not bad; I did not consciously break the rules; and yet I could never, not even for a week, get a pink ribbon, and this was something I could not understand, because I was trying as hard as I could. It was the same case as with the hated name; the nuns, evidently, saw something about me that was invisible to me.

The oddest part was all that pretending. There I was, a walking mass of lies, pretending to be a Catholic and going to confession while really I had lost my faith, and pretending to have monthly periods by cutting myself with nail scissors; yet all this had come about without my volition and even contrary to it. But the basest pretense I was driven to was the acceptance of the nickname. Yet what else could I do? In the convent, I could not live it down. To all those girls, I had become "Cye McCarthy." That was who I was. That was how I had to identify myself when telephoning my friends during vacations to ask them to the movies: "Hello, this is Cye." I loathed myself when I said it, and yet I succumbed to the name totally, making myself over into a sort of hearty to go with it—the kind of girl I hated. "Cye" was my new patron saint. This false personality stuck to me, like the name, when I entered public high school, the next fall, as a freshman, having finally persuaded my grandparents to take me out of the convent, although they could never get to the bottom of my reasons, since, as I admitted, the nuns were kind, and I had made many nice new friends. What I wanted was a fresh start, a chance to begin life over again, but the first thing I heard in the corridors of the public high school was that name called out to me, like the warmest of welcomes: "Hi, there, Si!" That was the way they thought it was spelled. But this time I was resolute. After the first weeks, I dropped the hearties who called me "Si" and I never heard it again. I got my own name back and sloughed off Clementina and even Therese—the names that did not seem to me any more to be mine but to have been imposed on me by others. And I preferred to think that Mary meant "bitter" rather than "star of the sea."

A good deal of stress has been laid on the unprepossessing appearance my classmates and I made. I felt the same way, on the whole, about my class in boarding school and even, to some extent, in college. That was why my eyes were always on the older girls, and why I courted a popularity with them which, in the nature of things (for of course they looked down on me), I could not have. I do not possess any photographs of my class in Forest Ridge, but recently some pictures have turned up of my class in boarding school which more than confirm my memory. Why this class, the class that graduated from school in '29 and from college in '33, should have been homelier than the classes preceding it is a mystery, perhaps there was something in the air. But it explains the feeling I had as a young girl of something unattainable, something just ahead of me—beauty, virtue, grace—that I could never catch up with.

My grades went to pieces in public high school, I nearly failed English, which was normally my best subject. The atmosphere in public high school was, in many ways, like that of the parochial school, except that the education was poorer and there was no discipline. It was the style to have crushes on boys, and I had a crush on the captain of the football team and on the captain of the track team, so that I spent my time following athletic events, as a member of the cheering section, instead of studying. The school was called Garfield High, and I was one of its most ardent rooters, I followed basketball too, back and forth across the city, to the various high schools we played. I was not allowed to go out with boys, but one night the captain of the track team drove up to my house in his roadster and honked for me to join him. My grandfather flashed on the front porch lights and thundered at him to go away, and that was the end of my conquest.

Another of the track man's admirers was a shy, intellectual Jewish girl named Ethel Rosenberg (she later changed her first name to Teya) who was also an enthusiast for Walter Pater. She and I became friends, we lived not far from each other. Through her family, who were typical Jewish intellectuals and very hospitable, though not well-to-do (the father was a tailor), I came to know the artistic colony in Seattle and to read serious books. But all this took place on a different plane from my other activities. The only point of fusion had been the track man.

After a year of public high school, my grandparents concluded that there was nothing to do but put me into boarding school, away from the distractions offered by the opposite sex. A convent, this time, was not considered, I was old enough, now, my grandfather said, to choose for myself in religious matters. An Episcopal boarding school in Tacoma, the Annie Wright Seminary, was selected, though I myself had wanted to go to the Anna Head School in California, because Helen Wills had gone there. But the family thought it wiser to keep me nearer home.

Meanwhile, my brothers remained in Saint Benedict's Academy, my youngest brother, Sheridan, had joined the other two. They were kept there, with the nuns, during Christmas and Easter vacations, in the summer, they were parceled out among relations or sent to camp. It was six years before we saw each other again, and then they were almost strangers to me, so different had been our

bringing-up. I was a child of wealth, and they were little pension-
ers on the trust fund that was left by my grandfather McCarthy
when he died. My share, which was equal to each of theirs, never
did more than pay my school board and tuition, the Prestons took
care of the rest. All my brothers' expenses, however, were item-
ized and deducted from the account. The Preston family "remembered" them with checks at Christmas and birthdays, but that was
all. Except on these occasions, their existence seems to have been
overlooked.

When I review my grandfather's character, I find this very
puzzling. He was not the man to neglect an obligation, his bills
were paid the day he received them—a habit still recalled by my
New York dentist with awe. Order, exactitude, fairness—these
were the traits my grandfather was famous for and the traits I
always found in him. How, especially knowing what he did of
the treatment we had received in Minneapolis, did he fail to concern himself with what happened later to my brothers? I cannot
explain this.

He was not an ungenerous or an unfeeling man. He had been
strongly attached to my mother. "The Preston family wanted all
of you," my mother's old friend writes me, as if in extenuation.
Failing to get all four of us, my grandfather may have responded
with a kind of masculine pique, holding himself stiffly aloof from
what had been refused him, i.e., my brothers. Or he may have
been angered by the slurs cast on him by the McCarthys: my
uncle Harry, a few years before, had written a bank in Seattle to
inquire into his financial position. Whatever the reason for this
surprising indifference, I cannot deny the fact of it. Nor can I
deny that I felt it, too. Until I was grown up, the idea never
crossed my mind that something might have been done by the
Prestons for my brothers as well as for me. The only persons,
evidently, to whom this idea occurred were the McCarthys.

The Figures in the Clock

NOT LONG AGO, hunting the rule for the formation of the vocative with my thirteen-year-old son, I pulled down from a top shelf my old Allen and Greenough Latin grammar. The worn green book fell open at the flyleaf, and I saw my name, school, and class written in ink, in the ornate handwriting I had been forming during my idle hours in Annie Wright Seminary in Tacoma. Three years before, I had been sent there despairingly by my grandparents, after a year in public high school. The Sacred Heart nuns, they thought, had made me an atheist; the public high school had made me boy crazy—what next? Peering over my shoulder, my young bantam crowed to find that his haughty mother had dotted her i's with circles; there they were, spattered over the page like bird droppings. Otherwise, the hand was my own, with its Greek e's, flamboyant scroll capitals, and narrow, precisian small letters; it dashed us both to perceive that already, in my senior year in boarding school, my present character had been set. Upside down on the same page, written in pencil in a far more careless style, was a list of some kind. I inverted the book and stared. Next to three crudely drawn cylinders (the influence of physics?) and enclosed in a rough bracket was the following:

Indianhead—Flame
Dishrags
Oilcloth
Gold Paint
Unbleached Muslin, 10 yds
Blue Indianhead 2½ yds

Ye gods, it was my Catiline costume for the Latin Club play,
"Marcus Tullius"!

Or, rather, it was the matrix from which gorgeous Catiline
would emerge: those dishrags, dipped in gold paint and sewed
together by our Latin teacher, Miss Gowrie, would be my chain-
armor breastplate; the oilcloth, gold, stiffened with cardboard and
crowned with a red plume, my helmet; the flame Indianhead my
military cloak, as I appeared in the fearsome scene of the Battle
of Pistoria, where I rushed into the ranks of the enemy and met
my death with great bravery. The blue Indianhead I could not
account for (perhaps a short military tunic?), but the unbleached
muslin would seem, by its length, to have been my toga, which I
flung around myself in the Senate scene as I turned on my prosing
detractor and strode exultant from the stage, promising to "extinguish the flames of my own ruin in the conflagration of all Rome."

And yet, stay, I said to myself, frowning. Why *unbleached*?
The senatorial toga was white, surely? And in my own recollection of that evening, the togas of my fellow senators were white,
with a "purple" stripe or band, this "purple" being in actual fact
scarlet, just like the Roman *purpura*, which came, said Miss
Gowrie, from the Greek *porphyra*. But unbleached the togas must
have been, for unbleached muslin is cheap, and Miss Harriet
Gowrie, a Highland Scotswoman, was a great relier on the power
of illusion. To an audience, natural muslin on a brightly lit stage
is supposed to look white, just as it now looked to me across the

footlit proscenium of time. I smiled ruefully to think of Miss Gowrie, with her tall, lean, doll-jointed "figger" and rustic, homely, frugal arts, so out of place amid our marcels and water waves, riding waistcoats and crops and bowlers, fur coats and Toujours Moi and Christmas Night perfumes. Her original drama "Marcus Tullius" is preserved in my memory as a fabulous example of the homemade.

> The Latin Club presents a drama in five acts, written and produced by Harriet Gowrie, B.A., M.A.
> Act I, the Senate at Rome, 63 B.C.
> Characters in the order of speaking: Cicero . . . Frances Berry.

The thronged scene still frames itself for me like a painting by David. The curtain is ready to go up. Black-haired Miss Gowrie, in a freshly steamed black velvet dress with a wide white bertha and a corsage of roses sent by the cast, is standing in the wings, her black eyes snapping, her apple cheeks afire. Cicero, an honors student in a boyish bob, is at the rostrum, tightening her toga over her large, firm bosom; foppish Caesar and sallow Cato and other *patres* are sitting on wooden benches, while I, in a tier apart, lounge with a scornful smile on my dark, ruined features. In the audience, programs in hand, sit the lady principal, the dean of the Episcopal church, the bishop and the bishop's wife; the publisher of the newspaper, the big and small fry of Puget Sound doctors, dentists, lawyers, insurance men, steamship-line owners, and lumber operators—our relations; the girls in their crepe de Chine dress uniforms; and a few of the town Lovelaces who have braved the principal's eye. With Miss Gowrie tugging, the curtain goes up, on time. Cicero scans her teacher, waits for the applause to die, receives a vigorous nod, opens her mouth, points her finger at me, swells the bellows of her lungs, and launches on the first Catiline oration: "How far, at length, O

Catiline, will you abuse our patience? To what ends does your audacious boldness boastfully display itself?"

How far, at length, Miss Gowrie, could you abuse their patience? Cicero's oration lasted thirty-one minutes by Miss Gowrie's watch. The white column of Frances's throat from time to time trembled faintly from strain, but her steady, clear first soprano had been trained by years in the choir. As the bobbin of words in her was unreeled, she grew paler, like a patient undergoing a long extraction, while the audience sat hushed and respectful, as if in the presence of death or of one of those harrowing athletic feats, tests of endurance, that were popular during the era. There was no coughing or rustling; the only movement was on the stage benches, where the other senators, in character, drew farther away from Catiline, shaking their heads and registering dismay, disbelief, horror, or what-did-I-tell-you, according to the part they were supposed to have played in history. Cato nodded grimly to Catulus and Caesar scratched his pate. As the arraignment of Catiline proceeded, I could feel the curiosity of the first rows slowly transfer itself to me—Lucius Sergius Catilina, adulterer, extortioner, profligate, bankrupt, assassin, suspected wife-killer, broken-down patrician, democrat, demagogue, thug. The wearisome indictment made this person smile. He glanced shruggingly at his fingernails and carelessly loosened his toga, to reveal a glimpse of his tunic, with the broad scarlet *clavus* of the patriciate running down the middle. As a libertine and man of deeds, he found the womanish rhetoric of republican institutions oppressive; at prescribed intervals, his heavy brows jerked up and his ringed fist tightened in a gesture of menace. At long last, it was over. Cicero rounded off her peroration and stepped from the rostrum. There was a great burst of applause. Miss Gowrie signaled. My moment had come.

From my lonely bench, I surveyed them in superb isolation, the

damned soul, proud and unassimilable, the marked, gifted man.
I paused, as though hesitating to waste my words on these gentry,
and then leapt to my feet and delivered Catiline's speech, *in toto*,
as recorded by Sallust—a short tirade, unfortunately, highly colored but stiff, ending in the *défi* "I will extinguish the flames of
my own ruin in the conflagration of all Rome." Now this speech,
from the start, had bothered me. With its threats and bombast, its
Senecan frigidity, it sounded guilty and rather stupid. Even making allowances for Sallust's prejudice and Miss Gowrie's buckram
translation, the effect of repeating it night after night in rehearsal
had awakened a tiny doubt: Was the Catiline I admired so much
merely a vulgar arsonist, as Cicero and his devotees contended?
These first stirrings of maturity were very unwelcome. To my
mind, Catiline was not only a hero—he was me. Not that I was
a misfit in our school; quite the contrary. It was senior year and
I was a big shot: the very oddities that had made me an object
of wonder in my first years had, with time's passing, won me
fame and envy. And yet this victory did not satisfy me, for it had
come about too naturally, in accordance with orderly processes—
one senior class and its leaders graduated and the next came up in
succession, like a roller towel being pulled. So it happens in real
life, but there is something irritating in this slow unfurling of the
generations, each with its roster of poets and politicians gradually
moving into the ascendancy, by sheer virtue of staying power; the
question of value is begged.

And for me at sixteen, sure now of my authority in the school,
sure that I would be forgiven and admired no matter what I did,
whether I ran away from school, or smoked, or met boys on the
afternoon walks, or was cruel and saucy to a young teacher—sure
of this empty freedom, I could not be content till I had imposed
not only myself but my whole pantheon on the Seminary. The
vindication of Catiline appeared to me a task of consummate im-

portance; on the momentous evening, the verdict of history was to
be reversed. And unsuspected, I pridefully thought, by Miss
Gowrie, I had been working up an "interesting" reading of my
brimstone speech. I was going to play Catiline straight, which
meant that I would have to "throw away" the greater part of my
lines, to speak them coldly and limply, like a man too disillusioned
to descend to oratorical effects. And then with my very last words,
I was going to step forward, dismissing Cicero and the Senate,
and levelly hurl my *défi* at the optimates of the audience—at the
spectacled dean and the bishop, at the old pussy-footed teachers,
at the principal and my grandparents and the mild, obedient girls.
This plan I had only adumbrated in rehearsals, for I feared Miss
Gowrie's correction, and I could almost feel her tighten in the
prompter's seat as I spoke my lines into a hush, swept my toga
over my shoulder, and strode off the stage, out of Rome to Etruria,
to my destiny, to death. But thunderous applause broke out before
the curtain could tumble down on my exit. The seventh and
eighth grades, always susceptible, were stamping. "Bravo!" cried
several male voices.

Other scenes followed while I was hurried into my costume
change: a scene among the secondary conspirators; a domestic
scene betwen Cicero and his pretty freshman daughter Tullia, at
home in the evening; a scene between Cicero and Fulvia, mistress
of the conspirator Curius and Cicero's spy; another scene in the
Senate (the third Catiline oration?); and a scene in which some
whiskered Gauls, the Allobroges, visit Cicero at his house. Following still another oration by Cicero and Caesar's plea for clemency,
sharply answered by Cato, came a barbaric scene in a dungeon,
where the remaining conspirators (some supers, plus rude Len-
tulus and bloody Cethegus) were throttled at Cicero's instance.
Then came the big scene of the Battle of Pistoria, where I entered
at the head of my army of malcontents, fought fiercely, and gave

up the ghost. The curtain went down as the Republic was saved.

In the audience, there was a veritable tumult. The school was taking sides in a clash of partisan feeling that recalled the Capulets and the Montagues or the Blues and Greens of Byzantium. Underneath its Episcopalian surface, our school was terribly factious and turbulent; the annual electioneering scandals during the voting for May Queen would have made Milo and Clodius blanch. Now curtain call followed curtain call; thanks to the eighth grade, Catiline's applause swelled above Cicero's as he waved his plumed helmet to his supporters. Girls were crying, and elderly doctors and lawyers pressed up to the stage to congratulate the two principals and Miss Gowrie, declaring with moist eyes that it had done them good to see it. It was pronounced the best play the Seminary had ever put on. The fervid quality of the response, indeed, took the cast by surprise. Our painted eyes interrogated each other over the heads of the swarming citizenry. The whole milling scene in the gymnasium had for us on the stage an unfamiliar, almost pioneer character, as though it had been taking place in Alaska or Virginia City in some old opera house thirty or forty years before. What we failed to take account of was the spell of the educational on the middle-aged Western heart. To these men in business suits, Miss Gowrie's fossilized play had the wondrous note of the authentic, like a petrified forest or the footprint of the giant sloth, and Miss Gowrie herself, stiffly bobbing to their congratulations, with a tight rubber band of a smile framing her false teeth, was something of a marvel in her own right: a genuine British Empire product, like the plaid woolen scarves you bore home from a steamer excursion to Victoria.

Our school specialized in such imports and relics. We had a fat old Austrian known as "Madam," and Frenchwomen, of course, and Swiss, and widows of the Episcopal clergy, a tall actress, and

two Virginia gentlewomen, and a beautiful blond goddess of an
Englishwoman with a nose like the reversed prow of a viking ship,
but none was so redoubtably foreign to us as the author of
"Marcus Tullius," who, once the curtain had been rung down
that night, stood, with her arms folded and a dry, remote look in
her eyes, rebuffing all pleasantries and nodding tersely as she
watched the scenery struck and the costumes piled in order. In
Miss Gowrie's round head was a Big Ben that warned her when
any moment was over. Cicero and I, coming up for praise, received an absent nod of commendation and an admonition to
hurry on to bed that dismantled our historical personalities like
so much canvas scenery. My "brilliant" reading, I saw, was going
to pass without comment. The short triumph of Catiline, if she
was even aware of it, had already been assimilated into the long
triumph of the classics, the marshaling of ablatives, and the rule
of law. It was a mistake—an American mistake—to think that
success could thaw Miss Gowrie. Only work could do that, as I
should have had reason to know. And yet, toward the end of
rehearsals, I could have sworn there was something, some faintly
sour warmth emanating toward us all, like the warmth of her
breath as she bent over you and penciled your face carefully
with the make-up stick.

I claimed Miss Gowrie as my discovery. Among the normal
Seminary girls, it was thought affected to take Latin unless you
"had to" for Eastern college boards or because your parents insisted. You were supposed to groan as you entered her chilly classroom, where the windows were kept open to obviate sleepiness.
Miss Gowrie herself wore a maroon cardigan buttoned down over
her thin chest winter and fall and spring, and those who sat near
the window huddled in their coats during the greater part of the
year. If we did our sight poorly, the windows were poked open

farther; the long pole with the hook on the end of it came to seem a part of her personality, like Saint Joseph's crook. And her chilblained nature had a queer, raw, stiffened sensitiveness. Like many spinsters in foreign countries, she suffered dreadfully from ideas of reference: any remark delivered in an undertone she took to concern herself and flushed up darkly, like a mulberry. She was touchy about a misdone translation, and the capillaries of her blood system seemed to tell her when you were not primed to recite, even though your hand was waving boldly. And when you knew your lesson, she peremptorily cut you short.

At this time, she must have been about thirty-eight or forty years old. A graduate of Girton and Edinburgh, she had come, probably by way of Canada, to our little church boarding school in the Pacific Northwest. Doubtless she had taught elsewhere, in the outposts of empire; it was her first stay in the States, and she took being Scottish *personally*, just as she took our mistakes in translation. So far as we could determine, she had no private life or history and consisted totally of national attributes (thrift, humorless hard work, porridge-eating, and tea-drinking), like one of those wooden dolls dressed in national costume that they show at fairs and expositions. And her appearance was like an illustration to an anthropologist's textbook. She was extremely dark, with brown skin, brown-black eyes, shiny, straight black hair, and a round skull, on which the hair grew in circular fashion. Her face was round also, with cheekbones like an Eskimo's or a pygmy's. She had a tall frame, stiffly articulated and curiously jerky in its movements. In short, as I now know, she belonged to that ancient Celto-Iberian or possibly Pictish strain that survives in the northern Highlands, and the foreignness we noticed in her may have been proof of the scholar's contention that the British Isles in prehistory were inhabited by non-Aryan aborigines, whose descendants, known to the Roman writers, were the little dark men who worked in tin. Her face, hands, and neck had an almost unnatural cleanness, and her red lips drew back from a set of very white false teeth. This glistening sign of early poverty awed us, as a sign of consecration, like a monk's tonsure.

For the out-of-doors, she wore a very old, but real, sealskin coat, of the same color and texture as her hair; from its unfashionable cut, it seemed to have been inherited from her mother, or even her grandmother, as did her long, flat black shoes. Her diction had an odd distinctness; she spoke with a Cambridge accent, but every syllable was formed concisely and separately, as though English were a prized foreign language she had learned young, by the phonetic method. This effect was heightened when she spoke Latin; her teeth clinked and sometimes the draft from the window seemed to whistle through them.

It was Scotland's pride, she told us, to have been throughout the darker ages a center of classical learning, and her very digestion evoked a dour history of Scottish letters and philosophy; like Carlyle, whom we were studying about in English, and like Carlyle's wife, she was dyspeptic. Her brown skin sometimes paled to a yellow hue, and after the school luncheon she often had gas on her stomach.

Yet Miss Gowrie was not an unpleasant person. The school admitted that she meant well, probably. But she did not understand about the rules. Our principal was a stout executive with the prejudices of an old chatelaine. Fountain pens were forbidden because girls had spotted the walls and floors by shaking the ink down in the pen. No food but fruit was permitted in the rooms, and we were forbidden to eat between meals on our walks or shopping trips, so that we would be sure to do justice to the school table. Each girl came with a list of ten approved correspondents, signed by her family, and she was supposed to get letters from no one else. All packages received through the mail were subject to inspection. None of these rules, however, was enforced, except by Miss Gowrie. There was a tacit understanding, shared even, I think, by the principal, that many of the rules existed for artistic reasons, for form's sake. They gave tone to the school. Candy and cookies and modern novels and love letters from unauthorized individuals poured in through the mails; inspection was cursory; fountain pens were rife. Our first stop on our walks was the corner luncheonette, whose main revenue derived from the Seminary, as everybody knew. The Saturday-morning shopping trip and the Saturday-night movie excursion ended, by immemorial custom, at the downtown Puss 'n Boots or Green Lantern, with the girls treating the chaperones to the latest fancy sundaes. The group of us who rode, on Friday afternoons and Saturday mornings, had our cigarettes tucked in our breeches as we drove out to the riding academy with the chaperone, who usually took advantage of the occasion to have a cigarette herself, privately, with the riding master's wife, and there was a standing order for hamburgers for the whole party at a barbecue place on the highway. When we were taken out Sunday afternoons by "a person designated by the family," many of us went out with undesignated men and came back with liquor on our breath. The vice-principal, who signed us in, was careful not to come too close to us, and in my time no girl was ever reported for drinking, though sometimes we must have reeked of gin. A teacher, meeting us downtown on a Sunday with our "brothers" and "cousins," hurriedly tacked off in another direction. All but Miss Gowrie, who felt it her duty to report.

The young teachers sighed, the girls tapped their heads, the vexed principal wept and took the offender on her lap. Austere and sensible, she hated to impose drastic punishments, because this interfered with the smooth running of the school. In the case of her best students, she was usually satisfied with mere repentance; any clever girl could cry her way out of a jam. Meanwhile, poor Miss Gowrie, rigid and bewildered, pursued her solitary course, deaf to the timid hints of friendly colleagues, who tried to set her on the right course. She was always the last chaperone to be chosen on all-school expeditions, and the ragtail group that got her was looked on with freshened pity: no smoking, no eating, no private jokes would be permitted. At the annual school picnic, hers was the last rowboat to be pushed off from the dock, with a disconsolate trio aboard, while she sat upright, facing the maneuvering oarsman, wearing a bright excursion smile clamped about her teeth. M.C.G. (Make Conversation General), the school rule for table talk, was Miss Gowrie's buoy still as she floated about the waters, never allowing her boat to be guided into one of the charming little shaded coves, out of the principal's sight, where you could catch at the weeping-willow branches and broach the idea of wading. It was sad, for when you got to know her, you found that she was a very simple being, a sort of atrophied girl, fond of an outing and what she considered wholesome fun. But she could not grasp at all our American conception of an outing, which consisted in a sort of mass truancy; on any kind of pleasure party, Miss Gowrie's first concern was to establish an idea of the official. It required character to be a spoilsport on a privileged day, but she rose to the painful occasion with a sort of pathetic, sporting determination, like a trout jumping to the cruel hook.

A cough and a tobacco stain on the second finger of her right hand told us that she was a heavy smoker, but we learned from the riding master's wife that Miss Gowrie steadily refused to take a cigarette anywhere near the Seminary and blinked with disapproval when she heard that other teachers did it. This watchfulness of conscience brooded likewise over her favorites; that is, her better students, for she knew no other measure. You could tell you were in Miss Gowrie's good graces by the bad-conduct marks she set firmly opposite your name in the school record book. In fact, in all her ways she was a stoic of the Roman mold, recalling that matron cited in Pliny, the terrible Arria, who, to encourage her husband to commit suicide, plunged a dagger into her own breast, drew it out, saying, "It doesn't hurt, Paetus," and handed it to him.

It was the whim of oddity, doubtless, that first decided me to "like" Miss Gowrie. And the other class stars, who happened that year also to be taking Latin, quickly fell in with the notion. The rest of the school, we thought, had been unjust to Miss Gowrie, and it delighted us to watch them marvel as they watched *us* forgo our cigarettes and our hamburgers and our sundaes and invite Miss Gowrie to chaperon us to the movies and the riding academy, where, *mirabile dictu*, heated by the fire and tea, she unbent a little with the shy English major and his wife who ran it, gentlefolk and exiles like herself. We could see by the way the conversation broke off when we tramped into the little sitting room after our hour's ride that Miss Gowrie had been confiding in the major's wife. This filled us with indulgent emotions; we were determined to bring Miss Gowrie out and see her round face shine with awkward pleasure. At the same time, we wanted to show the school that we had been right, that there was "another" Miss Gowrie underneath, just as we had been proclaiming. And to display this other Miss Gowrie in her proper setting we revived the moribund Latin Club, elected ourselves officers, proselytized among the freshmen and sophomores, and encouraged Miss Gowrie to start writing "Marcus Tullius."

It did not, of course, occur to me that there was also "another" me, behind the Catilinarian poses—that my discovery of Miss Gowrie was disclosing, unbeknownst to me, certain strange landscapes in myself. And yet something unforeseeable had happened early in senior year. Not having started Latin until the year before, I was tutoring with Miss Gowrie in Caesar to meet college requirements and at the same time taking Cicero in classwork. The very first day, as we sat at her desk with the *Commentaries* between us and learned the divisions of Gaul, the fantastic thing occurred: I fell in love with Caesar! The sensation was utterly confounding. All my previous crushes had been products of my will, constructs of my personal convention, or projections of myself, the way Catiline was. This came from without and seized me; there was nothing that could have warned me that Caesar would be like *this*.

Probably it might have happened with another—with Thucydides, say, if Greek had been offered at Annie Wright. I can experience today the same inner trembling when I read, "Thucydides of Athens has written the history of the war between the Peloponnesians and the Athenians." But, as it came about, the first piercing contact with an impersonal reality happened to me through Caesar, just, laconic, severe, magnanimous, detached—the bald instrument of empire who wrote not "I" but "Caesar." The very grammar was beatified for me by the objective temperament that ordered it, so much so that today I cannot see an ablative absolute or a passage of indirect discourse without happy tears springing to my eyes. Classicist friends laugh when I say that Caesar is a great stylist, but I think so. I know the *Gallic War* is regarded by historians as simply a campaign document, but in my heart I do not believe it. The idea that critics exist who pretend to tell you, at a distance of two thousand years, what "really" happened at Gergovia or in Britain fills me with Olympian mirth. For me, Caesar's word is sufficient; he did not palliate his cruelties or stain the names of his opponents.

It needed only a few days for me to discover that Miss Gowrie shared this passion; two lovers of the same person always find each other out. And like two lovers, precisely, we used to tell over the virtues of the beloved in a shared, incredulous delight. We *liked*, we said to each other, that bridge across the Rhine that students had been cursing for centuries; we liked the fortifications and the legions' feats of engineering. Above all, we liked that mind that was immersed in practical life as in some ingenious detective novel, that wished always to show you how anything was done and under what disadvantages. We liked the spirit of justice and scientific inquiry that reigned over the *Commentaries*, the geographer's curiosity and the Roman adaptiveness that circumvented the enemy by a study of his own techniques, as when the halyards of the Veneti's warships were caught in the long Roman hooked poles.

And, as usual in true love, there were obstacles to be surmounted, which gave Miss Gowrie, as a person of conscience, more difficulty than they gave me. For years, it would seem, her imagination had been tethered in the little patch of history that stretched from 58 to 51 B.C., and her moral faculty had been poring over this period with a sort of heavy intensity, seeking justification for the relentless course of history, for the northward march of the legions, pillaging and slaying. Miss Gowrie, after all, was a Celt, like me, and to her literalist mind those old whiskered Gauls were her kinsmen. The conquest of Gaul chafed her; as she sat beside me at her desk, her feet in their flat shoes planted straight before her on the floor, a nervous frown puckered her brow whenever the war shifted from the Swiss, the Germans, and the Belgians to deal with dissension in Gaul. As we neared the great rising of Book VII, she began, by slow degrees, to prepare me for something painful that was coming, like an aunt who is going to have to break the news of divorce or death in the family.

To her, this rising was a tragedy, a tragedy that Caesar anticipated and tried to avert up to the very last moment. It was a tragedy not only in the sense that a high civilization was crushed, to the accompaniment of many casualties, when a peaceful assimilation might have been managed, but because a noble nature was brought to dust in it. I mean Vercingetorix the Arvernian. If Caesar was Miss Gowrie's master, this young Romanized nobleman, *"summae potentiae adulescens,"* was her beau ideal. She never tired of dwelling on Caesar's praises of him, on the fact that Caesar called him "friend." It was a point of great significance to her that his conduct in leading the last great conspiracy of the Gauls was never reprobated by his conqueror. In his place, declared Miss Gowrie, warming, Caesar would have done the same thing. Did not Caesar himself say, *"omnis autem homines natura libertati studere et condicionem servitutis odisse"* ("however, all men by nature are zealous for liberty and detest the condition of slavery")? Caesar, to our minds, must have borne him a manly love, and it must have grieved Caesar's heart, we both thought, to see the young Gaul, most accomplished of all his opponents, who had won a round from him at Gergovia, ride down the hill from the starved fortress town of Alesia and make the chivalrous submission that saved his people from death. We saw moisture in Caesar's marble eyes as he waited there and the handsome Arvernian dismounted, as described in Plutarch, and seated himself gently at his feet. And yet, six years later, Vercingetorix was brought out of a Roman jail, driven in Caesar's triumph, and then executed. . . .

It was hard to forgive Caesar this deed, especially as Miss Gowrie recounted it, with a clink of her teeth and a sharp little shake of her head. According to her, Vercingetorix, in the triumph, was mounted on the same black charger on which he had come, in all his youth and generosity, down the hill at Alesia—the horse, too, had been preserved for the occasion and led out, a bag of bones, to mock the wretched captive. This was one of the odd fictional touches that Miss Gowrie's troubled imagination sometimes invented. History yields no horse and hence no savage stroke of irony to cap a pretty tale.

In Miss Gowrie's eyes, however, the blame accrued not to Caesar but to the bad Gauls. She had worked up a typical Foreign Office version of the conquest of Gaul, which divided the natives into two categories: good Gauls and bad Gauls. It was the bad Gauls who made Caesar's task hard and trying by continually playing him false. And it was these same bad Gauls who let Vercingetorix down and thus bore responsibility for the triumph. Vercingetorix eluded these categories by being an honorable opponent, like His Majesty's Loyal Opposition. The good Gauls, generally, were exemplified by a certain Diviciacus the Haeduan and the bad by his brother, Dumnorix.

These two Haeduans, who actually play a rather minor part in the *Commentaries*, occupied for Miss Gowrie the very center of the picture. And in my own memory of the Gallic Wars their presence dominates. Diviciacus, the druid, friend of Caesar, principal statesman of the Haedui, a grave and prudent and honorable man who had once made a trip to Rome and stayed the night with Cicero, received Miss Gowrie's special approbation. He stood for the spirit of the south, the Romanized province; he was capable of keeping sworn oaths, and for Caesar he was the first warning beacon on the hilltop signaling the descent of the northern invader. To Miss Gowrie and me, it was always a comfort to think of Diviciacus, with his reliable Latinized name, and to know that Caesar was not alone there, in turbulent, untrustworthy Gaul, where friends strangely turned into enemies and a Roman defeat sustained at dawn in the north would be celebrated in the south at sundown or before the end of the first watch. Caesar had Quintus Cicero, of course, and Labienus, the legates, but Quintus, like poor Marcus Tullius, was unstable, and the solid Labienus in the civil war was going to go over to Pompey and had, we thought, a coarse, crude personality, quite lacking in the grace and dignity that Caesar required in a friend. It was Diviciacus, Miss Gowrie emphasized, with a stern whistle of the teeth, who had for Caesar *"summam voluntatem, egregiam fidem, iustitiam, temperantiam,"* and for the Roman people *"summum studium."*

Justice, good will, moderation, and *uncommon fidelity*—why should these substantives of virtue have stirred the Seminary's Catiline? At the time, I was sublimely unaware that my fortifications had been breached, that the forces of law and order were pacifying the city while the rebel standard still waved on the ramparts. When I took Miss Gowrie's midyear, I answered the question "Contrast the two Haeduan brothers" with an account of political affairs within the Haeduan tribe that greatly pleased Miss Gowrie but that Caesar, the impartial historian, would have eyed askance. "Good!" wrote Miss Gowrie opposite the passage in which I described the perfidious Dumnorix as embodying all the worst qualities of the American Indian. If the voice of Diviciacus always sounded grave and cautionary in the Roman councils, the sly hand of Dumnorix was always discovered at the bottom of every intrigue, every defection, every difficulty. If the Haeduans failed to supply the promised grain, it was Dumnorix who was back of it; if the Sequani allowed the Helvetians free passage, it was because they had been prompted by Dumnorix, who had married a daughter of Orgetorix, the Helvetian chieftain. Dumnorix's light-fingered touch, like that of a savage, was everywhere. He had a clannish matrimonial eye; he matched a half sister here, a female cousin there, and even went so far as to marry off his mother to a chief of the Bituriges. Caesar was always forgiving him, "for the sake of the love he bore his brother, Diviciacus," but in the end Dumnorix went too far. On the eve of the second invasion of Britain, he ran off with the Haeduan cavalry, and Caesar sent his own horsemen after him, with instructions to kill him if he resisted. "The death of Dumnorix is ironic," I wrote (we had been studying irony in English), "because a fickle man dies adjuring his followers to keep faith with him." "Very good," commented Miss Gowrie. And yet Dumnorix died screaming that he was a free man and the son of a free state—"*saepe clamitans liberum se liberaeque esse civitatis.*"

In later years, those screams of a cornered man have echoed reproachfully in my mind, particularly during the recent war, when they merged with the screams of other Gauls, other patriots and Resistance leaders who failed to keep faith with the conqueror. I saw the "good" Diviciacus as the archetypal quisling and felt the keenest vexation with my old Latin teacher for having steered me, as I conceived it, in a false direction. Today, I look at things in a more "balanced" perspective and find certain merits in Miss Gowrie's point of view. We, too, have our expedient Diviciacuses, who, we are assured, are loyal to the democratic cause. The Pax Romana (in democratic hands, of course) once again appears to have its virtues, and we see the point of justice, moderation, and uncommon fidelity. If Caesar invented Caesarism, he had a distaste for blood. He shuddered and burst into tears when they brought him Pompey's head, unsolicited, and in the Gallic Wars only three atrocities, minute by modern standards, defaced his record of clemency: the flogging to death of two chiefs and the cutting off of the hands of the defenders of Uxellodunum. Hail Caesar!

One thing, however, I now think I know for certain: Catiline was a gangster and a ruffian, just as that old bore, Cicero, said. I believe I already knew it that night in the gymnasium. What puzzles me is an eerie sense that Miss Gowrie, unsuspected by me, was my co-conspirator, that our predilections that year kept alternating, like the two little wooden weather figures in a German clock, one of which steps out as the other swings back into the works, in response to atmospheric pressures. I suddenly remember the curious pains that were taken over every detail of my outfitting—how the flame Indianhead was stenciled with gold to make my military cloak far more glorious than history would have permitted, while the outfits of the generals of the Republic were rented in a tawdry lot from a theatrical costumer. A recollection of my own surprise comes back to me, surprise that Miss Gowrie, the pedant, should have let me wear a costume that even I knew was wrong. And I recall, too, how the finest white kid ballerina slippers, used only by professionals, were purchased and dyed crimson to make my *calcei patricii mullei* (red leather shoes worn by the highest magistrates), with crisscrossed red tapes that Miss Gowrie herself bound up my calves. I was the only performer who had these; even Cicero wore sandals. Everything Catiline wore was of the finest and most costly; he was dressed like a statue in a primitive religious festival—no wonder the seventh and eighth grades applauded.

I have only to summon up Miss Gowrie's tall, doll-like figure, with its rigid, jerky movements, and remember the mechanical pivoting of the round head and the short blink of the staring eyes to recognize the possibility of mild, clinical symptoms of the disease that adjusts itself to routine, to the performance of monotonous tasks, while the "real" patient, withdrawn, lives in a world of garish fantasies and symbols. I suspect, suddenly, that my childish rebelliousness and demagogic vanity may have been the tools of some absolutist world-dream of Miss Gowrie's, just as these qualities, matured in the real Catiline, had been the tools of Caesar. Little as it meant to me then, I cannot get it out of my mind today that Catiline, in his brilliant costume, was a murderer, who slew his own brother-in-law and tortured a man to death.

In any case, Miss Gowrie certainly repented "Marcus Tullius" with all her Presbyterian conscience. A few days after the performance, she denounced me to the principal for some small infraction of the rules. Next, Caesar was reported, then Cicero. By exam week, the leaders of the Roman republic had virtually all been proscribed. Within the classroom, she was unaltered, patient, and even kindly in her arid, abrupt way. But in the dormitory that peculiar *Doppelgänger*, her duty, seemed to have taken total possession of her, like an evil spirit. Her drawer was filled with confiscated fountain pens; she tightened up the bath schedule and rapped on the door if you lingered; she seemed to stay up half the night listening for voices talking after lights out.

But I, too, had a duty, or so I thought—a duty to break the rules and take all offered risks, in order not to graduate in an orderly, commonplace fashion, and as spring advanced into early summer and the last week of school was on us, I had a sense that these two opposed duties were rushing inflexibly toward each other, like two trains on the same track. It happened one night in June; she caught me coming in the gym window on my way back from meeting a boy. We stood staring at each other in sorry recognition, Miss Gowrie in a brown bathrobe and I in my dew-dampened dress uniform. She was a poor sleeper; she had heard a noise and thought somebody was trying to get in to the swimming pool. We both knew that what I had done was the only crime that was considered serious by the principal. Miss Gowrie did not ask where I had been but sent me up to my room, where I could not sleep for wondering whether she would report me in the morning. School was as good as over, but I doubted whether that would deter Miss Gowrie. And if she told, I was finished, I supposed, for it was against my code of honor to lie when you were directly accused.

The next day, after lunch, I was called into the principal's office. Miss Gowrie had reported me. After the first few minutes' colloquy, in which the principal did *not* ask what I had been doing, I saw that I could graduate after all if I would make the concession of lying: I was the top student in my class, and the school, I perceived, was counting on me to do it credit in my college boards. We assessed each other steadily; we both understood the position and understood that the lie was a favor being asked of me, not only for my own sake and the school's but on behalf of poor, misguided Miss Gowrie, who ought to have known better than to prowl about at night in her bathrobe in the last week of school. A sense of power and Caesarlike magnanimity filled me. I was going to equivocate, not for selfish reasons but in the interests of the community, like a grown-up, responsible person. I hesitated, seeking a formula that would not compromise principle too greatly. "I went out to smoke," I finally proposed; this was true in the sense that at any rate I *had* smoked. The principal sighed, accepting this farfetched explanation. In a moment, I was on her lap and we were crying, chiefly from relief but partly, or so I sensed, in farewell to my childhood; I suddenly felt old and tired, like the principal herself. A few days later, our class graduated, and Miss Gowrie, in an old silk print dress, sat in the audience watching us with a hurt, puzzled expression as we pronounced our triumphant salutes and valedictions in our white caps and gowns, wearing our new pearls and wrist watches and pendants, surrounded by baskets of roses and irises sent by our relations and admirers.

Miss Gowrie did not return to the school, and I saw her only once more—that summer, following the college boards, when I asked her to lunch with me in a department-store tearoom in Seattle. It was a queer, empty meeting. She bore me no grudge for graduating, but I could see that she could find nothing to say to me now that the context of work and discipline was gone. She blinked at me bewilderedly as I smoked and talked showily about modern literature and college and tried to gossip about the school. I had brought my Caesar along, and together, at Miss Gowrie's demand, we went over the translation that had been set in the college-board exam. I had not done as well as we had hoped. She ate a crackly dessert called "frange" that was popular in our city and experienced a slight indigestion. Filled with guilt, boredom, and a sense of helpless treachery to this mysterious individual who seemed to be wanting something I did not know how to give, I became confused and left my Caesar on the luncheon table. But if Miss Gowrie saw it as we were leaving, she said nothing and went her terse way, back to Canada and Empire. When I called for the book later, at the store Lost and Found, they told me it had not been turned in. Aside from the Latin grammar, the only souvenir of our acquaintance left to me was the pair of ballet slippers of the very finest kid that remained in my closet for fifteen years.

There are some semi-fictional touches here. My midyear exam paper for instance: I do not really know whether or not I was asked to contrast the two Haeduan brothers or whether I wrote, "The death of Dumnorix is ironic because a fickle man dies adjuring his followers to keep faith with him." But this was the kind of question Miss Gowrie would have given and the kind of answer I might have made. At some time, certainly, during the term I was asked to contrast the two Haeduans. The notion that Dumnorix was like an American Indian came to me much later, when I happened to be reading about the rising of Pontiac. This Indian chief had a brother who reminded me, at once, of Diviciacus. It is true that those two Gauls stuck in my mind like burrs. At one time, during the war, I had the idea of writing a novel, with historical interludes, about divided allegiances, one interlude was going to be devoted to the two brothers, and another to Parnell.

Miss Gowrie was always reporting her favorites for breaking the rules. She did report me for smoking, but I don't think this happened the day after "Marcus Tullius." This is an example of "storytelling", I arranged actual events so as to make "a good story" out of them. It is hard to overcome this temptation if you *are in the habit of writing fiction, one does it almost automatically.*

I was discovered coming into the gymnasium after meeting a boy one spring evening, shortly before graduation. I think it was Miss Gowrie who caught me, but I am not positive. Sometimes I feel it was and sometimes I feel it wasn't. I recall the sequel more clearly. The principal did invite me to equivocate as to what I had been doing. She was a great crier, and she cried again when I graduated, calling me "Cousin Mary" (she had the same name, Preston, as my grandfather, and they had done their genealogies together), and predicting that I would be an "ornament" to the Seminary. I cried, too, and our joint tears persuaded me that I had been a model pupil all along.

Miss Preston would have had to expel me, though, if the truth had come out, for the boy I had been meeting, in the woods back of the Seminary, was a strange person, a juvenile delinquent. He had lost one leg in a hunting accident and gone to the bad, his sister, I believe, had been a day girl at the Seminary, so that his case was well known to the principal. In reality, our meetings were innocent. We only smoked and talked, but no one would have credited that. I tried to put a darker complexion on it myself and wrote him a poem in study hall that showed the influence of Swinburne, Edna Millay, and possibly Dowson. I still know the first lines by heart:

> Oh, boy that I have loved and shall not see again,
> Be this to you a last and sweet farewell.
> You are too young for me and far too evil.
> Oh, boy whose beauty proved too great for me,
> Smile but a little now and let me go.

The only truth in this poem was that I was slightly afraid of this good-looking boy. I was touched by his empty trouser leg and fascinated by the stories I had heard of his criminality, it was rumored that he had been in reform school. His actual age was seventeen—one year older than I was.

This episode, now that I examine it, does reflect the two themes of "The Figures in the Clock": juvenile delinquency versus maturity. The crippled boy was, to me, a sort of Catiline, that is, a wild, defiant mirror image that I was reluctantly outgrowing. This was why I felt old in comparison to him, though when I made myself an Older Woman in the poem, I thought it was only to give a sad effect. His name was Rex (king), which made a funny link with my Latin studies. I noticed this at the time. That name was part of the charm he had for me, as we sat, side by side, on a little hill, his crutch thrown down, while younger members of his outlaw band circled the woods behind us, to warn us if anyone were coming. The poem was false, and yet it was true. It "tells the same story" as "The Figures in the Clock."

My grandfather was enthusiastic about "Marcus Tullius." He declared, quite seriously, that it was the best play he had ever seen. I understand why a lawyer would like it; no doubt, he was on Cicero's side. He stood up and clapped long and loud, and as I pick out his spare figure now in the audience, another piece in the pattern falls into place. Caesar, of course, was my grandfather: just, laconic, severe, magnanimous, detached. These are the very adjectives I might use to describe Lawyer Preston, who was bald into the bargain. Catiline was my McCarthy ancestors —the wild streak in my heredity, the wreckers on the Nova Scotia coast. To my surprise, I chose Caesar and the rule of law. This does not mean that the seesaw between these two opposed forces terminated; one might say, in fact, that it only began during my last years in the Seminary when I recognized the beauty of an ablative absolute and of a rigorous code of conduct. I was not prepared for this recognition; it was like an unexpected meeting.

That is the reason, I suppose, for the flood of joyful emotion released in me by Caesar and the Latin language and for the fact that I feel it still.

The injustices my brothers and I had suffered in our childhood had made me a rebel against authority, but they had also prepared me to fall in love with justice, the first time I encountered it. I loved my grandfather from the beginning, but the conflicts between us (the reader will hear of them presently) somewhat obscured this feeling, which poured out with a rush on Caesar, who, in real life, would have been as strict as my grandfather ("Caesar's wife must be above suspicion"), but whom I did not have to deal with personally.

In the Seminary, we had Sacred Study under the widow of a bishop. As a Catholic, I had come to know the New Testament well—it is not true that Catholics do not read the Bible. In the Episcopalian school, we concentrated on the Old Testament. The sentence that still rings in my ears is one from Micah: "And what doth the Lord require of thee, but to do justly, and to love mercy, and to walk humbly with thy God?" This moved me powerfully when I first heard it in Mrs. Keator's classroom (I believe she also wrote it on the blackboard), and it seemed to me that a new voice had spoken, the plain protestant voice of true religion.

At the same time, I took advantage of the fact that I was still, officially, a Catholic to get out of going on Sundays with the rest of the girls to the Episcopal church, where the dean regularly delivered an hour-and-a-half sermon. The Catholic mother of some of our small day pupils took me with her to the Catholic church, where the noon Mass lasted only fifteen minutes. The school chapel services, morning and evening, I greatly enjoyed, in spite of being an atheist. I loved the hymns and the litanies and hearing our principal intone at nightfall: "We have left undone

*those things which we ought to have done, And we have done
those things which we ought not to have done, And there is no
health in us."*

*My grandfather, during this period, used to express the hope
that I would be a lawyer. But I still dreamed of becoming an
actress; I had starred in three school plays, and the summer after
I graduated from Annie Wright, the family let me go to drama
school (the Cornish School in Seattle), which was a sorry disappointment to my ambitions, for I only learned eurythmics and
played the wordless part of a pirate in a scene that, for some
reason, was supposed to take place under water: we pirates, all
girls, made strange, rhythmic movements to create a subaqueous
effect. In college, my hopes revived; I was in several plays and
took the role of Leontes in A Winter's Tale during my senior year.
But the actor I later married came to see my performance and
told me the truth: I had no talent. I had begun to feel this myself,
so without further discussion I gave up the dream that had been
with me thirteen years, ever since I had been Iris in a parochial
school play about the kingdom of the flowers. I started to write
instead, which did not interest me nearly so much, chiefly because
it came easier. At the very time I was renouncing the stage, unknown to me Kevin at the University of Minnesota was beginning
his acting career.*

Yellowstone Park

THE SUMMER I was fifteen I was invited to go to Montana by Ruth and Betty Bent, a pair of odd sisters who had come that year to our boarding school in Tacoma from a town called Medicine Springs, where their father was a federal judge. The answer from my grandparents was going to be no, I foresaw. I was too young (they would say) to travel by train alone, just as I was too young (they said) to go out with boys or accept rides in automobiles or talk to male callers on the telephone. This notion in my grandparents' minds was poisoning my life with shame, for mentally I was old for my age—as I was also accustomed to hearing from grownups in the family circle. I was so much older in worldly wisdom than *they* were that when my grandmother and my great-aunt read *The Well of Loneliness*, they had to come to ask me what the women in the book "did." "Think of it," nodded my great-aunt, reviewing the march of progress, "nowadays a fifteen-year-old girl knows a thing like that." At school, during study hall, I wrote stories about prostitutes with "eyes like dirty dishwater," which my English teacher read and advised me to send to H. L. Mencken for criticism. Yet despite all this—or possibly because of it—I was still being treated as a child who could hardly be trusted to take a streetcar without a grownup in attendance. The argument that "all the others did it" cut no ice with my grandfather, whose lawyer's mind was too precise to deal in condonation. He conceived that he had a weighty trust in my upbringing, since I had come to him as an orphan, the daughter of his only daughter.

Yet like many old-fashioned trustees, he had a special, one might say an occupational, soft spot. Anything educational was a lure to him. Salesmen of encyclopedias and stereopticon sets and Scribner's classics found him an easy prey in his Seattle legal offices, where he rose like a trout to the fly or a pickerel to the spoon. He reached with alacrity for his pocketbook at the sight of an extra on the school bill. I had had music lessons, special coaching in Latin, tennis lessons, riding lessons, diving lessons; that summer, he was eager for me to have golf lessons. Tickets for civic pageants, theater and concert subscription series, library memberships were treated by him as necessities, not to be paid for out of my allowance, which I was free to devote to freckle creams and Christmas Night perfume. Some of the books I read and plays I saw made other members of the family raise their eyebrows, but my grandfather would permit no interference. He looked tolerantly over his glasses as he saw me stretched out on the sofa with a copy of *Count Bruga* or *The Hard-Boiled Virgin*. I had been styling myself an atheist and had just announced, that spring, that I was going east to college. The right of the mind to develop according to its own lights was a prime value to my grandfather, who was as rigid in applying this principle as he was strait-laced in social matters.

The previous summer had been made miserable for me by his outlandish conduct. At the resort we always went to in the Olympic Mountains (my grandmother, who did not care for the outdoors, always stayed home in Seattle), he and I had suddenly become a center of attention. The old judges and colonels, the young married women whose husbands came up for the week end, the young college blades, the hostess with the Sweetheart haircut who played the piano for dancing, the very prep-school boys were looking on me, I knew, with pity because of the way my grandfather was acting—never letting me out of his sight, tapping me on the dance floor to tell me it was my bedtime, standing on the dock with a pair of binoculars when a young man managed to take me rowing for fifteen clocked minutes on the lake. One time, when a man from New York named Mr. Jones wanted me to take his picture with a salmon, my grandfather had leapt up from the bridge table and thundered after us down the woodland path. And what did he discover?—me snapping Mr. Jones' picture on a rustic bridge, that was all. What did he think could have happened, anyway, at eleven o'clock in the morning, fifty feet from the veranda where he and his cronies were playing cards? The whole hotel knew what he thought and was laughing at us. A boy did imitations of Mr. Jones holding the salmon with one hand and hugging me with the other, then dropping the salmon and fleeing in consternation when my grandfather appeared.

My grandfather did not care; he never cared what people thought of him, so long as he was doing his duty. And he expected me to be perfectly happy, taking walks up to the waterfall with him and the judges' and colonels' ladies; measuring the circumference of Douglas firs; knocking the ball around the five-hole golf course; doing the back dive from the springboard while he looked on, approving, with folded arms; playing the player piano by myself all afternoon: torn rolls of "Tea for Two" and "Who" and one called "Sweet Child" that a young man with a Marmon roadster had sung into my radiant ear on the dance floor until my grandfather scared him off.

Sweet child, indeed! I felt I could not stand another summer like that. I had to go to Montana, and my grandfather, I knew, would let me if only I could persuade him that the trip would be broadening and instructive; that is, if in my eyes it would be profoundly boring.

It did not take divination on my part to guess what would fit these requirements: Yellowstone Park. The very yawn I had to stifle at the thought of geysers, Old Faithful, colored rock formations, Indians, grizzly bears, pack horses, tents, rangers, parties of tourists with cameras and family sedans, told me I had the bait to dangle before his kindly-severe grey eyes. It was too bad, I remarked casually, in the course of my last school letter home, that the trip was out of the question: the girls had been planning to take me on a tour of Yellowstone Park. That was all that was needed. It was as simple as selling him a renewal of his subscription to the *National Geographic*. The ease of it somehow depressed me, casting a pall over the adventure; one of the most boring things about adolescence is the knowledge of how people can be worked.

I *ought* to go to Montana, said my grandfather decidedly, after he had looked up Judge Bent in a legal directory and found that he really existed: a thing which slightly surprised me, for in my representations to my grandparents, I always had the sensation of lying. Whatever I told them was usually so blurred and glossed, in the effort to meet their approval (for, aside from anything else, I was fond of them and tried to accommodate myself to their perspective), that except when answering a direct question I hardly knew whether what I was saying was true or false. I really tried, or so I thought, to avoid lying, but it seemed to me that they forced it on me by the difference in their vision of things, so that I was always transposing reality for them into terms they could understand. To keep matters straight with my conscience, I shrank, whenever possible, from the lie absolute, just as, from a sense of precaution, I shrank from the plain truth. Yellowstone

Park was a typical instance. I had not utterly lied when I wrote that sentence. I entertained, let us say, a vague hope of going there and had spoken to the Bent girls about it in a tentative, darkling manner, *i.e.*, "My family hopes we can see Yellowstone." To which the girls replied, with the same discreet vagueness, "Umm."

At home, it was settled for me to entrain with the girls shortly after school closed, stay three weeks, which would give us time to "do" the Park, and come back by myself. It would only be two nights, my grandfather pointed out to my grandmother; and Judge Bent could put me on the train in care of the conductor. The two girls nodded demurely, and Ruth, the elder, winked at me, as my grandfather repeated these instructions.

I was mortified. As usual, my grandfather's manner seemed calculated to expose me in front of my friends, to whom I posed as a practiced siren. My whole life was a lie, it often appeared to me, from beginning to end, for if I was wilder than my family knew, I was far tamer than my friends could imagine, and with them, too, as with my family, I was constantly making up stories, pretending that a ring given me by a great-aunt was a secret engagement ring, that I went out dancing regularly to the Olympic Hotel, that a literary boy who wrote to me was in love with me— the usual tales, but I did not know that. All I knew was that there was one central, compromising fact about me that had to be hidden from my friends and that burned me like the shirt of the Centaur: I could not bear to have anyone find out that I was considered too young to go out with boys.

But every word, every gesture of my grandfather's seemed designed to proclaim this fact. I perceived an allusion to it in the fussy way he saw us off at the Seattle depot, putting us in our drawing room with many cautions not to speak to strangers, tipping the Pullman porter and having a "word" with the conductor, while my grandmother pressed a lacy handkerchief to her eyes and my uncle grinned and the old family gardener and handy man advised me not to take any wooden nickels. During this degrading ordeal, the Bent girls remained polite and deferential, agreeing to everything (it was always *my* tendency to argue). But as soon as the train pulled out of the station, Ruth Bent coolly summoned the conductor and exchanged our drawing room for two upper berths. They always did this on boarding the train, she explained; two could fit very comfortably into an upper, and the money they got back was clear profit.

Ruth Bent was the boldest person, for her age, I had ever met. She was seventeen, two years older than her sister, and she looked, to me, about forty. She had reddish-brown frizzy hair and she wore earrings, eyeglasses, picture hats, printed chiffon dresses, a deep purplish red lipstick, and Golliwog perfume. Her voice was deep, like a man's; her skin was swarthy and freckled; her eyebrows, shaped with tweezers, were a dark chocolate color. She had a good figure, small, with a sort of shimmying movement to it. In school she had the name of being fast, which was based partly on her clothes and partly on the direct stare of her reddish-brown eyes, very wide open and rounded by the thick lenses of her glasses so that the whites had the look of boiled eggs. She made me think of a college widow.

Actually, she was a serious girl, in her own inscrutable way; she sang in the choir and was respected by the school principal. No one knew quite what to make of her. It was argued that she was common (I could not help thinking this myself) and that her sister, Betty, was more the school type. Betty was a boyish girl with a short haircut, a wide thin face, high cheekbones, and clear grey-green eyes. She had a broad flat mouth and a big elastic Western smile that disclosed shining teeth. Her lipstick was

Tangee. She had a lighter voice than her sister's and a light, scherzo touch on the piano; she played at school recitals.

Both girls were very good dancers. And they both liked to ride, which was how we had become friends. In the pocket of her black riding habit (Betty wore jodhpurs), Ruth always had a package of cigarettes, which she calmly took out as soon as we were mounted, right in front of the English major who was the school riding master. The major liked both girls and let them have the best horses and ride wherever they pleased. The Bent girls had some quality—levelheadedness, I suppose—that reassured older people. They never got into trouble, no matter what they did, while I was either in high favor or on the verge of being expelled. Unlike me, they did not seek to make a point; they merely did what they wanted, in a bald, impersonal way, like two natural forces—a sultry dark-browed wind and a light playful breeze. Their self-possession, I felt, must rest on an assured social position at home. In Montana, they said, they had a very lively crowd and their family gave them complete freedom. Their town was small, but there was always a party going, and they had friends all over the state. I would have plenty of dates, they promised me, in Medicine Springs.

Geography, in those days, left me cold; it reminded me of grade school, slide lectures, and the stereopticon. Consequently, I had not bothered to look up Medicine Springs on the map. It had once been a spa, the girls said, and this was enough for me to place it up in the north, near Canada, where I supposed the mountains were; I thought vaguely of Saratoga Springs, horse races, big rambling hotels in Victorian architecture, gamblers, mining men from roaring Butte. It astonished me to learn, in mid-journey, that Medicine Springs was in the center of the state and that we were going to have to change trains to get there. It was nowhere near Yellowstone Park, I discovered with a guilty tremor; in fact, it was not near any place I had heard of. It did not even figure on the railroad map on our timetable.

We changed—I forget where—and took a dusty little branch train with hard board seats. I had never seen a train like this, and a gloomy premonition overtook me as we jolted along across a prairie, the two girls in high spirits at the prospect of getting home. I kept looking out the window for scenery, but there was nothing, not a river, not a hill, not a tree—just a flat expanse of dry grass and gopher mounds, with a few houses strung along at the rare stations. Medicine Springs, when we reached it, was a small, flat, yellowish town set in the middle of nowhere. There was one wide dusty main street with a drugstore and a paintless hotel; several smaller streets crossed it, ran for a block or two, and then stopped. You could take it in at a glance. Behind the hotel there were the "springs" alluded to in the town's name; they consisted of a dirty, sulphurous, cement swimming pool with one half-dead tree leaning over it. The heat was awful, and the only shade apparent was provided by telephone poles. I could not believe that my friends lived here and supposed, to myself, that we must be going to a ranch somewhere out of sight on the prairie.

Judge Bent was at the depot, a sallow, middle-aged man with dark hair and a modified cowboy hat; he put our bags in his car, and I got set for a long drive. But in a trice we had arrived at the Bent home. It was somewhat larger than the other houses we had passed and it had a front porch and a tree. Another dwelling with a tree was identified by the girls as "The Manse"; I looked in vain for mosses. These two frame houses and one other, which professed to be haunted, constituted the town's "residential" quarter.

Mrs. Bent came to the door, and I tried to put on a pleased and excited expression. But everything I saw shocked and almost frightened me; the modest size of the house, the thin walls, the absence of books and pictures, the lack of any ornament or architectural feature, the table already set in the middle of the afternoon without a flower or a centerpiece, the fact that Mrs. Bent evidently did her own work, that there was no guest room and that I was to share a room and closet with Betty and a bath with the whole family. This feeling on my part was not precisely a snobbish reaction; if the Bents had been poor, I would not have felt so ill-at-ease and indeed paralyzed. What struck me here was a sense of disorientation. Knowing the Bents not to be poor, I could not "place" them. The girls, I perceived, were unaware of my difficulties. They did not catch even a glimpse of their home refracted from my glazed eyes. This was a relief, but at the same time it amazed me. In their place, I would have died of mortification.

This disregard was typical of the Bent household. The two girls, while perfectly affectionate, took no notice of their parents, who might as well have been a pair of mutes at the family board. I had been trained not to talk at table until drawn out by my hosts, but neither Judge nor Mrs. Bent appeared conscious of a social duty to find out who I was, where I came from, what my parents did. I was there, simply, and they accepted my presence. The only fact I ever elicited about them was that Judge Bent had taken his law degree at Madison, Wisconsin. My provenance, theirs, were as indifferent to them as that of the baked potato that the judge silently helped onto my plate.

Mrs. Bent's function seemed to be to answer the telephone and iron the girls' summer dresses. She never wanted to know who was calling or where the dresses were to be worn. I wished she *would* ask, that first night at dinner, for this was a question that interested me. Despite what I had seen of Medicine Springs, my hopes began to stir again when I perceived that we were to have dates that night. The girls were talking of a dance, out of town, on the prairie; someone named Frank was coming to call for us with his car. I was too uppity to dream of cowboys, even if the girls had not warned me that they were all dirty, spitting old men. But from casual bits dropped by the girls, I was piecing together, once more, an image of what the true West must have in store for me—smooth, sleek boys whose fathers owned sheep or cattle ranches, who wore white linen suits and drove roadsters and probably went east to college. I imagined a long piazza, a barbecue pit, and silver flasks glinting in the moonlight.

But there were no boys in Medicine Springs; all the men in Medicine Springs were married.

This bitter news came to me slowly, and it was prefaced by other information that slightly blunted its effect, like a preliminary dose of Novocain. They were not *all* married; there was one dim exception, the "Frank" who had come to fetch us in an old Ford. He was a young man of twenty with glasses and hair that stood straight up; he clerked in the hotel in the summer and in the winter he went to the state college at Bozeman. His father, Mr. Hoey, was the hotelkeeper. The Hoeys and the Bents and the people who owned the drugstore made up the local aristocracy. That was all there was. There had once been a clergyman, but he had died, and a circus family, but they had gone away. I now say to myself that there must have been a doctor, at least, and an undertaker, but memory shakes its head. No. Probably the pharmacist combined these functions.

At any rate, I was so dashed by this lesson in small-town sociology, which the girls imparted on the way down to the hotel, and by the sight of the hotel lobby, which contained three straight-backed chairs, three cuspidors, a desk with a register, some fly-paper, and Mr. Hoey in his shirtsleeves, that I could hardly take in the next tidings: on my first official date, I was going to have to go out with a married man. Betty too. There they stood, the husbands, waiting for us beside their cars: a small black-haired man called "Acey," who did automobile repairs (he was Betty's), and a tall wavy-haired blond named Bob Berdan, who worked in the drugstore (he was mine).

Later, Ruth explained that the men here married early or else went away to work. That winter there had been several marriages, which left only Frank, who belonged to her, as the elder sister, and Acey, who belonged to Betty and was practically single since he was getting divorced from a wife who had run away from him. Usually, there were boys staying in the town, but this summer they had been lucky to get Bob Berdan, whose wife was away visiting her relations. Every single girl was after him; he was the handsomest man in Medicine Springs and very hard to please.

Of the three men, he was certainly the best looking; I had to admit that, as he put out a large hand with a ring on it and stood looking down into my eyes. He was common; his hair was too wavy; his skin was too dark for his hair; and he had a white toothpaste-ad smile that made me think of his work in the drugstore. But from a distance he could pass. He had an old touring car, which he was waiting for me to get into; Betty had already joined Acey in his salesman's coupé.

What was I to do? My grandfather would have told me to say good night, politely, and ask to be taken home. Just because the others had fixed it up for me was no reason for me to fall in with their plans. Today, in my grandfather's place, I would give the same counsel, which shows how out of touch, how impractical, older people are. In reality, I had no choice but to get into the car, which I did, seating myself nervously in the far corner. The three cars, with Frank and Ruth in the lead, started out in procession across the prairie. I could see that in the car ahead of us Betty's head was on Acey's shoulder. Was I expected to follow this example too? My date, I was glad to find, was busy manipulating the wheel and singing last year's love songs in a croony voice. Peering at his arrow-cut profile, I began to feel a little less terrified.

Before long, the first car stopped and we all followed suit. I thought there was something wrong; the road was very bad, almost a wagon trail. But it seemed that we were pausing to have a drink. Frank got out of the first car and came back with a pint bottle, which he passed to Acey and Betty and then to Bob and me. I took a mouthful and gagged. It was the first time I had ever tasted hard liquor, but I did not want them to guess that; the few sips of champagne and half-glass of Canadian beer that had been allowed me at home, on special occasions, had prompted me to boast of my drinking prowess. With Frank and Bob watching, I tried once more to swallow the burning stuff in my mouth; instead, I gagged again and the liquor spilled out all over my face and neck. Bob got out a handkerchief and advised me to try again. I could not get it down. By this time, the whole party had joined us. "Is that whisky?" I asked cautiously; it did not smell like the whisky my grandfather drank. It was moonshine, they said; corn whisky, but the very best; Bob always tested it at the drugstore. One by one, they tilted the bottle and drank, to show me how to do it. It was no use. My throat simply rejected it; I gagged until the tears came. Ruth proposed that I should hold my nose, and in this way I managed to get down a large gulp, which made my stomach rock.

I did not like it at all; the lift they spoke of did not come; I would rather have had my throat painted with Argyrol by the doctor. But they kept passing me the bottle; we stopped repeatedly on the way to the dance to have another swig; eventually, to my horror (for I thought at last it was over), Bob produced a fresh pint from the side pocket of the car. They did not force me to drink; I was free to refuse, as my grandfather could have pointed out. They just watched while I did it and they noticed if I merely put my lips to the bottle. I was ashamed to keep holding my nose, but there seemed to be no other way to swallow, until at length I discovered that I could take a gulp and hold it in my mouth and work it down gradually, when no one was looking, a few drops at a time. This prevented me from talking for long periods. Bob Berdan sang, and I rode along tight-lipped beside him, with a mouth full of unswallowed moonshine, which washed around my teeth as the car bumped along the rutted road. After a while he threw his arm lightly over the back of the seat.

I must have choked down more than I would have thought possible for I can hardly remember the dance. It was in a sort of shed—not even a barn; and there were a lot of rough-looking, unshaven, coatless men pushing and grabbing and yelling while an old woman played the piano. I was frightened, and we did not stay there very long. There was nobody of our own sort or age present, only hands from a ranch and a few older women. The men in our party seemed very white and civilized and out of place in this setting. I stuck close to Bob Berdan, who appeared much more attractive than he had an hour or so before. I could almost imagine that he had been to college.

Perhaps we bought another pint there.

Some hours later, I woke up in a strange room and found there was a man in bed with me. It took me a minute or two to recall who he was: Bob Berdan, of course. My date. We were in a double bed; overhead, hanging from a cord, an unshaded electric light bulb was burning. I had no idea what time it was; probably it was morning, the morning after. And I had no recollection of the room or how we had got there. As everything whirled around me, I felt a wan relief in being able to recognize *him* at least. I had only known him a few hours, but at any rate I knew him.

And it could have been anybody. I was undressed, I could tell
from the touch of the sheet on my bare shoulders, and I was
afraid to raise the covers to explore any further. I lay absolutely
still, staring up at the unfinished beams of the ceiling. In the next
room, I could hear a phonograph and voices. I felt that my life
was over. Bob was asleep; one of his arms was around me. As I
lay there, grimly taking stock, he woke up and his arm tightened;
he started muttering tenderly. Men, I had heard, were like that
after. . . . I was too horror-stricken to finish the thought. The
very first night, the *very* first man, I said to myself, paying no
attention to him, absorbed in my own stolid woe. I did not blame
him, but I would have blotted him out if I could.

He was offering me reassurances, I slowly realized. Nothing
had happened, he kept murmuring; he had not harmed me. I
dared not believe him. But he pulled off the blankets to show me
and, sure enough, I was not really undressed. It was only my dress
and shoes that were gone. I was in my slip and underclothes, and
he was dressed too, except for his coat and shoes.

I had been sick, he explained, and the girls had taken my dress
to try to wash it. We were in his house; they had put me to bed
and I had passed out there. This was not all, I was certain; it did
not explain what *he* was doing there, with his arms around me.
I decided not to inquire. If there had been a certain amount of
necking (which now began to come back to me, hazily), I did not
want to hear about it. The main thing, the miraculous thing, was
that my age had spared me. His voice was full of emotion as he
told me that he would never take advantage of a sweet kid like
me. He had fallen for me, the girls declared, teasing; the sound
of our voices had brought them in from the next room to corrobo-
rate what he was telling me. Nothing had happened, they attested;
they had been there all the time.

Had I drawn a blank, they inquired, solicitously. I had to ask the meaning of this expression. Was it different, I wished to know, from "passing out"? Oh, very different, replied Ruth: you walked around and did and said things which you could not remember afterward. A peculiar smile, reminiscent, flitted across the assembled faces; I buried my head in the covers. It was all right, said Ruth, kindly: Betty used to draw blanks too, when she was younger. ("Younger?" I cried to myself. How much younger? Twelve?)

Matter-of-factly, just as though this happened every day, the girls helped me into my dress, which they had sponged out and ironed. Wasn't it lucky, they commented, that Bob was a married man? Bob kissed me good night, tenderly, and Frank Hoey, who seemed a trifle embarrassed, drove us home in the dawn. I was nerving myself to face Judge and Mrs. Bent, irate, on the stairway, in their night clothes, but no one was up at the Bent house. When we came down to breakfast, finally, Mrs. Bent was busy with the iron. The only question she asked was an absent one: "Did you have a good time?" "Bob Berdan took a tumble for Mary," Ruth vouchsafed, with a laugh. "Oh," said Mrs. Bent, incuriously. "Bob's a nice fellow; is his wife still away?"

During the next weeks, I worried about what Mrs. Bent thought. She must have known that Betty was with Acey and that I was with Bob Berdan nearly every night. But in her mind, apparently, we were out with what she called "the crowd," which included Frank Hoey's sister and the pharmacist's daughters. She must have felt there was safety in numbers or that a married man was a chaperon; that seemed to be how she viewed Bob Berdan, who was nearly twenty-five. Yet what did she suppose the crowd did, from eight until three in the morning? She must have heard me being sick, time and again, in the Bent bathroom and noted my green face at breakfast.

That was the awful thing. Virtually every night was a repetition of the first one. I could not learn to drink their liquor, but I would not stop trying, so that I was either passed out or sick on every one of our dates. We were forever driving somewhere (or, rather, nowhere), and the parade of cars was forever halting for me to throw up by the roadside. As soon as I had done so, the bottle would be passed again. When I was conscious, I was frequently speechless, owing to the fact that there was a gulp of moonshine in my mouth that I had not yet been able to swallow; it would sometimes take ten minutes to work it down. It was all a matter of practice I told myself; look at Ruth and Betty. They never got sick or passed out. And they were always able to tell me what I had done during the hours I could not remember, or rather what I had *not* done, which was all I cared about hearing. Half the town, I think, knew about me and Bob Berdan, down to the detail that he was not "taking advantage" of me, on account of my age and inexperience. He was sweet on me, everyone said, and I accepted it, though I could not imagine why he should be, considering.

It seemed to me, often, that I was taking advantage of *him*. I grew a little tired of his kisses, which did not excite me, perhaps because they were always the same, leading nowhere but to more kisses. I felt he was sentimental, which made me impatient. When I saw him in the drugstore, with his white coat and ripply hair, I was embarrassed for him, just because I could see him so clearly *from the outside*, as a clerk, who would always be a clerk, limited, like his kisses, flat, like the town.

And yet I liked him. I think it was that I was sorry for him, in some faraway part of myself, the part that was already back in Seattle while the rest of me was locked in his arms. I really looked on him, though I was not aware of it, as I did on other adults, seeing him as circumscribed and finite and yet encumbered, like all the rest of them, with a mysterious burden of feeling. In the back of my mind, I had a child's certainty that I was moving, going somewhere, while the grownups around me were standing still. I was only precocious mentally and lived in deadly fear of losing my virtue, not for moral reasons, but from the dread of being thought "easy." Bob's restraint on this score was his sole source of fascination for me, paradoxically. Here, his being older and married put him somehow beyond me.

Yet I was glad, I know, of the respite, when, after ten days of Medicine Springs, the girls grew restless and we went off with Frank and his sister on overnight trips to Helena and Great Falls. I had suggested Yellowstone, hopefully, but the girls temporized. If we went to Yellowstone, they said, the family would want to go too. We could do that later, when we got back. The idea of sightseeing had begun to appeal to me. In Medicine Springs, the only things we had done that would bear repeating were an afternoon visit to a sheep ranch, where they were slaughtering some lambs, and a morning visit to a cow ranch, where I rode for five minutes on a mutinous old horse and tried in vain to trot in a Western saddle. One night, in the car's headlights, we had seen the red eyes of a loco horse reflected. That was all, except for the thunderstorms that took place every evening at dinner time and left the sky on the horizon a pale green. In a word, nothing to write home about.

In Helena and Great Falls, we stayed at hotels, ordering gin from the bellboy to drink in our rooms. I liked the gin quite well, mixed with lemon soda and ice. Nothing to write home about, either, though on the ride up to Helena I had had an odd experience. As usual, we had a bottle of moonshine with us when we started out and we passed it back and forth, as usual, while we drove along. The road was rough and once, when it was my turn,

I spilled a few drops on my silk stockings. That night when we were changing for dinner I found little holes in my stockings everywhere the liquor had spattered. I showed them to the girls, who positively could not understand it. The liquor, they pointed out, had been analyzed by Bob in the drugstore.

We made jokes about it and kept the stockings for a trophy; yet the incident, so to speak, burned a hole in our minds. In Great Falls, Ruth suddenly decided that she did not like the looks of the bellboy who had brought us the gin. It tasted all right; it smelled all right; but Ruth remained suspicious, her dark brows drawn together, as we had one drink and started on a second. About halfway through the second, with one accord we set down our glasses. Ruth packed the bottle to take back to Medicine Springs for analysis. It was wood alcohol, sure enough, Bob Berdan told us a few days later. If so, we should have been dead, since we had each had two or three ounces of it. In fact, we felt no ill effects; perhaps the local moonshine had developed a tolerance in us—a tolerance not shared by my stockings. But the two incidents made us warier and tamer. That night, in Great Falls, we went respectably to the movies and then back to bed. The next morning I found a book store and while the others waited in the car I hurried in to make a purchase: the latest volume, in a boxed de luxe edition, of James Branch Cabell.

I was tremendously excited by this act. It was the first expensive book I had ever bought with my own money. The whole trip to Montana for a moment seemed worthwhile, as I stood in the wide dull main street with the book, wrapped, in my hands. I was in love with Cabell and had written him many letters that I had not had the courage to mail. Why, it would change my grandmother's whole life, I used to tell her, if she would only let herself read a few pages of Cabell or listen to me recite them. Now, as the owner of a limited edition, I felt proudly close to him, far closer than to Bob Berdan or to the girls, who were already honking the horn for me to get in and join the party. They could never understand—only Cabell could, I supposed—what finding this book in this out-of-the-way place meant to me. That was the way it went, in Cabell; horns honked, alarm clocks shrilled, cocks crowed, to bring the ardent dreamer back to the drab, mean routines of middle-class reality.

And yet a strange thing happened when I finally opened the book, taking it carefully from its waxy wrapper. I was disappointed. I told myself that it was not a very *good* Cabell; perhaps he had written himself out (I knew about that, of course). But all the while I suspected that it was not the book, which was no different from other Cabells; it was me. I had "outgrown" Cabell, just as older people had said I would. For the second time in Montana, I felt that my life was over. I put the book aside quietly and now I cannot remember whether I ever finished it.

The next thing I recall is being on the train, going home. We had never got to Yellowstone, naturally, and my conscience was bothering me. I felt I had nothing to show for the visit—not even a proper array of lies, for the Bent household possessed no encyclopedia in which I could have boned up on the Park, while the girls, for their part, had only the haziest memories of Old Faithful and bears. My grandfather, in his youth, had been a geodetic surveyor during college vacations, and he would be bound to ask a lot of questions that I had no means of answering. Were there mountains there, for instance? What tribes of Indians? What kind of rock? Did we stay in a hotel or camp out and if so, where? Yellowstone was a big place. The paucity of my information made me conscious of the enormity of the deception I was going to have to put over. It was not the fear of being found out, even, that was troubling me as the train brought home nearer and nearer. Not being the kind of person who took refuge in monosyllables, I felt I owed my grandparents the courtesy of a well-put-together and decently documented lie.

Fortunately, a party of tourists, two men and two women, fresh out of Yellowstone, boarded the train. They had a bottle with them in the observation car and were very lively and friendly, treating me as an equal, though they must have been around thirty. They were able to help me a little, when I explained my predicament, but they did not have the grasp of detail that my grandfather expected from a narrative. To my critical ear it sounded as if they had hardly been in Yellowstone at all. I attributed it to drinking; they were having too good a time, on the train, to put their minds on scenery and Indians and what kind of bears.

A fatherly old conductor kept watching them as they bought me lemonades. On the second day out I was sitting with them in the observation car when the conductor stuck his head in the doorway and beckoned to me. He led me into an empty drawing room, asked me to sit down and, looking at me gravely through steel-rimmed glasses, told me that I must not talk to those people any more. "Steer clear of them," he said. "Give them a wide berth." Why, I wanted to know; but instead of answering this question he swerved off on a tangent and announced that he had been studying me and that I was one of the cleanest, sweetest, truest young girls it had ever been his pleasure to observe. It was because of this he was speaking to me now, as he would to one of his own daughters or granddaughters. There were tears in his eyes, I saw, as he warmed to his subject. "Stay that way," he said. "Clean and sweet and wholesome." I dropped my eyes, abashed and yet touched by this notion. I did not get exactly what he was driving at, but I supposed my friends in the observation car must be cardsharps or something of the kind. Even so, I did not see what harm they could do me and my curiosity was roused. "What's wrong with them?" I said bluntly. "Don't ask me," said the old conductor. "Just take my word for it and stay away from them." I persisted, and at last he told me, lowering his voice and glancing away from me. "They changed berths," he said. "Last night." I did not take in his point at first, for I had supposed they were married. Thinking it was my innocence, he elucidated. When they had got on at the Park, he said solemnly, the two women were together and the two men were together. "During the night . . ." He broke off.

"Oh," I said, flatly, meaning, "Is that all?" "Do you understand?" he asked. I nodded. "So you see why you mustn't talk to them?" I supposed I did, from his point of view, and I nodded again, reluctantly. A month before I might have argued the issue, for how could I have been safer than with two men and two women who only had designs on each other? Or I might have defied him. But now I did not have the heart to go against his instructions. It would crush him if he caught me talking to them after what he had told me; he would see that he had been duped in me. And I felt too old and weary to explain why I was not shocked.

On the other hand, it seemed rather mean to drop my new friends out of hand just to spare the conductor's feelings. I felt caught in a dilemma that was new to me then but which since has become horribly familiar: the trap of adult life, in which you are held, wriggling, powerless to act because you can see both sides. On that occasion, as generally in the future, I compromised. That is, I steered a zigzag course between the conductor and the two couples, talking to them when the conductor was not looking and leaving them abruptly, with some unlikely excuse, when I would glance up and find his old eyes on me. This jerky behavior, and the copious, dazzling smiles with which I tried to mitigate it, must have made both parties think I was deranged.

Back in Seattle, I found myself still serving out my sentence of childhood, which had three more years to run yet: I was eighteen, a freshman home from college, before I was able to sweep down the staircase, dressed in the height of fashion, and find a boy waiting, in uneasy conversation with my grandparents. Even then, my grandfather, as he raised his soft cheek for a kiss, would mortify me by the inevitable question: "Home by eleven?"

The trip to Montana left no outward scars. Indeed, it was educational, in that I could not bear the taste of whisky for years afterward; even now I cannot take it straight—I gag. And my ardor for dates was somewhat subdued, for the time being; more than a year passed before I began meeting boys on the sly, in the afternoons. I do not know whether my grandparents guessed that I had never been to Yellowstone. I think they must have, eventually, for they did not ask too many questions. In a gloomy way, I was happy to be home again. At home, at least I could be romantic, lying on the sofa in the evenings, reading and dreaming, and looking out across our terraces to where the moon made a path on the lake, a path that beckoned to suicide, as I wrote in a school composition. Across the room, my grandparents played double solitaire, and when my grandmother lost she would send me upstairs to fetch her petit-point handbag out of the drawer that contained her handkerchiefs, her pearl opera glasses, and her pearl-handled revolver. The phone seldom rang, and I was almost glad of it, because if it were a boy, I would have to make some excuse to explain why I could not go out that night or any other night he proposed. At home, nothing ever happened, but it was an atmosphere in which one could think that the unknown, the improbable, might occur in the depths of the familiar, like the treasures I could find in my grandmother's bureau drawer.

And in fact this proved to be true. Two summers later, when I was going to drama school, I first beheld what we then called my Dream Man (an actor whom I later married), at, of all places, a Bar Association pageant on the Magna Charta that my grandfather had made me go to, sulky and protesting. As for the Bent girls, I do not know what has become of them. The last time I saw Ruth Bent was when I was a junior at Vassar and she telephoned me from a small town in the Hudson River Valley to ask me to come and see her. She was twenty-one then and a widow, very well to do; she was running a chocolate factory which her husband, who had been killed in a plane crash, had left her. I had the sense that she had fulfilled her destiny: she still looked about forty, a poised, competent executive, with a furrow between her brows. And she was not a bit wild any more.

Except for the name of the town and the names of the people, this story is completely true. The only point that worries me is the business of Ruth's changing the tickets, I know she did it, but it seems odd to me that the Pullman conductor let her. Possibly he issued her a voucher and she got a refund later, at the company offices in Seattle.

Technically, this ought to precede "The Figures in the Clock," since it happened a year and a half before Miss Gowrie's play. But I have placed it here because in "Yellowstone Park" I seem older. This may have been because I was not in school. Also, in Medicine Springs, I was having to live up to a role that "grew me up" overnight. Once I was out of that curious wonderland where all the men were married, I shrank back to my normal age. There is another explanation too. In my first years at the Seminary, I finally achieved my wish of making friends with older girls, except for Betty Bent, all my intimates were juniors and seniors. Their talk was mostly of men, dances, and fraternity pins, one of them, a girl of eighteen, was engaged. When they graduated, all this changed, my friends, now, were my own classmates, who, if anything, were rather young for their age. The fact that there were no beauties among them may account for this. Their inter-

ests were sports, studies, and eating. Most of them had never been
out with a boy, and many of them did not even smoke. As it
turned out, being with my contemporaries was more fun than I
had expected, it was less of a strain, for one thing. I did not have
to pretend to greater experience than I had. We were busy too, as
seniors, running the school, two of us were studying for college
boards. This absorbed most of our energies and drew us closer
to our teachers.

The reader has heard a great deal of my grandfather and very
little of my grandmother. One reason for this is that she was living
while most of these memoirs were being written. Sooner or later,
however, I knew I was going to have to touch on her, or the story
would not be complete. Even when she was dead, I felt a certain
reluctance toward doing this, as toward touching a sensitive
nerve. It meant probing, too, into the past, into my earliest, dim-
mest memories, and into the family past behind that. The sense
of a mystery back of the story I had already told traced itself
more and more to the figure of my grandmother, who had appeared only as a name, a sob, a lacy handkerchief, a pair of opera
glasses, a pearl-handled revolver. The McCarthy family, great
talkers and romancers, revealed their secrets readily enough, even
if some of their revelations were dubious as fact. As a man, my
grandfather Preston was an open book. His history was a matter
of public record, for the most part, and if it contained hidden
chapters, those chapters occurred, precisely, I found, at the point
where his history met or merged with my grandmother's.

They met, one story has it, at a military ball, he was in gala
uniform, and they fell in love at first sight. But this cannot be
right, because, so far as I know, my grandfather was never in the
army, nor does "love at first sight" jibe with my grandmother's
account of their courtship. "Their relations opposed the mar-

riage." Possibly so, but I never heard this from any member of the family, on this subject, the principals were silent. As a man, my grandfather was an open book, as a husband, he is an enigma. My grandmother is the key, in her character too may lie the key to that strange favoritism shown to me and the cold reserve with which my brothers were treated.

All I know of her is told in the following, final chapter. She and my grandfather had three children. Both of her sons are living, and neither have had any issue. After them, the Preston name will be extinct.

Ask Me No Questions

THERE WAS something strange, abnormal, about my bringing-up; only now that my grandmother is dead am I prepared to face this fact. When she died, she had not divulged her age; none of her children knew it, and whatever figure they found in her papers has remained a secret to me. She was well over eighty, certainly, and senile when she finally "passed away," three years ago, in her tall Seattle house—under her gold taffeta puff, doubtless, with her rings on her fingers and her blue-figured diamond wrist watch on her puckered wrist. Probably she herself no longer knew how old she was; she was confused the last time I saw her, six years ago, when I flew west to be with her after she had broken her hip. Going over family photographs, which we spread out on her bed, she nodded and smiled eagerly, sitting up among her pillows like a macaw on its perch, in her plumage of black hair and rouge and eyebrow pencil and mascara. She recognized the faces—her husband with a mustache, her husband clean-shaven, her son in a World War I uniform, her nephews, her younger son in a sailor suit, my mother dressed as a Spanish dancer, my mother in a ball gown—but she was vague about the names. "My father," she decided after studying an obituary photograph of Grandpa, clipped out of a newspaper. "Son," "hus-

band," and "father" were all one to her. She knew who I was,
right enough, and did not mix me up with my dead mother, but
this was not very flattering, since it was usually the people she
had loved that she could not keep apart, melting them into a
single category—father-son-husband—like the Mystery of the
Trinity. One relation whom she had quarreled with she picked
out instantly, while I was still fumbling for the name. "That's
Gertrude!" she proclaimed victoriously. Then she made a face—
the same face she made when the cook brought her something
she did not like on her tray. I reminded her that she had made up
with Gertrude years ago, but she shook her head. "Bad," she said
childishly. "Gertrude said bad things about me."

"You," she said one day, suddenly pointing. "You wrote bad
things about me. Bad." It was not true; I had never written about
her at all. But when I told her so, she would not listen, nor would
she say where she had derived her notion. This was exactly like
her; she collected stray grudges like bits of colored ribbon and
would never tell where they came from. Nobody had ever known,
for instance, the exact cause of her falling-out with Gertrude.
Now, sitting by her bed, I tried to coax her into a better frame of
mind. She turned her head away on the pillow and shut her eyes;
long, sharp lines ran down, like rivulets of discontent, from her
nose to the corners of her mouth. A hopeless silence followed. It
troubled me to see her like this; those deep, bitter lines were new
to me, yet it must have taken years to indent them. I did not know
whether to leave or stay, and I wished the nurse would come in.
"You wrote about my husband," she abruptly charged, opening
her eyes and frowning over her high-bridged nose. This was a
sign that she was far away; in her clear moments, she spoke of
him to me as "Grandpa." "Yes," I agreed. "I wrote about
Grandpa."

It transpired that this had made her very angry, though she had never alluded to it in any of her letters. But why, precisely, she was angry, I could not find out from her. Certainly I had not said anything that she could call "bad" about Grandpa. It occurred to me that she was jealous because she had not been included in these writings; moreover, my grandfather had been shown with other women—a Mother Superior, a fictional aunt, myself. When she accused me of putting her in, did she really mean that she felt left out? She was capable of such a contradiction even before her mind had clouded. Or did she suppose that *she* was the aunt —a disagreeable personage? Hopeless, hopeless, I repeated to myself. It had always been like this. You could never explain anything to her or make her see you loved her. She rebuffed explanations, as she rebuffed shows of affection; they intruded on her privacy, that closely guarded preserve—as sacrosanct as her bureau drawers or the safe with a combination lock in her closet —in which she clung to her own opinion. "Look, Grandma," I began, but then I gave it up.

I was going to say that (a) I had not written about her in any shape or disguise, and (b) if I had not, it was not because I considered her unimportant but because I knew she would hate to have her likeness taken. For nearly forty years, she had refused to be photographed. The last picture made of her, a tinted photograph, stood on her chiffonier; it showed an imperious, handsome matron in a low-cut beaded evening dress and a gauzy scarf, with her hair in a pompadour and her young son at her knee. This remained her official image, and nothing would persuade her to let it be superseded. In the four-generations pictures made when my brothers and I were children—my great-grandfather, my grandfather, my mother, and the babies—my grandmother is absent. The last time I had come to visit her, with my own baby, I had begged her to let us take pictures of this new family group. But she would not allow it. In the snapshots I have of that summer, in 1939, just before the war, my grandmother again is absent; a shadow on the lawn, near the playpen, in one of them may indicate where she was standing. Yet I dared not draw these facts to her attention, for there was a story behind them, the story of her life—a story that was kept, like her age, a secret from those closest to her, though we all guessed at it and knew it in a general way, just as we all knew, in a general way, calculating from our own ages and from the laws of Nature, that she had to be over eighty.

Starting to tell that story now, to publish it, so to speak, abroad, I feel a distinct uneasiness, as though her shade were interposing to forbid me. If I believed in the afterlife, I would hold my peace. I should not like to account to her in whatever place we might meet—Limbo is where I can best imagine her, waiting for me at some stairhead with folded arms and cold cream on her face, as she used to wait in her pink quilted Japanese bathrobe or the green one with the dragons when I turned my key softly in the front door at two or three in the morning, with a lie, which I hoped not to need, trembling on my lips. She would never forgive me for what I am about to do, and if there is an afterlife, it is God who will have to listen to my explanations.

My first recollection of her is in her grey electric, her smartly gloved hands on the steering bar or tiller. How old I was, I am not sure, but it was before my family left Seattle when I was six. The grey box would glide up to the curb in front of our brick house on Twenty-fourth Avenue, and we would see her step out, wearing a dressy suit, braided or spangled, and a hat with a dotted veil that was pulled tight over her high-bridged nose, so that the black furry dots against her skin looked like beauty patches. On her feet, over her shoes, were curious cloth covers fastened with pearl buttons; my father said they were called "spats" and that some men wore them, too. She had come to see my mother, and smelled of perfume. The electric would be parked for a long time outside our house; one day, my brothers and I climbed in and got it started rolling. My mother spanked us with her tortoise-shell comb, but my father boasted of the exploit. "How did the little tykes do it?" he would say, laughing; we must all have been well under six.

Next, I think I see her in our bathroom, telling my mother that we must each have our own towel with our name above it, so that we would not keep catching colds from each other. When she left, that afternoon, there was a brand-new towel for each of us hanging folded on the towel rack, with our names written out on a little label pasted on the wall behind each towel: "Roy" and "Tess" for our parents, and "Mary," "Kevin," and "James Preston" for us; my little brother Sheridan was too young to have one. I was impressed by this arrangement, which seemed to me very stylish. But the very next day my father spoiled it by using one of our towels, and soon they were all scrambled up again and the labels fell off. This was the first (and, I think, the only) time I felt critical of my debonair father, for I knew the strange lady would be cross with him if she could see our bathroom now.

On Sundays, sometimes, we were taken to lunch at her house, out by Lake Washington. Two things we loved to do there. One was to crawl under the table while the grownups were still eating and find the bulge in the carpet where there was a bell she stepped on when she wanted the maid to come in. The bulge or little mound in the carpet was rather hard to locate, with all the feet and the women's skirts in the way, but eventually we found it and made the bell ring. It was nice under there, with the white table-cloth hanging down all around us like a tent. The carpet was thick and soft and furry, and if we peered out, we could see exotic birds on the wallpaper. I don't remember anyone's telling us not to get under the table, but one Sunday, perhaps the last time we went there, we could not find the bulge at all, and I remember the strange, scary feeling this gave me, as though I had been dreaming or making up a story and there had never been any bulge or bell in the first place. It did not occur to us that the bell must have been removed to keep us from annoying the maid, and the mystery of its disappearance used to plague me, long after we had left Seattle, like some maddening puzzle. I would lie awake in my new bed, thinking about the bell and wishing I could be given another chance to look for it. Five years later, when I was brought back to that house to live, a girl of eleven, I had the great joy, the vindication, of finding the bell just where I thought it should be, between her feet and mine.

The other thing we liked to do was, after lunch, to roll down her terraces, which dropped in grassy tiers from her tall house right down, I remembered, to Lake Washington. We rolled and rolled, almost into the water, it seemed, and nobody stopped us until it was time to go home, our white Sunday clothes smeared with green stains. The grass was like velvet, and there were flower beds all around and a smell of roses; a sprinkler was going somewhere, and there were raspberries that we ate off bushes. Alas, when I came back, I found I had been dreaming. The grounds did not go down to the lake but only to the next block, below, and there was only one grass bank; the second one was wild, covered with blackberry prickers, and it had always been so, they said. I rolled a few times down the single green slope, but it was not the same; only five or six turns and I had reached the bottom; I could not recapture the delicious dizzy sensation I remembered so well. And the raspberries, which I had been looking forward to eating, did not belong to us but to the people next door.

The strange lady was supposed to be my grandmother, but I did not think of her that way when I was little. She did not have white hair, for one thing, like my other grandmother—the real one, as I considered her. Nor did she do embroidery or tapestry work or stare at us over her glasses. She did not have glasses, only a peculiar ornament on a chain that she put up to her eyes when she wanted to look at something. With her queer electric car that ran soundlessly and was upholstered inside in the softest grey like a jewel case, her dotted veil, her gloves, which had bumps in them (made by her rings, I discovered later), her bell, and her descending terraces, she was a fairy-tale person who lived in an enchanted house, which was full of bulges, too—two overhanging balconies, on the lake side, and four bays and a little tower. (She had a fairy-tale sister, different from herself, tall, with white hair piled on top of her head in a long, conical shape, a towering mountain peak or a vanilla ice-cream cone; we were taken to see her one day and her house was magic also. She had a whole polar bear for a rug, and her floor shone like glass and made you slip when you walked on it; her house was like a winter palace or like the North Pole, where Santa Claus came from.) I did not love the strange lady in the electric but I loved the things she had.

The last time I saw her, in this pristine, fairy-tale period, was in the elevator of the Hotel Washington, where we were staying because our house had been sold and we were moving away from Seattle. She was wearing a funny white mask, like the one the doctor had worn when they took my tonsils out; I heard the word "epidemic," and I think she told my mother that we should have masks, too, when we rode up and down in the elevator—a thing we were fond of doing. But I did not like the masks.

We were very sick on the train. Then, one day, I saw her again, in a place where she did not belong, a place called Minneapolis, where my other grandmother lived. I was sick and just getting better, lying in an iron bed in my other grandmother's sewing room, when the strange lady came in, with a different kind of veil on, a black one, which hung all the way down over her face.

She flung it back, and her face looked dreadful, as if she had been crying. Then she sat down on my bed, and her husband, Grandpa Preston, sat on a straight chair beside it. She sobbed and her husband patted her, saying something like "Come now, Gussie," which appeared to be her name. She wiped her tears with a handkerchief; they went away on tiptoe, telling me to be a good girl. I did not understand any of this; my reason was offended by her turning up here in Minneapolis when I knew she lived in Seattle. No one enlightened me; I heard the word "flu," but it was months before it dawned on me that the occasion had been my parents' funeral. Yet when I surmised, finally, that Mama and Daddy were not coming back, I felt a certain measure of relief. One mystery, at least, was cleared up; the strange lady had come and cried on my bed because her daughter was dead. I did not see her again till five years later, when she was standing in the depot in Seattle in a hat with a black dotted veil, pulled tight across her face, which was heavily rouged and powdered. By this time, I knew that she was my grandmother, that she was Jewish, and dyed her hair.

The last of these items was a canard. Her hair was naturally black, black as a raven's wing and with a fine silky gloss, like loose skeins of embroidery thread. When she was over eighty and bedridden, the first sprinkling of white hairs began to appear in her thick, shining permanent. Brushing it, the nurses used to marvel ("Wonderful, isn't it? You'd swear, at first, it was dye"), but this triumph over her calumniators came too late. The nurses could testify, my uncles and their wives could testify, I could testify, but whom were we to tell? Within the immediate family, we had always given her the benefit of the doubt, though I recall my grandfather's uneasy face when she went to have her first permanent, for in those days dyed hair did not take well to the process and was reputed to turn green or orange. It was the outsiders—the distant in-laws, the ladies who bowed to my grandmother in the shops and then turned aside to whisper something—whom I should have liked to make eat their words now, in particular my other grandmother, with her reiterated, crushing question "Who ever saw natural hair *that* color?" But she was in her mausoleum, unavailable for comment, and the others were gone, too. My grandmother had outlived them all—an unfortunate state of affairs. Moreover, she herself was no longer in a condition to appreciate or even understand her victory; on her energetic days, she would ask me to fetch her hand mirror from her bureau and, frowning into it, would set herself to plucking out those stray white hairs, not realizing that they were the proof she had long been needing to show that her hair was truly black.

She had been a beautiful woman, "the most beautiful woman in Seattle," my friends' mothers used to tell me, adding that my mother, in her day, had been the most beautiful woman in Seattle, too. I can see it in the case of my mother, but my grandmother does not appear beautiful to me in the few photographs that exist of her as a young woman. Handsome, I would say, with a long, narrow, high-nosed, dark-eyed, proud, delicate face, the pure forehead topped by severe, somewhat boyish curls, such as the Romantic poets used to cultivate. A Biblical Jewish face that might have belonged to the young Rachel when Jacob first saw her. Her ears were pierced, and in one photograph she is wearing a pair of round, button-style earrings that lend her, somehow, a Russian appearance; in another, where she is posed with my mother as a little girl, her hair is caught in a big dark hair ribbon that gives her the air of a student. She has a gentle, open, serious mien—qualities I would never associate with the sharp, jaunty woman I knew or with the woman of the mature photograph on her chiffonier. Perhaps fashions in photography are responsible for the difference or perhaps her character changed radically during the early years of her marriage. The long, dreamy countenance became short, broad, and genial; the wide eyes narrowed and drew closer together. The change is so profound as to evoke the question "What happened?" The young woman in the photographs looks as though she could be easily hurt.

She came to Seattle from San Francisco, where her father had been what she called a "broker." Whether she meant a pawnbroker, I never could discover. He was a Forty-niner, having gone out to California in the gold rush, after a year in Pennsylvania. He had left Europe during the troubles of '48, and I like to think he was a political *émigré*, but I do not know. I do not know, though I once asked her, what part of Europe he came from. Poland, I suspect; her name, however, was German: Morganstern. Her first name was Augusta. These few sketchy facts were all she seemed to know of her early life and family history, and it puzzled her that anyone should want to find out more. "All those old things, Mary," she would say to me half grumpily. "Why do you keep asking me all those old things?" Like many great beauties, she had little curiosity; for nearly ten years, she did not know the name of the family who had moved into the house next door to us.

Her parents had died when she was quite young—in her teens —and she and her younger sister, my Aunt Rosie, came to live in Seattle with an older sister, Eva, who had married a fur importer named Aronson; this was the lady with the polar-bear rug. The girls had had some private education; my grandmother, at one time, used to play the piano—rather prettily, I imagine. She had a pleasing speaking voice and a surprising knowledge of classical music. "Were you rich or poor?" I asked her once, trying to learn the source of these accomplishments. "My father had a nice business," she replied. She had read the Russian novelists; when I sought to introduce her to Tolstoy and Dostoevski, she gave her dry laugh and said they had been the popular writers of her youth. All her life, she retained a taste for long novels that went on from generation to generation, on the model of *War and Peace*. She hated short stories, because, she said, just as you got to know the characters, the story ended; it was not worth the trouble. Her sister Rose was fourteen when the two arrived in Seattle; Aunt Rosie went out and inspected the University of Washington, which had just been started, and decided she knew more than the professors did, a fact she faced up to ruefully, since she had been yearning for a higher education.

Aunt Rosie was a very different person from my grandmother, yet they talked together on the phone for nearly an hour every day and often went "downtown" together in the afternoon, my grandmother stopping by at her house to pick her up in the electric, later in the Chrysler or the La Salle. Aunt Rosie was a short, bright, very talkative, opinionated woman, something of a civic activist and something of a Bohemian. She had married an easy-going New York Jew, Uncle Mose Gottstein, a juicy, cigar-smoking man who ran a furniture store, subscribed to the New York *Times*, and liked to chat about current events, his cigar tilted at a reflective angle, upward, in his cherry-red mouth. He and Aunt Rosie often sat up all night, in their first-floor bedroom, with its big walnut double bed, Uncle Mose in his nightgown reading the newspapers, and Aunt Rosie playing a solitaire, which she would not leave till it came out. Uncle Mose had fond recollections of Luchow's and of Jimmy Durante, whom he remembered as a singing waiter, and their big bedroom, strewn with newsprint and playing cards and smelling of cigar smoke, was like a club or a café. Aunt Rosie and her husband and two sons always sat there, even in the daytime, instead of in the living room or the little par-

lor, which was lined with signed photographs of opera stars and
violinists and pianists. Aunt Rosie had "known them all"; in her
youth, she had been a vocal soloist, much in demand for weddings
and special services in Seattle's Protestant churches. Later, she
had managed the musical events at Seattle's Metropolitan Theatre; the high point of her life had been a trip she took to Van-
couver with Chaliapin, about whom Uncle Mose liked to twit her,
his small, moist eyes (he later developed cataracts) beaming behind his glasses, his apple cheeks flushed. Aunt Rosie had met
other artistes besides Chaliapin and the various divas, including
Mary Garden and Galli-Curci, who had inscribed their photographs to her; thanks to her theater connection, she had known
Houdini and the Great Alexander and could explain the magi-
cians' acts by the fact that there was a trapdoor on the Metropolitan Theatre's stage. When I knew her, she was running the Ladies'
Musical Club.

Aunt Rosie was poor, compared to her sisters. Her husband
was the kind of man who is chronically unsuccessful in business—
the genial uncle nearly every Jewish family possesses who has
to be helped out by the others. Aunt Rosie had a plain "girl" to
give her a hand with the housework; she dressed very unmodishly
and lived in a somewhat run-down section in a smallish frame
house that needed painting. She was active in the temple as well
as in the musical world. The cookbook of the Ladies' Auxiliary of
the Temple de Hirsch, a volume got up for charity and much
used in our family—I still own a copy—has many recipes contributed by Mrs. M. A. Gottstein. Her chicken stewed with
noodles, hamburger in tomatoes, and rhubarb pie are quite unlike
the recipes contributed by Mrs. S. A. Aronson, my other great-
aunt, which begin with directions like this: "Take a nice pair of
sweetbreads, add a cup of butter, a glass of good cream, sherry,
and some *foie gras*." Or her recipe for baked oysters: "Pour over

each caviar and cream, and dot with bits of butter. Serve hot."

Aunt Rosie, with her energy, her good heart, and rattling, independent tongue, was a popular woman in Seattle, among all classes and kinds. Society ladies fond of music gushed over "the wonderful Mrs. Gottstein"; poor Jewish ladies in the temple praised her; Protestant clergymen respected her (they used to try, she told me, to convert her when she was younger, because she sang their anthems with such feeling); judges, politicians, butchers, poor tailors, clerks in bookstores all knew Aunt Rosie. She had not let the Protestant ministers tempt her away from her religion, but she was a truly open person, able to cross barriers naturally because she did not notice they were there. Most of the Jews in Seattle lived a life apart, concerned with *bar mizvahs* and weddings, and family and business affairs; a few, with German-sounding names, managed to cross into the Gentile world and get their sons pledged to regular fraternities at the university, leaving temple and observances behind them. Aunt Rosie was a unique case. Her Jewishness—that is, her bounce and volubility—was a positive asset to her in her dealings with the Gentile ascendancy. If my grandmother's marriage (to a Gentile) had made it a little easier for Aunt Rosie to get around, Aunt Rosie, I think, never suspected it; she had a lively self-conceit and no social envy or ambition. To her good-humored mind, being Jewish was simply a matter of religion.

Each of the three sisters had a different attitude toward their Jewish heritage, perhaps in each case conditioned by the man they had married. Aunt Eva—Mrs. Aronson, whose husband, Uncle Sig, had long ago passed on—was a typical wealthy widow of Jewish high society. She traveled a good deal, with a rather hard, smart set who had connections in Portland, San Francisco, New York, and even Paris; she gambled, and went to resorts and fashionable hotels in season; when she was in Seattle, she was an habituée of the Jewish country club, where they golfed in the day-time and played bridge for very high stakes at night. The scale of living of these people—widows and widowers, bachelors and divorcees, for the most part—was far beyond anything conceived of by the local Christian *haute bourgeoisie*, which was unaware of their existence. This unawareness was mutual, at least in the case of Aunt Eva, who, gyrating with perfect aplomb on her roulette wheel of hotels, yachts, race tracks, and spas, her white hairdress always in order, seemed ignorant of the fact that there was a non-Jewish society right under her nose, whose doings were recorded in the newspapers, daily and Sunday, whose members were "seen lunching" at the Olympic Hotel on Mondays, or golfing at the Seattle Golf Club next to the Highlands, or sunning at the Tennis Club on the lake.

Aunt Eva, I think, hardly realized that the world contained persons who were not Jewish. She, too, never knew envy; her nature was serene and imperturbable. My grandmother's mixed marriage never seemed to give her a qualm; her tall unawareness was sublime, a queenly attribute. If my grandfather was not "of the tribe," as my Irish relations used to call it suggestively, she did not give any sign of perceiving it. The "unpleasant" was barred by Aunt Eva, who seldom read anything and talked in magnificent generalities. She was fond of the theater, and when she was not traveling, she used to go every week to see the Henry Duffy stock company in Seattle. My grandmother, Aunt Rosie, and I had strong opinions about these players ("He's a perfect stick," my grandmother almost invariably complained of the lead-ing man), but to Aunt Eva there were no distinctions. Every play she saw she pronounced "very enjoyable." And of the actors: "They took their parts well." We used to laugh at her and try to get her to acknowledge that the play was better some weeks than others. But Aunt Eva would not cross that Rubicon; she smelled a rat. To her, all the plays and players were equal, and equally, blandly good.

Toward the end of her life, she suffered cruelly from indigestion (the *foie gras* and the cup of butter, doubtless), and it was an awful thing to watch her, after a Sunday luncheon at our house, majestic and erect, walk about our back living room, her lips bubbling a little and her face pale-vanilla-colored and contorting slightly from spasms of pain. "Gas," she would say, with dignity. It tortured me to see this highly aristocratic lady reduced by her stomach to what I felt must be a horrible embarrassment for her, but her unawareness seemed to extend to the "unpleasant" aspect of her sufferings; she entertained them, as it were, graciously, like a hostess. My grandfather showed her great sympathy during these ordeals of hers; she was his favorite, I think, among my grandmother's relations. Having helped her with her business affairs, he must have come to realize that Aunt Eva, unlike her sisters, was extremely stupid. Perhaps this regal stupidity, like that of a stately white ox, elicited his chivalry, for he was a gallant man, or perhaps the slow measured pace of her wits allowed him to forget that she was one of the Chosen (another classic epithet dear to my Irish relations).

How did my grandfather feel about the Jews? Again, I do not know; this was one of the many mysteries that surrounded our family life. He almost never attended church, except to be a pallbearer at a funeral, but he was by birth a Presbyterian Yankee, the son of a West Point man, who was head of a military college in Norwich, Vermont, commanded a Negro regiment during the Civil War, and was retired as a brigadier general. Simon Manly Preston was my great-grandfather's name (wife: Martha Sargent, born in New Hampshire), and he lived to be ninety-nine; his last years were passed in Seattle, where he was one of the local curiosities. All his progeny, including Uncle Ed, another West Point man, who died in his fifties, were eventually drawn to Seattle; my grandfather Harold, my great-uncle Clarence, and my great-aunt Alice, who married a law partner of my grandfather's, Eugene H. Carr, and lived for a time in Alaska. My grandfather first came west working as a geodetic surveyor during his college vacation (he started at Cornell and finished at what is now Grinnell College, Iowa), and when he had his A.B. degree, he decided to read law in Seattle. It was then that he must have first met my grandmother, aged circa seventeen, who was living in the house of the fur importer, Sigismund Aronson. Did this name ring strangely on my grandfather's Yankee ears? Possibly not. Seattle was a frontier town, where you could expect to meet all kinds—French and Dutch and Germans, aristocrats and plebeians. Many of our first families had aristocratic pedigrees (the de Turennes, the von Phuls), yet it used to be said of every first family that the great-grandfather "came here with his pack on his back." My grandmother was courted by a number of suitors, including one, George Preston, who had the same last name as my grandfather. She had Jewish beaux also, I discovered, and, as far as I could make out, she did not distinguish between the two kinds. They were assorted young men who took her driving; that was all.

"As far as I could make out—" this matter was impossible to probe with my grandmother. I don't think I ever used the word "Jewish" in any connection when talking with her. I sensed she would not like it. I used to think about the word a lot myself, when I first came back to Seattle and was sent as a five-day boarder to a Sacred Heart convent. I thought about it partly because of the ugly innuendoes dropped by my father's people, but chiefly because I was in love with my cousin, Aunt Rosie's tall, ravishing son Burton, who was twenty-one, ten years older than I, and I worried, being a Catholic, about the impediments to our marriage: the fact that he was my first cousin once removed, and the difference in religion—would he have to be baptized? This passion of mine was secret (or at least I hope it was), but even if it had not been, I could not have discussed the problem with my grandmother because of that unmentionable word.

I myself had a curious attitude, I now realize, in which the crudest anti-Semitism ("Ikey-Mose-Abie," I used to chant, under my breath, to myself in the convent) mingled with infatuation and with genuine tolerance and detachment. I *liked* Uncle Mose and Aunt Rosie far better than any other older people I knew, and "Ikey-Mose-Abie" represented what I supposed others would think of them. It was a sort of defiance. If I identified a little bit of myself with those others, my dead mother had gone much further; one day, I found a letter she had written to my grandmother Mc-Carthy in which she spoke of an evening "with the Hebrews." Finding this letter was one of the great shocks of my adolescence. It destroyed my haloed image of my mother, and the thought that her mother must have read it, too (for there it was, in my desk, put away for me with other family keepsakes), nearly made me ill.

Perhaps I was too sensitive on my grandmother's behalf. No secret was ever made of the family connection with Aunt Rosie and Aunt Eva, and whenever my grandmother gave a tea, it always appeared in the paper that Mrs. M. A. Gottstein and Mrs. S. A. Aronson poured. I used to hear about some distant cousin having a *bar mizvah*, and once I was taken to a Jewish wedding, which fascinated me because it was held at night in a hotel ballroom. Nevertheless, there was *something*—a shying away from the subject, an aversion to naming it in words—so much so that I was startled, one morning, when I was about sixteen, to hear my grandmother allude to "my faith." I had been talking to her about my disbelief in God, and to my surprise she grew quite agitated. She no longer practiced her faith, she declared, but she was certain that there was a kind God Who understood and Who watched over everything. She spoke with great feeling and emphasis—a rare thing in our relations.

It was characteristic of her queer, oblique nature that I chanced to find out that she had had Jewish suitors by idly asking her the names of the young men she had driven out with. She gave them with perfect readiness, but without any indication that such a name as Schwabacher or Rosenblatt would tell a story to me. If it had been a major step to marry outside her own people, she did not seem to recall this any more, and, of course, I could not ask her.

Yet in other respects she was remarkably frank. "How did you come to marry Grandpa?" I asked her one night, when I was home on a visit after I myself had married. "Rosie and I didn't get along with Uncle Sig," she answered matter-of-factly.

So that was all; I could hardly believe my ears, and wondered whether she realized the enormity of what she was saying. "But why did you pick Grandpa instead of one of the others?" I pressed her, determined, for Grandpa's sake, that she would answer that it had been because of his eyes or his mustache or his intellect. She appeared to search her memory, in vain, "Oh, I don't know, Mary," she said, yawning. "You *must* know," I retorted. She thought he would be good to her, she finally conceded.

This archaic view of the function of a husband astonished me. But to her, as I soon learned, it was the prime, the only, consideration. "Is he good to you?" she asked me, another night, on that same visit, speaking of my new husband. I had to stop and think, because marriage had never presented itself to me in this light. "Why, yes, I suppose so," I said slowly. "Yes, of course he is." My grandmother nodded and reopened her evening newspaper. "That's all right, then." The subject was closed. "Grandpa was always good to me," she resumed tranquilly, turning to the racing column and beginning to mark her selections for the next day's parimutuel.

What did these words mean? Kindness, patience, forbearance —or fur coats and jewelry? Or was it all the same thing? Love, evidently, was as foreign a concept to her as this "goodness" was to me. She did not want to hear about love; it irritated her. The words "I love him" were meaningless sounds to her ears: if I uttered them in her hearing, which at length I had the sense not to do, I might as well have been talking Chinese. She did not care for love stories, which she pronounced trash, and she used to make fun of the movie actors who were my heroes as a young girl. "He has such thick lips," she used to say of Ronald Colman, mimicking his expression by thrusting out her own lower lip. "And that mustache! Think of kissing that bristly mustache!" Ricardo Cortez, she said, mimicking his expression, looked "as if he had a stomach ache." Yet her own favorite was Adolphe Menjou. My grandfather liked Lewis Stone.

She was not so much cynical as prosaic. She made fun of the young men who used to come to take me out when I was home from college on vacations by seizing on small detail about their appearance and relentlessly exaggerating it: curly hair, rosy cheeks, full lips, large ears. This was not done maliciously but in high-humored jest, as though *she* were the young girl mocking her suitors behind their backs to her audience of sisters. I never minded it (though I had minded about Ronald Colman), but it struck me as unfair in the abstract; the part was always greater to her than the whole, and some of the things she noticed would have escaped the attention of anyone but a phrenologist.

Her marriage had been successful, and she attributed this to a single simple recipe, like one of the household hints in the back of the Temple de Hirsch cookbook, on how to clean ermine (rub with corn meal) or how to extract grease from papered walls (flannel and spirits of wine). She had never let a quarrel continue overnight. No matter how mad she was at Grandpa, she told me, she always kissed him good night. And, a corollary, no matter how mad she was in the morning, she always kissed him good-by before he went to the office. She passed this recipe on to me gravely after I had been divorced; if I would just follow it, I would never have any more trouble, she was certain. This advice made me smile; it was so remote in its application to my case. But she shook her head reprovingly as she stood in front of her mirror, undoing her pearls for the night. "Remember, Mary," she enjoined. "All right," I said lightly. "I'll remember. 'Always kiss him good night.'" She had felt the moment as a solemn one, like the time she had spoken of "my faith"; yet in an instant she, too, was smiling broadly. An anecdote had occurred to her, and she began to tell me, acting out both parts, of a morning when Grandpa had left for his office without the usual morning salute. . . . From one point of view, her entire married life was a succession of comic anecdotes, of which she was both butt and heroine.

These anecdotes began before her marriage, with the time the horse ran away with her and George Preston in the buggy, and Grandpa was terribly jealous. Then there was her honeymoon: how he had taken her back to Iowa, to visit his family, who had settled there after the Civil War. It was winter, and before they left, my grandfather had kept asking her whether she had enough clothes. She answered yes each time, but the question puzzled and offended her, for she took it as a criticism of her wardrobe. "I had very nice clothes," she explained. What he meant, it turned out, was long underwear, but he was too delicate to name it, so she went ignorantly on to Newton, Iowa, in her fine batiste-and-lace underclothing—she could never tolerate anything else next

to her skin; silk was too coarse. In the barbarous midwestern climate, she nearly froze to death, she declared, and she came out in chilblains all over. She nearly died of boredom also.

The provinciality of her in-laws horrified her. She had never met people like this, whose idea of a social evening was to stand around the stove, clad in long underwear and heavy dark clothing, the men cracking one joke after the other. She could see that her in-laws, with the exception of Great-Grandpa Preston, did not like her. "They thought I was fast and stuck-up." She could not eat their food or put on the union suit they offered her. They were displeased by her elegant clothes and by her smiles and laughter. They only laughed, shortly, at the humorless jokes they told. Alone in her bedroom with her husband, she cried and cried, and finally she made him have a telegram sent to himself calling him back to Seattle. After the telegram came, her father-in-law, the General, took them to Chicago, which was supposed to be a treat. But they put up at an awful boarding house, where she could not eat the food, either. The two men stayed out all day, looking at sights like the stockyards, and the other boarders scared her, they were so rough and crude in their manners. That was the end of her honeymoon, and on the train going back she made my grandfather promise that he would never take her to Newton again.

Later, they went to Chicago for the World's Fair with my Aunt Eva, and this was the subject of another anecdote. She and Aunt Eva were left at a stop in Montana, when the train drew out unexpectedly while they were buying post cards in the station. Another passenger, a man, seeing their predicament, jumped out of the train and said to my grandmother, "Can I be of assistance to you, Madam?" Somehow (I forget the details), he managed to get the train to come back for them or to wait at the next station for them to arrive by carriage. But my grandfather was terribly jealous; as soon as he saw them again, he accused my grandmother of having got off the train to be with the strange man. And she never could convince him differently all the rest of her life.

There was the time the house caught on fire while my grandmother was downtown shopping. When she boarded the Cherry Street trolley to go home (her house was way out, almost in the country, then), the conductor said to her, "Mrs. Preston, your house is on fire," and she arrived on the scene to find the fire engine there and (yes, she swore it) their one-eyed maid, Tilda, carrying the piano out of the house balanced, on one hand, like a tray; all the little boys in the neighborhood were sitting on the lawn, reading her love letters from my grandfather, which they had found in a bureau drawer. There was the time her riding horse ran away with her, down in Gearhart, Oregon, and there was an incident, I think, with a rowboat. There was the time she came to our house, when my mother had been taken to the hospital to have our little brother, and found the three of us sitting on the floor of the living room, making a bonfire of my father's law-books and pointing his loaded revolver at each other.

My grandmother was a gifted *raconteuse* when she could be induced to tell one of her stories. She acted out all the parts zestfully, particularly her own, and short trills of unwilling laughter proceeded from her as she spoke; when she had finished, she would have to wipe her eyes with a handkerchief. This power of being amused at herself, this perpetual dismay, made one see her in these disconcerting situations, which had a classic plot—the plot of a nightmare, really.

Someone, usually a man, laconically breaks her an untoward piece of news, or fails to break it successfully, as in the case of the long underwear. Or it is a runaway horse, a runaway train, a runaway buggy, a rocking boat, a loaded revolver; my grandmother is always helpless while some uncontrollable event unfolds before her eyes. (There was the story of the crazy piano tuner who without a by-your-leave walked into her parlor and took the piano apart as my grandmother watched, unable to stop him, bewitched by his flow of talk: "A beautiful instrument, Madam . . . So you have neglected your lovely musical gift [an imitation of him shaking his head]. Believe me, Madam, you owe it to the world and to your husband and family to take up the instrument again. . . ." At the end of the story, naturally, the dismembered piano was lying on the floor; he had forgotten how to put it together again.) She is always the loser in these anecdotes; she never gets the better of the situation with a biting retort, as she often did in real life. But because she is the heroine, she is usually rescued, in the nick of time.

In my grandmother's narratives, it is the other person who is self-possessed, full of an almost supernatural assurance—the stranger alighting from the moving train in a single airy bound, like an acrobat sliding down a rope to bow at her feet. She is forever disconcerted, put out of countenance, dumb-struck. In reality, *she* was the disconcerting one, short of speech when she was not telling a story (and to get her to tell a story usually took a lot of coaxing), impassive, forbidding. Most people, including all my friends, were afraid of her.

The first thing that would have struck an outsider about her in her later years—that is, when she was in her sixties and seventies —was the oddity of her appearance. If you saw her downtown, shopping in Frederick's or Magnin's—and she never did anything but shop any afternoon of her life, excluding Sundays, matinee days, and the days of the racing meetings—you would probably ask the salesgirl who she was: a woman of medium height, a little plump but not fat, wearing a small, high-crowned hat topped with ribbons or feathers, pumps with Cuban heels, fabric gloves, an onyx-and-diamond *lorgnon*, a smart dress in black or navy, printed or solid color, with a fur piece over it—silver fox or baum marten. This would be in summer. In the fall, she might be wearing a dark-green wool ensemble trimmed with leopard, or a black one trimmed with monkey, or a beige one trimmed with beige broadtail or caracul. In the winter, she would have on her mink or her Persian or her squirrel or her broadtail. She would be proceeding at a stately walk through the store, stopping to finger something at a counter, smiling at the salespeople, nodding. Her clothes in themselves should not have attracted attention. She disliked bright colors and never wore anything but black, navy, dark green, beige, or wine. Nor were the styles youthful or extreme. She was careful about her skirt lengths; her dresses were lavish in tucks and shirring, but the cut was simple and discreet. She wore small pearl earrings and a short string of pearls; her rings were concealed by her gloves. Underneath the gloves, her nails were natural color, polished with a buffer. Nor did her toilet table contain a lipstick. Yet the whole effect she made was of an indescribable daring.

It was partly the black hair, so improbably black and glossy. It was partly the mascara and the eye shadow surrounding her black narrow watchful eyes, though these aids to beauty were not applied carelessly but with an infinite discretion. It was the rouge, perhaps, most of all, the rouge and the powder and the vanishing cream underneath. When she perspired, on a warm day, the little beads of sweat on her eagle nose under her nose veil and on her long upper lip would produce a caked look that seemed sad, as though her skin were crying. Yet not even her cosmetics and the world of consummate artifice they suggested could account for the peculiarly florid impression she made as she moved across the store, peering through her *lorgnon* at the novelties and notions, and vanished into the elevator, up to the lending library or the

custom-made or the hat department—her favorite purlieus—
where elderly salespeople, *her* salespeople, would hurry up to
greet her, throwing their arms around her, just as though they had
not seen her the day before.

"Have you got anything for me?" my grandmother would demand of Mrs. Slaughter, the red-haired hat lady at Frederick's,
surveying the premises with a kind of jesting coquetry, a hand on
her hip. This was the same tone she took with the clerks in the
circulating library or with the butcher on the telephone—a tone
of challenging banter, as though she defied these people, her suitors, to please her.

On a good day, Mrs. Slaughter would bring out two or three
hats she had "put away" for my grandmother in a special cupboard. "They just came in," she would whisper. "I've been saving
them for you." My grandmother would try them on before the
mirror, tilting her head sideward and back in an odd way she had,
at once vain and highly self-critical. If she liked one of them well
enough, she would walk to the full-length mirror and assay herself, thrusting one small foot forward and balancing back and
forth, seeming to weigh herself and the hat in the scales of judgment. To my disappointment, watching her, she never bought
on the spot. She would set the hat or hats back on the table, as
if she were through with them, and Mrs. Slaughter, who seemed
to be a mind reader, would whisk them back into the special
cupboard, where they would wait, out of sight of other cus-
tomers, for several days or even a week, while my grandmother
arrived at a decision. She was the same with her shoes and dresses;
she would even coquette with a piece of meat; it was as though
she would not give these things the satisfaction of letting them see
that she liked them. To her, every piece of merchandise, suing
for her favor, appeared to enter the masculine gender and to be

subject, therefore, to rebuff. Yet the salespeople were all eager to oblige her, for she was a good customer, and, more than that, underneath her badinage, always good-humored.

It pleased her to pretend to be cross with them; indeed, in all her relations, she had an air of just consenting to be mollified. Her veteran salespeople would flatter her ("You're looking younger every day, Mrs. Preston. Nobody would believe this young lady was your granddaughter. Make her pass for your daughter"), and my grandmother would hide her gratification in a short, tart, scathing laugh. Actually, they were proud of her, for she did look remarkably young, despite her blazonry of make-up; she *could* have passed for my mother. They were genuinely fond of her. "Take care of yourself," they would call after her, and some of them used to kiss her. My grandmother pretended to be suspicious of these manifestations; a muscle moved, like a protest, in her cheek while the kiss was being planted.

She was lonely. That was the thing that made her seem so garish and caused people to turn their heads when she went by. Loneliness is a garish quality, and my grandmother's wardrobe and elaborate toilette appeared flamboyant because they emphasized her isolation. An old woman trying to look young is a common enough sight, but my grandmother was something stranger and sadder—a hermit all dressed up for a gala, a recluse on stubborn parade. Tagging along, even as a little girl, I was half conscious of the bizarre figure my grandmother cut, and if I had not known her, my imagination might have woven some story around her for a school composition—the holocaust, at the very least, of all her nearest and dearest, her husband gone to prison, her children branded as traitors. . . .

But in fact, during the years I knew her best, the years after I had left the convent and was in boarding school in Tacoma, she had a husband; two sons, whom she saw every day (one of them lived at home and went to the University, and the other lived across the street with an exemplary wife); two sisters, whom she saw nearly every day; a sister-in-law, Aunt Alice Carr, who lived downtown in the Sorrento Hotel; a granddaughter (myself) who came home from school for vacations; a cook; and an old gardener who had been with her twenty-five years—the original family coachman. All these people were devoted to her. She was independent; she had her own investments and drove her own car. Every winter, my grandfather took her to California, where they ate at the best restaurants and lived at the best hotels and went to the races at Santa Anita and at Tia Juana, over the border. He was a distinguished citizen, with a prosperous law practice, a reputation for immense integrity, and countless friends and cronies. During my sophomore year in boarding school, he had taken her to New York, where they had seen nearly every play on the board and she had had an outfit made by a smart new designer in a new color called "kasha," an exact copy of an outfit worn by Katharine Cornell in *The Green Hat*, and he had taken her to Washington, where they had had an interview with Calvin Coolidge.

She had nothing to complain of in life. There was nothing wrong with her health, except for a mild diabetic condition that the best local specialist was controlling and a high blood pressure that was not dangerous but that gave her headaches in the afternoons. Nor did she complain; she was a little fretful sometimes when she was having her headaches, but she possessed an equable temper, the result, no doubt, of self-discipline. She and I used to quarrel, and she had much to find fault with in my conduct. She worried a good deal about her younger son's late hours. But she was never cross or nagging. It was only much later, when she grew senile, that she became difficult to deal with, capricious and fault-finding, sending the cook downtown to return a mascara applier that dissatisfied her, pushing her food away, soughing, and making faces.

But until she reached her second childhood, she seemed, on the surface, a contented woman, well situated in life, self-contained, unemotional. The only blights she had suffered, so far as I knew, were the unseasonable death of my mother and a mastoid operation that had left her with some scars, just under her ears, in her neck and lower cheeks. If she was cold to me for a few days, or stopped speaking, abruptly, to Gertrude, or feuded with my grandfather's brother, Uncle Clarence, these were mere quirks—the privileges of beauty—that did nobody any harm. She was not a demonstrative person, but neither were her sons or her husband or her daughter-in-law; they all seemed to have been cut from the same bolt of cloth. I was the only member of the family—not counting Aunt Rosie—who was excitable.

When I was first brought back from Minneapolis to live with my grandparents (and this remained my official home until I was twenty-one and married), I was impressed by our house and its appurtenances, much as I had been as a young child: the bay-window seat in the parlor, the cabinet with opaline Tiffany glass and little demitasse cups, all different, the grass wallpaper, the pongee-silk curtains, the sleeping porches upstairs, the hawthorn tree in front of the house, the old carriage block with the name "PRESTON" carved on it, the date "1893" over the front door, the Kelvinator in the kitchen, the bell system, the generator in the garage that charged the electric, the silver samovar, the Rhine-wine glasses (never used), with green bowls and crystal stems. To me, the house was like a big toy, full of possibilities for experiment and discovery; I was constantly changing my sleeping quarters—out to the sleeping porch behind my bathroom, upstairs to the little room under the eaves on the cook's floor, back again to my green-and-violet bedroom; once, I even got permission to sleep outdoors, in the moonlight, on the back lawn, overlooking the lake.

The room I was given had been redone for me; I had lots of pretty new clothes, made by my grandmother's own dressmaker; the gardener drove me about in the electric and let me practice steering; I did not have to wear glasses any more, as I had had to in Minneapolis, and I could read anything I wanted to in the family library: Dickens and Frank Stockton and Bulwer-Lytton and Sienkiewicz, and the Elsie Dinsmore books, which had belonged to my mother. I could look through the stereopticon, or play an old record of "Casey at the Bat" on the new Victrola. Everything we had seemed superior to anything anyone else had—the flowers in our garden, the vegetables on the table, which we grew ourselves in the lower back yard, instead of getting them from the store, as other people did. We had strawberry beds, too, and rows of currant bushes, a crab-apple tree and two kinds of cherry trees, black and Royal Anne, and, something very special for Seattle, my grandmother's favorite, an apricot tree. At Christmas, we had our own holly, cut from a tree in the front yard; the idea that this was better than other holly persisted in my grandmother's mind until the very end, for every year until she died, a box would arrive for me, just before Christmas, in New England, from Seattle, packed full of holly from the Preston tree. My grandmother's gardening was a distinguished, personal thing; she never joined a garden club or pored over seed catalogues, or exchanged slips or compared notes with other gardeners. Every morning after breakfast, she gave directions to the old gardener, descending from the back porch in a straw farmer's hat and a smock, with a basket over her arm, to pick flowers for the day's bouquets and supervise the new asparagus bed he was laying out or the planting of the new variety of sweet corn they were trying.

She was greedy, in a delicate way, picking daintily at her food, yet finishing off a whole bowl of fresh apricots or a dozen small buttered ears of the tenderest white corn. She had a cormorant's rapacity for the first fruits of the season: the tiniest peas, the youngest corn, baby beets cooked with their greens. This emphasis of hers on the youth of the garden's produce made her fastidious appetite seem a little indecent—cannibalistic, as though she belonged to a species that devoured its own young.

"Take a spring chicken," many of her recipes began, and the phrase often salted her conversation. "She's no spring chicken," she would say of another woman. Baby beets, new potatoes, young asparagus, embryonic string beans, tiny Olympia oysters, tiny curling shrimps, lactary ears of corn—like my grandmother's clothes, our food was almost too choice, unseemly for daily use. The specialties of our table were like those of a very good hotel or club: Olympia oyster cocktail and deviled Dungeness crabs; a salad, served as a first course, that started with a thick slice of tomato, on which was balanced an artichoke heart containing crabmeat, which in turn was covered with Thousand Island dressing and sprinkled with riced egg yolk; a young salmon served in a sherry sauce with oysters and little shrimps; eggs stuffed with chicken livers. We ate this company food every day; every meal was a surprise, aimed to please some member of the family, as though we were all invalids who had to be "tempted." On Sundays, the ice cream, turned by the gardener in the freezer on the back porch, was chosen to suit me; we had strawberry (our own strawberries), peach, peppermint (made from crushed candy canes), and the one I was always begging for—bisque. Our icebox always contained a bowl of freshly made mayonnaise, a bowl of Thousand Island dressing, and usually a chicken or a turkey and a mold or *bombe* with maraschino cherries, whipped cream, and macaroons or ladyfingers in it. My grandmother's own palate was blander than the rest of the family's. I associate her with sweetbreads, with patty shells, and with a poulette sauce.

Or, if I shut my eyes, I can see her at the head of the table, on a summer morning, wearing her horn-rimmed reading glasses, the newspaper before her on a silver rack; there is a bowl of fresh apricots in the middle of the table, and as she reads, her bare, plump white arm, as if absently, stretches out toward this dish; her slender, tapering fingers pinch the fruit, and she selects the choicest, ripest one. The process is repeated until the bowl is empty, and she does not look up from her paper. I had a tremendous appetite myself ("If she assimilated all she ate, she'd be a mountain," my uncle's wife used to comment after a Sunday-night supper), but my grandmother's voracity, so finical, so selective, chilled me with its mature sensuality, which was just the opposite of hunger. I conceived an aversion to apricots—a tasteless fruit, anyway, I considered—from having watched her with them, just as though I had witnessed what Freud calls the primal scene. Now I, too, am fond of them, and whenever I choose one from a plate, I think of my grandmother's body, full-fleshed, bland, smooth, and plump, cushioning in itself, close held—a secret, like the flat brown seed of the apricot.

This body of hers was the cult object around which our household revolved. As a young girl, I knew her shoe size and her hat size and her glove size, her height and weight, the things she ate and didn't eat, her preferences in underwear and nightgowns and stockings, the contents of her dressing table in the bathroom, down to the pumice stone which she used for removing an occasional hair from under her arms; one of her beauty attributes was that her white, shapely arms and legs were almost totally hairless, so that she never had to depend on a depilatory or a razor. No other woman has ever been known to me in such a wealth of fleshly, material detail; everything she touched became imbued for me with her presence, as though it were a relic. I still see her clothes, plumped to her shape, hanging on their velvet-covered hangers in her closet, which was permeated with the faint scents of powder and perfume, and the salty smell of her perspiration; she comes back to me in dress shields, in darned service-sheer stockings (for morning), in fagoting and hemstitching, in voile and batiste, in bouclé and monkey fur, in lace, dyed écru with tea.

I never saw her undressed. Once, when she was in her seventies, I did catch a disturbing glimpse of her thighs, which were dazzling, not only in their whiteness and firmness but in the fineness of the skin's texture—closer to a delicate chiffon than to silk or satin. Disturbing, because I knew she would not want to be looked at, even in admiration. She shared with my grandfather the mysteries of the big bathroom, but until she became bedridden, no one else, I think, ever saw her in less than her corset, camisole, and petticoat.

The big bathroom, which had a sofa covered with worn Oriental carpeting and an old-fashioned deep tub with claw feet, was the temple of her beauty, and I never went into it, even as a grown woman, without feeling as if I were trespassing. For me, as a young girl, it had all the attractions of the forbidden, and as soon as my grandmother left the house in the afternoon, I would fly in to examine her salves and ointments, buffers and pencils and swabs, brushes and tweezers, her jars and bottles from Elizabeth Arden, Dorothy Gray, Marie Earle, Helena Rubinstein, and Harriet Hubbard Ayer, her skin food, neck lotion, special astringent, and antiwrinkle emollient, Hind's Honey and Almond, cucumber lotion, Murine, special eye lotion, Velva cream, mascara, eye shadow, dry rouge, paste rouge, vanishing cream, powders, chin strap, facial mask. One day, I found a box of something called

Turkish Delight, which I took, from its name, to be a beauty preparation used in harems.

The room had a queer, potpourri smell; my grandmother seldom threw anything away, and some of her cosmetics were so old they had gone rancid. Another odor, medicinal, sometimes hung about the room in the morning; I smelled it on the days when I was allowed to have my hair washed in the basin there, by my grandmother's "woman." Actually, as I learned many years later, what I smelled was bourbon whisky; my grandfather, though a temperate man, was accustomed to have two shots of bourbon before breakfast. The only other sign of his presence was a bottle of Eau Lilas Végétal—a purple cologne—on my grandmother's dressing table and some corn plasters in one of its drawers. He kept his shaving things, as I recall, in a small dressing room that opened off the big bathroom. You could find almost anything there: medicine, bath salts, an unopened bottle of Virginia Dare, family photographs, fishing tackle, Christmas presents that were being hidden, newspaper clippings that dated back to the time when my grandfather had been running for United States Senator (he was defeated by Levi P. Ankeny, of Walla Walla).

The temptation to try out some of my grandmother's beauty aids got the better of me when I was twelve. Unfortunately (like her household hint for a successful marriage), most of them had no bearing on my particular problems. "Not for the Youthful Skin," cautioned one astringent, and there was nothing in her crowded drawers for freckles. I did not need eyebrow pencil; my eyebrows were too thick already, and I had recently performed the experiment of shaving half of them off in the convent, while my grandparents were in California. My nose was my chief worry; it was too snub, and I had been sleeping with a clothespin on it to give it a more aristocratic shape. Also, I was bowlegged, and I was wondering about having an operation I had heard about that involved having your legs broken and reset. The dressing table offered no help on these scores, and, failing to find a lipstick and being timorous of the curling iron, I had to be satisfied with smearing a little paste rouge on my lips, putting dry rouge on my cheekbones (to draw attention away from the nose) and pink powder all over my face. I myself could see little change, but my grandmother could, and as soon as she came home that afternoon, a terrible scene took place, for I felt so guilty at what I had done that I would not admit that I had been "into" her dressing table, even when confronted with the proof in the disarrayed drawers and the rouge that came off on the handkerchief she applied firmly to my cheek.

She did not actually, as I learned later, think that what I had done was so bad; it was the lying that offended her. But I was convinced that I had committed a real crime, so terrible that I might be sent away from home. The idea that I was not to touch my grandmother's things had impressed itself on my excitable mind like a Mosaic commandment. I had left the well-codified Catholic world in which my young childhood had been spent, and in this new world I could no longer tell what was a mortal and what was a venial sin. The bathroom figured to me as the center of everything in the Preston family life from which I was excluded. I had begun to wonder about this family life a little; it was not as much fun as I had thought at first. In spite of the glamour that lay on it like a spell, I was not having as good a time, nearly, as my schoolmates had. Yet when I tried to determine what was different, the only thing I could put my finger on then was that, unlike other people, we did not have a regular lunch at home, and that at the time most people were lunching, my grandmother was in the bathroom with the door shut.

This seems a small complaint, but the clue to everything was there. When I think of our house now, the strongest memory that comes back to me is of shut doors and silence. My young uncle, five years older than I was, had his own apartments, reached by a dark set of stairs that branched off the main staircase at the landing; my grandmother and grandfather had their separate chain of rooms, connected with each other by a series of inner doors; the cook had her own, on the third floor, though she had to tiptoe down to share my bathroom; the gardener lived over the garage in rooms I never saw. There was no guest room.

During the greater part of the day, the upstairs hall was in gloom, because every door opening off it, except mine, was shut. The common rooms downstairs—the library, parlor, and living room—were seldom used in the daytime by anyone but me. The rest of the family kept to their own quarters; you would have thought the house was empty when everyone was home. I remember those summer mornings during school vacations. These mornings of the long years of my teens were so alike that they might have been one morning. The silence was profound. Every member of the family, except me, was taciturn—the cook and the gardener, too. After a wordless breakfast (my grandfather had already gone to the office), I was left to my own devices while my grandmother went out to the garden, picked flowers, then arranged them in the pantry; every vase in the house was renewed daily, but I was not allowed to help with the bouquets. Then she climbed the stairs to her bedroom; the door was shut and stayed shut for an hour or more while she talked on the telephone to her sisters and the butcher. During this period, the stillness was broken only by the hum of the vacuum cleaner and the sound of the mail dropping through the slot in the front door.

There was never any interesting mail, just the *National Geographic, Vogue,* and the *American Boy* (which my grandfather, for some reason, had subscribed to for me), some ads and charitable appeals addressed to "The Honorable Harold Preston," and perhaps a letter from Aunt Eva or Aunt Alice Carr. After a time that seemed interminable, while I lay on the sofa reading and waiting for something to happen, the door to the old nursery upstairs, where my grandfather slept and my grandmother did her sewing, would open—a signal to me that I could come up if I wanted. Then, for another hour, we would sit opposite each other in the bay window, my grandmother mending, or looking through the latest copy of *Vogue*, I staring out the window and trying to start a conversation.

"What did Aunt Rosie have to say?" I would begin. "Oh, nothing," she would answer. "Just talk. You know Rosie." Or, "Uncle Mose isn't feeling so well." Or, "She had a letter from Mortie in New York." Silence. When she was finished with the magazine, she would pass it on to me, and I would study the society notices of weddings and engagements, but there was never anything from Seattle. New York, Chicago, Boston, San Francisco —that was all. You would think, to read *Vogue*, that nothing ever happened in Seattle, a supposition which, from where I sat, was true. Yet I never lost hope; I think I somehow expected to find my own name in these columns, just as I somehow expected that, down below, a roadster would turn the corner with a boy in it who had discovered that I existed. My interest in boys was one of the many subjects I could not discuss with my grandmother; I was not supposed to be aware of them until I was in college. Indeed, the only topics we had in common were clothes and movie actors and actresses. She disliked the kind of books I read and would have disliked the girls I saw if she had had any inkling of what they were like. She would never give her opinion of any member of the family, even those she was "mad" at. For all my fishing, I could never find out even a simple thing, such as what she thought of me.

The liveliest time we had, in all the mornings we sat opposite each other in the nursery, was when I wrote in for a *Vogue* pattern to make a tennis dress. If I could have learned to sew, or she had had the patience to teach me, we might have found a medium in which we could communicate. The tennis dress, thanks to her help, did not come out too badly, and, encouraged, I wrote for another pattern, a model far too old for me, in tiers of crepe de Chine that were supposed to shade from a pale yellow, through apricot, to flame. This dress was never finished; I found the blushing remains of it in a hall cupboard on my last visit home.

The dressmaking phase, of which my grandfather entertained great hopes, was a failure. We could never be "like mother and daughter" to each other, in spite of what people said. She could not bear to watch me sewing without a thimble and with a long thread with a slightly dirty knot on the end of it. If I started on a piece of mending, my ineptitude always drove her to finish it.

Much of my adolescent boredom and discontent sprang from the fact that I had absolutely nothing to do but read and play the Victrola. I was not allowed in the kitchen, except to fix a sandwich for my lunch, because of an historic mess I had made with a batch of marshmallows; as with the dawn-colored dress, I had been too ambitious for a beginner. All I know today of sewing I learned in boarding school and, earlier, from the nuns in the convent, and the only person who was willing to show me anything about cooking was the old gardener-chauffeur, who used to come in and make German-fried potatoes for his lunch. On the cook's day out, he would let me watch him and then try it myself. In our family now, we have a dish called, in his memory, chauffeur-fried potatoes; they are very good.

My grandmother herself did not eat lunch as a regular thing, and at twelve o'clock every day, and sometimes earlier, my audience was over. She would get up from her chair and retire to the bathroom, shutting the door behind her. In a minute, her bedroom door closed, the nursery door closed. From then on till a time that varied between two and three o'clock, she was invisible; no one was allowed to disturb her. She was getting ready to go downtown. This sortie was the climax of her day. Her bedroom door would open, revealing her in festive array—every outfit she wore, like every meal, was a surprise. The car would be waiting, in front of the old carriage block, and we would set off, sometimes stopping for Aunt Rosie. The next two or three hours would be spent in the stores, trying on, ransacking counters. My grandmother was not much interested in bargains, though we never missed a sale at Helen Igoe's or Magnin's; what she cared about was the "latest wrinkle" in dresses or furs or notions—news from the fashion front. During these hours, she reached her highest point of laconic animation and sparkle; she shopped like an epigrammatist at the peak of form, and the extravagance of her purchases matched her brilliant hair and bobbing feathers and turkey walk and pursy pink cheeks.

But at a quarter of five, wherever we were, my grandmother would look at her watch. It was time to pick up Grandpa, in front of his club, where he always played a rubber of bridge after leaving the office. At five o'clock, punctually, he would be on the sidewalk, anxiously surveying the traffic for us. The car would draw up; he would climb in and kiss my grandmother's cheek. "Have a good day?" he would ask. "All right," she would reply, sighing a little. We would get home at five-thirty; dinner was at six, punctually. During the meal, my young uncle would be queried as to how he had passed his day, and he would answer with a few monosyllables. My grandmother would mention the names of any persons she had seen on her shopping tour. My grandfather might praise the food. "Allee samee Victor Hugo," he would say, referring to a restaurant in Los Angeles. After dinner, my married uncle would drop in with his wife, perhaps on their way out to a party. My other uncle, yawning, would retire to his quarters. The doorbell might ring. I would run to answer it, and two or three of his friends would tramp past me upstairs to his rooms. The door on the landing would shut. In a little while, he would lope down the stairs, to say that he was going out. He would kiss his mother and father, and my grandfather would say to him, "Home by eleven, son." My grandfather and grandmother, having finished the evening papers, would start playing double Canfield, at which my grandmother nearly always won. "I'll have to hitch up my trousers with a safety pin," my grandfather would say to me, jesting, as he paid her over her winnings; this expression signified to him the depths of poverty.

Then he might go downtown to his club for a game of poker, or he might stay in his deep chair, smoking a cigar and reading a book that always seemed to be the same book: *The Life and Letters of Walter Hines Page*. My grandmother would take up her library book, I would take up mine, and silence would resume its way over the household. The only sound would be the turning of a page or the click of the door on the kitchen landing as the cook went upstairs to bed. Rarely, the telephone would ring, and I would rush to get it, but it was never anything interesting—someone for my uncle or a girl for me, asking what I was doing. Or my grandmother would glance over at me as I lay stretched out on the sofa with my copy (disappointing) of *Mademoiselle de Maupin*: "Mary, pull your dress down." At ten o'clock, she would close her book, sighing, and start out to the front hall, on her way to bed. "Going up, Mama?" my grandfather would say, if he were at home, raising his gray eyes with an invariable air of surprise. "I think so, Harry," she would reply, sighing again, from the stairs. The stairs creaked; her door closed; the bathroom door closed. Soon my grandfather would put down his book and his paper knife, offer his cheek to me for a kiss, and follow her up the stairs. The nursery door would shut.

Occasionally, we would all go to the movies, or to the theater if a New York company was in town; my grandfather did not care for stock. We saw *The Student Prince* and *No! No! Nanette!* I remember, and *Strange Interlude*, which my grandmother pronounced "talky." On Thursday nights, we might go out to dinner at my grandfather's club. On Sundays, the cook left a supper prepared for us; my married uncle and his wife always came to this meal, no matter how many invitations they had to turn down, and sometimes Aunt Eva or Aunt Alice. These suppers usually ended with our going to the movies afterward; we were always home by eleven.

About once a year, or possibly every two years, my grandmother gave a tea and we had the caterer in. That was the only entertaining we did. Except for Aunt Alice and Aunt Eva (both widows), we never gave anyone dinner outside the immediate family. We never had Uncle Mose and Aunt Rosie or Uncle Clarence and Aunt Abbie (a vegetarian pair) or any of my cousins and their wives or my grandfather's partners and theirs. My grandmother's brother Elkan, whom she saw rarely but was not on bad terms with, was never, to my knowledge, in our house, nor were his wife and his numerous progeny. This leads me to wonder whether it was not the Jewish connection that had put the bar on entertaining. "If we have one in the house, we'll have them all," my grandfather may have said. But we did have Aunt Eva, frequently, and once, a great exception, her daughter from Portland to Sunday lunch. The only other exception that comes back to me was a dinner we gave for old Judge Gilman, of the Great Northern, and his wife, a stout lady who called herself Little Eva; I remember this because the men were served whisky before dinner, the only time this ever happened in our house. But why we had Judge and Mrs. Gilman I do not know; I think it puzzled me at the time by introducing into my head the question of why we did not have other people, since, on this occasion, a good time was had by all.

Up to then, it had never occurred to me that my family was remarkably inhospitable. I did not realize how strange it was that no social life was ever planned for me or my young uncle, that no young people were invited for us and no attempt made to secure invitations on our behalf. Indeed, I did not fully realize it until I was over thirty and long a mother myself. If I did not have an ordinary social set but only stray, odd friends, I blamed this on myself, thinking there was something wrong with me, like a petticoat showing, that other people could see and I couldn't. The notion that a family had responsibility for launching the younger members was more unknown to me than the theorem of Pythagoras, and if anybody had told me of it, I think I would have shut my ears, for I loved my family and did not wish to believe them remiss in any of their obligations. The fact that they would not let me go out with boys was an entirely different case; I saw their side of it, even though I disagreed violently—they were doing it for my own good, as they conceived it.

And yet I knew there was something odd about my grandmother's attitude toward outsiders. She would never go up to Lake Crescent, in the Olympic Mountains, with my grandfather and my young uncle and me in the summertime, where, amid my grandfather's circle of friends and their descendants, we had the only regular social life I ever experienced in the West. Life in the mountain hotel was very gay, even for the old people—Judge and Mrs. Battle, Colonel Blethen, Mr. Edgar Battle, Mr. Claude Ramsay, Mr. and Mrs. Boole—in my grandfather's set. They had card games on the big veranda and forest walks up to the Mary-mere waterfall; they took motorboat expeditions and automobile expeditions; they watched the young people dance in the evening and sent big tips to the chef in the kitchen. I could not understand why my grandmother preferred to stay in Seattle, pursuing her inflexible routine.

She was funny that way—that was the only explanation—just as she was funny about not letting my young uncle or me ever have a friend stay to dinner. In all the years I lived with my grand-mother, as a child and a woman, I can only recall two occasions when this rule was ever broken. The second one was when she was bedridden and too feeble, morally, to override my determina-tion to ask a poet who was teaching at the university to stay and have supper with me. I felt a little compunction, though the nurse and the cook assured me that it would be all right—she would forget about it the next minute. But her pretty voice, querulous, was heard from upstairs at about eight-thirty in the evening: "Mary, has that man gone home yet?" And all through the rest of my visit, she kept reverting crossly to the subject of "that man" who had stayed to supper; it was no good explaining to her that he had no means of getting home, that he lived in rooms way out at the University and took his meals in diners and tearooms, that he was an old friend to whom some hospitality was owing in my native city. Nor could I laugh her out of it. "Why didn't he go home for his dinner?" she reiterated, and those dark, suspicious words were very nearly the last I heard from her.

This ungraciousness of my grandmother's was a deeply con-firmed trait. It was not only that she resisted offering meals to anyone outside the immediate family; she resented a mere caller. There was a silver tray for calling cards on the hall table, but most of the cards in it were yellow with age; my grandmother was always downtown shopping at the hour when calls were normally paid. If I had a girl in for the evening, we could not really talk until my grandmother had gone to bed, and often she would outstay the guest, sitting in a corner with her book and glancing at us from time to time as we sat on the sofa endeavoring to improvise a dialogue. We could tell she was listening, but she did not talk herself. Suddenly, looking up, she would make the gesture to me that meant "Pull your skirt down."

My uncle's situation was the same, but he had the advantage of having his own sitting room, where his friends could congregate. For the most part, my grandmother ignored their presence; she would nod to them curtly if she chanced to meet them in the hall. The girls he knew were never asked to the house; he could never give a party.

Yet she was not an unkindly woman. She was good to her servants and their families, and on some occasions, if she were persuaded to unbend and tell an anecdote, she could be positively cordial. Her house, with its big rooms and wide porches, had been built, it would seem, with a hospitable *intention*. And in my mother's day, so I was told, things had been very different; the house had been full of young people. The silver and crystal and cut glass had not always been put away in the cupboard; there had been music and dancing, and my mother's school and college friends had spent night after night on the sleeping porches (which served as guest rooms) without even the necessity of a permission.

My mother had been my grandmother's darling. The fact that we did not entertain, I was given to understand, was related to my mother's death. My grandmother had resented her marriage to my father; according to my Irish relations, she would not have a priest in the house, and so the ceremony had been performed on the lawn. I do not believe this story, which is contradicted by other accounts, but it is true that my grandmother resented the

Catholic Church, to which my mother was eventually converted. Dr. Sharples, the family physician, had told my father, it seems, that my mother would die if she had another child, and my father went right ahead anyway, refusing to practice birth control. Actually, my mother's death had nothing to do with childbearing; she died of the flu, like so many young women of her age during the great epidemic. But this would not have deterred a woman like my grandmother from holding my father and the Church responsible. That was perhaps the reason she took no interest in my three brothers, who were still living with my father's people in Minneapolis; she sent them checks and gifts at birthdays and Christmas, and remembered them later in her will, but during the years I lived with her, the three little boys who had been born against her judgment were very remote from her thoughts. Possibly, I was enough of a handful for a woman of her age; nevertheless, it seems odd, unfeeling, that dry lack of concern, when she well knew that their lot was not happy. But happiness, like love, was a concept she had no real patience with.

As for the impassibility or aloofness she showed sometimes toward me, this may have been due to an absence of temperamental sympathy (could she have thought I had my father's traits?), or it may have been because I reminded her painfully of my mother. (I was always conscious of a resemblance that did not go far enough; everyone was always telling me how "good" my mother had been.)

For three years after my mother's death, one of her friends told me, my grandmother did not go out socially. Five years, said another. And this prolonged mourning was always offered as the official explanation of any oddities in our household. My grandmother, people said, lowering their voices, had never recovered from the shock of my mother's death. As a child, I could not quite believe this; it was impossible for me to imagine this contained, self-centered woman overcome by a passion of grief. Without being a psychologist, I felt somehow that her obdurate mourning was willful and selfish.

Children generally feel this about any adult emotion which is beyond their ken, but in this case I think I was on the track of something real. My grandmother's grief had taken a form peculiar to herself, stamped, as it were, with her monogram—the severe "AMP," in scroll lettering, that figured on her silver, her brushes and combs, her automobile. Her grief had the character of an inveterate hostility. One of my mother's friends recently wrote me a letter describing how my grandmother had hurt her feelings by refusing to speak to her whenever they met in the stores for a year after my mother's death. "Your grandmother could not bear the sight of me," she sadly decided.

And that is how I see my grandmother, bearing her loss like an affront, stubborn and angry, refusing to speak not only to individual persons but to life itself, which had wounded her by taking her daughter away. Her grief was a kind of pique, one of those nurtured *grievances* in which she specialized and which were deeply related to her coquetry. If I had only her photographs to go on, I might doubt the legend of her beauty; what confirms it for me is her manner of grieving, her mistrust of words, her refusal to listen to explanations from life or any other guilty suitor. Life itself was obliged to court her—in vain, as it appeared, for she had been mortally offended, once, twice, three times.

What the first offense was, I do not know, but I imagine it had something to do with her Jewish pride and sensitiveness; some injury was dealt her early in her marriage, and it may have been a very small thing—a chance word, even—that caused her to draw back into an august silence on this topic, a silence that lasted until her death. The second one I know about. This was the tragic face lifting that took place, in 1916 or 1917, I imagine, when she was in her forties and my mother was still living. Perhaps she really did have a mastoid operation at some later period (I rather think she must have), but the pouchy disfiguring scars I have spoken of that started on her cheeks and went down into her neck were the work of a face-lifter, who, as I understand the story, had pumped her face full of hot wax.

Such accidents were common in the early days of face lifting, and the scars, by the time she was sixty, were not especially noticeable. It was only that her cheeks had a puffy, swollen appearance, which her make-up did not conceal—in fact, if anything, enhanced, for though she did not know it, she always looked better in the morning, before she put on the rouge and the powder that made her skin's surface conspicuous. But when the scars were new, they must have been rather horrifying, and that was surely the reason for the dotted veils she wore, pulled tight across her face. The photographs break off at the time of the operation. That was when she stopped speaking to the camera, and, according to one informant, my grandmother left Seattle for a year after the tragedy.

"According to one informant"—the story of the face lifting was well known in Seattle, and yet in the family no mention was ever made of it, at least in my hearing, so that I learned of it from outsiders—my father's people, friends of my mother's, who naturally were unable to supply all the details. I was grown up when I learned it, and yet that same unnatural tact that kept me from ever using the word "Jewish" to my grandmother kept me from prying into the matter with the family. "Your grandmother's tragedy"—so I first heard the face lifting alluded to, if I remember rightly, by one of my friends, who had heard of it from her mother. And I will not query the appropriateness of the term according to the Aristotelian canon; in this case, common usage seems right. It was a tragedy, for her, for her husband and family, who, deprived of her beauty through an act of folly, came to live in silence, like a house accursed.

My grandmother's withdrawal from society must have dated, really, from this period, and not from the time of my mother's death, which came as the crowning blow. That was why we were so peculiar, so unsocial, so, I would add, slightly inhuman; we were all devoting ourselves, literally, to the cult of a relic, which was my grandmother's body, laved and freshened every day in the big bathroom, and then paraded before the public in the downtown stores.

I was living in New York when my grandfather died, from a stroke, one morning, when he was seventy-nine, in the big bathroom. My grandmother's ritual did not change. She still dressed and went downtown at the same hours, returning at the time when she would have picked him up at his club. She was cheerful when I saw her, a year or so after this; she went to the races and had a new interest—night baseball; we went to the ball park together. Once in a great while, she would lunch and play bridge with a group of women friends, with whom she had resumed connections after twenty years. But she did not, to my knowledge, ever have them to her house; they met at the Seattle Golf Club usually, the best (non-Jewish) country club.

Like many widows, she appeared to have taken a new lease on life; I had never seen her so chatty, and she was looking very handsome. I remember an afternoon at the races, to which she drove Aunt Rosie and me in her car, at a speed of seventy miles an hour; she herself was well over seventy. The two sisters, one a lively robin and the other a brilliant toucan, chaffed and bantered with the sporting set in the clubhouse. Conscious of their powers and their desirability, they were plainly holding court. Aunt Rosie did not bet but advised us; my grandmother, as usual, won, and I think I won, too. That night, or in the small hours of the morning, Aunt Rosie died.

It was something, Dr. Sharples thought, that she had eaten at the races; an attack of indigestion caused a heart block. He believed at first he could save her, and I had persuaded my grandmother to go to bed, confident that Aunt Rosie would be almost herself the next day. But in the middle of the night, the phone rang. I ran to get it; it was Uncle Mose. "Rosie just went." My grandmother understood before I could tell her, before I had set down the telephone. A terrible scream—an unearthly scream—came from behind the closed door of her bedroom; I have never heard such a sound, neither animal nor human, and it did not stop. It went on and on, like a fire siren on the moon. In a minute, the whole household was roused; everybody came running. I got there first. Flinging open her bedroom door (even then with a sense of trepidation, of being an unwarranted intruder), I saw her, on her bed, the covers pushed back; her legs were sprawled out, and her yellow batiste nightgown, trimmed with white lace, was pulled up, revealing her thighs. She was writhing on the bed; the cook and I could barely get hold of her. My uncle appeared in the doorway, and my first thought (and I think the cook's also) was to get that nightgown down. The spectacle was indecent, and yet of a strange boudoir beauty that contrasted in an eerie way with that awful noise she was making, more like a howl than a scream and bearing no resemblance to sorrow. She was trying, we saw, to pull herself to her feet, to go somewhere or other, and the cook helped her up. But then, all at once, she became heavy, like a sack full of stones. The screaming stopped, and there was dead silence.

Eventually, I forget how, but thanks chiefly to the cook, we got her calmed down to the point where she was crying normally. Perhaps the doctor came and administered a sedative. I sat up with her, embracing her and trying to console her, and there was something sweet about this process, for it was the first time we had ever been close to each other. But all at once she would remember Rosie and shriek out her name; no one could take Rosie's place, and we both knew it. I felt like an utter outsider. It seemed clear to me that night, as I sat stroking her hair, that she had never really cared for anyone but her sister; that was her secret. The intellectual part of my mind was aware that some sort of revelation had taken place—of the nature of Jewish family feeling, possibly. And I wondered whether that fearful insensate noise had been classic Jewish mourning, going back to the waters of Babylon. Of one thing I was certain: my grandmother was more different from the rest of us than I could ever have conceived.

Uncle Mose was taking it well, I learned the next morning. It was only my grandmother, so unemotional normally, who had given way to this extravagant grief, and the family, I gathered, were slightly embarrassed by her conduct, as though they, too, felt that she had revealed something, which, as far as they were concerned, would have been better left in the dark. But what *had* she revealed, as they saw it? Her essential Jewishness? I could never find out, for I had to take the train east that very day, with my baby, and when I came back several years later, no one seemed to remember anything unusual about the occasion of Aunt Rosie's death.

"That's my sister," my grandmother would exclaim, eagerly pointing when we came to a photograph of Aunt Rosie. "My sister," she would say of Aunt Eva, in a somewhat grander tone. She always brightened when one of her two sisters turned up in the photograph collection, like a child when it is shown its favorite stuffed animal. I think she was a little more excited at the sight of Aunt Rosie. By that time, I imagine, she had forgotten that her sisters were dead, or, rather, the concept, death, no longer had any meaning for her; they had "gone away," she probably believed, just as children believe that this is what happens to their dead relations. I used to stand ready to prompt her with the names, but she did not seem to need or want this; her sisters' relationship to her was what mattered, and she always got that straight. "Aunt Rosie," I would observe, showing her a picture of a small, smiling, dark woman in a big marabou hat. "My sister," her voice would override me proudly, as if she were emending my statement.

The clothes in the old photographs amused her; she had not lost her interest in dress, and was very critical of my appearance, urging me, with impatient gestures, to pull my hair forward on my cheeks and surveying me with pride when I had done so; it gave a "softer" look. If I did not get it right, she would pull her own black waves forward, to show me what she meant. Though she could no longer go downtown, she still kept to the same schedule. Every day at twelve o'clock, the nurse would close my grandmother's door and the doors to the nursery and the bathroom, reopening them between two and three, when the beauty preparations had been completed. "You can come in now. Your grandmother is all prettied up." One afternoon, responding to the summons, I found my grandmother frowning and preoccupied. There was something the matter, and I could not make out what it was. She wanted me to get her something, the "whatchamacallit" from her bureau. I tried nearly everything—brush, comb, handkerchief, perfume, pincushion, pocketbook, photograph of my mother. All of them were wrong, and she grew more and more impatient, as if I were behaving like an imbecile. "Not the *comb*, the whachamacallit!" Finally, for she was getting quite wrought up, I rang for the nurse. "She wants something," I said. "But I can't make out what it is." The nurse glanced at the bureau top and then went swiftly over to the chiffonier; she picked up the hand mirror that was lying there and passed it silently to my grandmother, who at once began to beam and nod. "She's forgotten the word for mirror," the nurse said, winking at me. At that moment, the fact that my grandmother was senile became real to me.

Printed in the USA
CPSIA information can be obtained
at www.ICGtesting.com
LVHW031451230823
756063LV00006B/29

9 780156 586504